REGENTS RENAISSANCE DRAMA SERIES

General Editor: Cyrus Hoy
Advisory Editor: G. E. Bentley

CATILINE

BEN JONSON

Catiline

Edited by

W. F. BOLTON *and* JANE F. GARDNER

UNIVERSITY OF NEBRASKA PRESS · LINCOLN

MANUFACTURED IN THE UNITED STATES OF AMERICA

Regents Renaissance Drama Series

The purpose of the Regents Renaissance Drama Series is to provide soundly edited texts, in modern spelling, of the more significant plays of the Elizabethan, Jacobean, and Caroline theater. Each text in the series is based on a fresh collation of all sixteenth- and seventeenth-century editions. The textual notes, which appear above the line at the bottom of each page, record all substantive departures from the edition used as the copy-text. Variant substantive readings among sixteenth- and seventeenth-century editions are listed there as well. In cases where two or more of the old editions present widely divergent readings, a list of substantive variants in editions through the seventeenth century is given in an appendix. Editions after 1700 are referred to in the textual notes only when an emendation originating in some one of them is received into the text. Variants of accidentals (spelling, punctuation, capitalization) are not recorded in the notes. Contracted forms of characters' names are silently expanded in speech prefixes and stage directions, and, in the case of speech prefixes, are regularized. Additions to the stage directions of the copy-text are enclosed in brackets. Stage directions such as "within" or "aside" are enclosed in parentheses when they occur in the copy-text.

Spelling has been modernized along consciously conservative lines. "Murther" has become "murder," and "burthen," "burden," but within the limits of a modernized text, and with the following exceptions, the linguistic quality of the original has been carefully preserved. The variety of contracted forms (*'em, 'am, 'm, 'um, 'hem*) used in the drama of the period for the pronoun *them* are here regularly given as *'em,* and the alternation between *a'th'* and *o'th'* (for *on* or *of the*) is regularly reproduced as *o'th'.* The copy-text distinction between preterite endings in *-d* and *-ed* is preserved except where the elision of *e* occurs in the penultimate syllable; in such cases, the final syllable is contracted. Thus, where the old editions read "threat'ned," those of the present series read "threaten'd." Where, in the old editions, a contracted preterite in *-y'd* would yield *-i'd* in modern spelling (as in "try'd," "cry'd," "deny'd"), the word is here given in its full form (e.g., "tried," "cried," "denied").

Punctuation has been brought into accord with modern practices. The effort here has been to achieve a balance between the generally light pointing of the old editions, and a system of punctuation which, without overloading the text with exclamation marks, semicolons, and dashes, will make the often loosely flowing verse (and prose) of the original syntactically intelligible to the modern reader. Dashes are regularly used only to indicate interrupted speeches, or shifts of address within a single speech.

Explanatory notes, chiefly concerned with glossing obsolete words and phrases, are printed below the textual notes at the bottom of each page. References to stage directions in the notes follow the admirable system of the Revels editions, whereby stage directions are keyed, decimally, to the line of the text before or after which they occur. Thus, a note on 0.2 has reference to the second line of the stage direction at the beginning of the scene in question. A note on 115.1 has reference to the first line of the stage direction following line 115 of the text of the relevant scene.

CYRUS HOY

University of Rochester

Contents

List of Abbreviations

See also Alphabetical List of Sources, in Appendix B

F1	the second edition, in Jonson's first folio, 1616.
F2	the fourth edition, in Jonson's second folio, 1640.
Ff	Jonson's 1616 and 1640 folios, and readings common to them.
Gifford	*The Works of Ben Jonson.* Ed. William Gifford. 9 vols. London, 1816. Revised by Francis Cunningham. London, 1875.
H & S	*Ben Jonson.* Ed. C. H. Herford, Percy and Evelyn Simpson. 11 vols. Oxford, 1925–1952.
Lat.	Latin
(o)	the original, first setting of a forme or a portion thereof.
om.	omits, omitted
opp.	opposite
Q	the first edition, in Jonson's quarto, 1611
S.D.	stage direction
S.P.	speech prefix
Whalley	*The Works of Ben Jonson.* Ed. Peter Whalley. 7 vols. London, 1756.

Introduction

Catiline, Jonson admitted, received "all vexation of Censure" at its premiere in 1611; in the Restoration, the diarist Pepys thought it "the worst upon the stage, I mean, the least diverting, that ever I saw any"; in our own times, T. S. Eliot stigmatized it as "that dreary Pyrrhic victory of tragedy."[1] The way to an appreciation of the work its author thought "a legitimate poem . . . of this race . . . the best" is not, clearly, an easy one.

Yet Jonson was writing in a tradition long established and popular in England. Throughout the Middle Ages, the "matter of Rome" —tales from classical history and legend—had provided the subject for many of the most successful verse romances (including Chaucer's *Troilus and Criseyde* and "Knight's Tale") and indeed gave its name to "romance" as a long narrative fiction with a historical basis (compare Modern French and German *Roman*, "novel"). In Jonson's day, the plays of Shakespeare included *Titus Andronicus* (c. 1590), *Julius Caesar* (c. 1599), *Troilus and Cressida* (c. 1602), *Anthony and Cleopatra* (c. 1607), *Timon of Athens* (c. 1608), *Coriolanus* (c. 1608), and *Pericles* (c. 1608), the first three prior to Jonson's own tragedy *Sejanus his Fall* (1603) and his comedy with an ancient Roman setting, *Poetaster* (1601). Other examples include the lost tragedies on the Catiline theme by Stephen Gosson (c. 1578) and by Robert Wilson and Henry Chettle (1598).

Something of Jonson's consciousness of his place in this tradition can be seen in the re-use he made of some features of *Sejanus* when he came to write *Catiline*.[2] Both plays recount a Roman conspiracy

1 Samuel Pepys, *Diary*, ed. H. B. Wheatley (London, 1920), VIII, 172; T. S. Eliot, *Selected Essays 1917–1932* (New York, 1932), p. 129, reprinted in J. A. Barish, ed., *Ben Jonson: A Collection of Critical Essays* (Englewood Cliffs, 1963), p. 16. Yet for evidence that *Catiline* was the most respected play of its century, see G. E. Bentley, *Shakespeare & Jonson: Their Reputations in the Seventeenth Century Compared*, I (Chicago, 1945), 109–112.

2 Writers who have treated the two plays together include K. M. Burton, "The Political Tragedies of Chapman and Ben Jonson," *Essays in Criticism*, II (1952), 397–412; G. R. Hibbard, "Goodness and Greatness: An Essay on the Tragedies of Ben Jonson and George Chapman," *Renaissance and Modern Studies*, XI (1967), 5–54; G. Hill, "The World's Proportion: Jonson's

which, in a conspiratorial age like Jonson's, had great topicality (Jonson was briefly jailed for *Sejanus*); both depend heavily on historical sources (the quarto edition of *Sejanus* had copious learned marginal notes by Jonson); both present a hero—title character might be a better term—who attracts no sympathy from the audience and hence affords them no "catharsis" by his destruction; both do without the introspective portraits of changing personalities that we associate with English Renaissance drama (and, indeed, with the comedies of Jonson himself); in both, civil disaster is forestalled but left lurking in the wings at the final curtain; both make use of heavily rhetorical dialogue to adumbrate Jonson's view of politics as an amoral clash where the acquiescence of good, rather than its conquest, allows the prevalence of evil; both have striking boudoir scenes and make other use of sexuality both thematically and metaphorically; and both employ tags like "The night grows fast upon us" (*Sejanus*, IV.523; cf. *Catiline*, III.iii.1) and others that reveal some common stock of vocabulary and phraseology. To the extent that most of these points, except the last, are even more characteristic of *Catiline* than of *Sejanus*, it does seem that the later play is a re-working of the preoccupations and techniques of the earlier, as though Jonson had wrecked *Sejanus* in his disappointment with it and salvaged its best features for his new attempt in the same mode.

Even so, some important differences stand out. Unlike *Sejanus*, *Catiline* has a Chorus and a Prologue; *Catiline* shows evil seeking to destroy power, *Sejanus* evil in power; hence *Catiline* shows evil against good, *Sejanus* evil against evil; *Catiline* tells of "his conspiracy," a slow-moving cat-and-mouse tragedy of the hero's flight from law with the party he heads, whereas *Sejanus* tells of "his fall," a dynamic rise-and-fall tragedy of the solitary hero's soaring ambition; perhaps accordingly, in *Catiline* the supernatural portents appear in the first Act at a blasphemous oath-taking, in *Sejanus* in the last Act at a profane consultation of the auguries.

Modern critics of *Catiline* can be grouped into a large number who have sought to explain its failure,[3] and a smaller number who have

---

Dramatic Poetry in 'Sejanus' and 'Catiline'," *Stratford-upon-Avon Studies*, I (1960), 113–131; J. I. de Villiers, "Ben Jonson's Tragedies," *English Studies*, XLV (1964), 433–442; and L. C. Stagg, *Index to the Figurative Language of Ben Jonson's Tragedies* (Charlottesville, 1967).

[3] Notably M. J. C. Echeruo, "The Conscience of Politics and Jonson's *Catiline*," *Studies in English Literature*, VI (1966), 341–356; J. J. Enck, "Prodi-

tried to demonstrate its success.[4] Most have concentrated on the play as tragedy, some on its view of history. As a tragedy, it clearly departs from the Aristotelian canons; it elicits, we have seen, no pity for its central character, and, since he never really rises, he cannot be said to fall in a soul-stirring way. Moreover, classical notions of simplicity are contravened by the crowded stage with over thirty characters, the "dual plot" that traces both Catiline's defeat and Cicero's victory, and the passages of satire jumbled in among those of high drama. On the other hand, as we have also seen, it is unlike other English Renaissance tragedies in that it deals with its main characters only as public figures, not as private psychological studies; yet they are not really noble as even a villain like Marlowe's Tamburlaine undoubtedly is. Moreover, Jonson allows himself abundant overt didacticism and—except perhaps in the Choruses—no lyricism (the use of a lyric verse-form in the Chorus is in any case a convention of classical drama): the emphasis is on the rhetorical expression of such passions as the historical sources reveal or hint at, but his meticulous classicizing appears to make Rome foreign where Shakespeare made it universal. Even the supernatural element, which neither participates in the train of dramatic causes nor externalizes the inward thoughts of the characters, is remote from what we find in *Hamlet* or *Macbeth*.

Indeed, we may find more like *Catiline* in Jonson's comedies than in either ancient or Shakespearean tragedy (which might explain why Francis Meres, in *Palladis Tamia* of 1598, termed Jonson "one of our best for tragedy" long before either *Sejanus* or *Catiline*, although he may instead have been referring to Jonson's now untraceable contributions to a play like *The Spanish Tragedy*). The comedies, of course, are satirical, and make a special attack on veniality and the weaknesses of—and for—women. Catiline himself recalls at times the life-denying

---

gious Rhetoricke," *Jonson and the Comic Truth* (Madison, 1957), pp. 172–188; R. Ornstein, "Ben Jonson," in *The Moral Vision of Jacobean Tragedy* (Madison, 1960), pp. 84–104, reprinted in R. J. Kaufmann, ed., *Elizabethan Drama: Modern Essays in Criticism* (New York, 1961), pp. 187–207; and C. G. Thayer, "Interlude: The Tragedies," *Ben Jonson: Studies in the Plays* (Norman, Okla., 1963), pp. 112–127.

4 Notably, A. Schlösser, "Ben Jonson's Roman Plays," *Kwartnalnik Neofilologiczny*, VIII (1961), 123–159; R. E. Knoll, "Catiline," *Ben Jonson's Plays: An Introduction* (Lincoln, Nebraska, 1964), pp. 135–144; R. Nash, "Ben Jonson's Tragic Poems," *Studies in Philology*, LV (1958), 164–186; and J. A. Bryant, Jr., "*Catiline* and the Nature of Jonson's Tragic Fable," *PMLA*, LXIX (1954), 265–277, reprinted in Barish's *Collection*, pp. 147–159.

Morose of *Epicoene*, at times the carnal projector Sir Epicure Mammon of *The Alchemist*. Herford and Simpson were right to say that as the comedies are poor in laughter, so *Catiline* is poor in tears.[5] Neither Jonson's comedy nor his tragedy sends us away amused or purged, but rather both seek to disturb us and, by suspending us at the brink of chaos for five acts, turn us back to the disorder of our own lives with a new sense of disquiet and hence of purpose.

Jonson had admitted into his play three influences current in his day. One is of the Senecan drama, the devices developed from the practice of the first-century Roman dramatist, exampled in *Catiline* by the Prologue put into the mouth of a ghost, to create atmosphere and to foreshadow the horrors to come; by the dearth of rapid movement; by the dialogues full of aphorisms; by the Choruses disjoined from the dramatic action; by the depraved "hero" whose criminality is his glory and his power over men, but who proves to be ultimately obtuse; and by numerous verbal borrowings from half a dozen of the works of Seneca himself. In some aspects of the character of Catiline, indeed, the Senecan models played almost as great a part as the historical sources. Jonson also admitted the influence of his contemporary academic playwrights, whose productions, more poems than plays, were meant for study and not for performance—"closet dramas" like Milton's later *Samson Agonistes*. But in accepting the conventions of form, rhetoric, and concern for politics and statecraft that characterized academic drama of his time, Jonson sought to transform them for the popular stage and to write a "playable" play. To an extent he succeeded, for although *Catiline* was not well received at its early performances by the prestigious King's Men—Shakespeare's company—with the famous actor Richard Burbadge, probably as Cicero, it was more popular in the last years of Jonson's life and the remainder of the seventeenth century; yet Pepys' remark, quoted above, was prefaced by the qualification that the play is "of much good sense and words to read" (although he might have found more diversion in the 1669 production, to which Nell Gwyn read the Prologue and Epilogue), and Jonson himself had, in the first edition of 1611, turned his persuasion to the readers, in ordinary and extraordinary, and away from a theatrical audience. It is as a closet drama alone that the play has survived.

If the play has connections with the academic drama as a tragedy,

---

[5] C. H. Herford and Percy Simpson, *Ben Jonson*, II (Oxford, 1925), 127.

it has connections with the contemporary chronicle play as a stage version of historical material. Jonson himself had written at least part of a play on Mortimer, Earl of March, of which a fragment survives, and all but completed another about Henry V, destroyed in the fire in his library in 1623. He numbered antiquaries and historians among his closest friends, including the learned Camden, and called history "the light of truth" in his commendatory verses to Sir Walter Raleigh's *History of the World* (1614). The phrase recalls the first of the four requirements of tragedy that Jonson had stipulated in the address "To the Readers" at the beginning of *Sejanus*: "truth of argument, dignity of persons, gravity and height of elocution, fulness and frequency of sentence." (The last three can be paraphrased "characters of high social rank, dialogue in the highest rhetorical style, abundance of moral aphorisms.")

"Truth of argument," it becomes clear, means not only historicity, the kind of authenticity that Aristotle had shown would commit the audience's attention more than any imagined plot, but also verisimilitude. To preserve the illusion, the suspension of disbelief, it was necessary that nothing should be presented that the stage could not manage without undue artificiality: hence we do not see the battle in which Catiline dies, although the unity of place is varied often enough, from the Senate to Cicero's house, the Milvian bridge, and so forth. Though the play has an ethical rather than antiquarian impulse, history is necessary to ensure the audience's conviction of its truth to life, and history forms the basis of all true tragedy.[6]

Here Jonson was taking a position in a debate over the relative merits of the historian and the poet and their roles in mediating moral truth. Sidney, writing of course on behalf of the poet in the *Defense of Poesy* (1595), had claimed that imaginative handling would excel mere fidelity to the sources in presenting the past as a sequence of events of which the great were to be imitated and the base to be shunned; for the inconsistencies of human nature blurred the outlines of the models. Jonson has taken the poet's role by detracting from Catiline's reforming fervor—his populism becomes merely the revolt of a degenerate aristocrat against a degenerate society—and by giving Caesar a complicity in the plot that the sources only hint at. On the other hand, Cato does allow Catiline a measure of grudging credit in

6 See J. A. Bryant, Jr., "The Significance of Ben Jonson's First Requirement for Tragedy: 'Truth of Argument'," *Studies in Philology*, XLIX (1952), 195–213.

the closing lines of the play, and Caesar, in Act V, speaks vehemently in defense of a law for the breaking of which Cicero was, a few years after the time covered in the play, disgraced and exiled. And indeed Cicero is by no means a figure after Sidney's simplicity. Although he opposes Catiline in the struggle for the safety of Rome, he adopts many of the conspirator's methods in a wholly pragmatic way, and accomplishes his mission only by the accidental advantages provided through a whore's envy and the chance intercession of a few minor Gaulish tribesmen. So circumscribed is he by his methods and by chance that he becomes unable to deal with Caesar, who receives the reassurance "Caesar, be safe" (V.vi.163) and remains to foreshadow the next stage of the disintegration of Roman civilization. Cicero is alone in his lofty ideals, a "new man" who sees virtue as the standard of nobility rather than, as the conspirators do, the other way around; but in attempting to deal with the corruption in his society he is after all doing no more than the Catilinarians claimed they were doing, and he is reduced to embracing many of their means as well, to the extent that even his brother is capable of questioning his courses (III.iv.14–16). Cicero's oratory in praise of the whore Fulvia is a cynical echo of the praise heaped on him by Cato as the savior of Rome, and he knows it.

Such features of Jonson's handling of his material go a long way to neutralizing the ethical conflict inherent in the struggle for Rome and to equivocating the moral polarities it might have elucidated. Along with the failure to adopt the traditional procedures of any established tragical drama, this historical approach—whether it arose from Jonson's skepticism or from his uncertainty—undoubtedly dispels much of the unity of vision and art that the four requirements outlined in *Sejanus*, plus the Prologue and Choruses, might have secured for *Catiline*.

When we turn our attention to the language of the play, Cicero again appears to be equivocated. In the tradition of rhetoric he had an undimmed reputation during the Renaissance, whatever his political history may have been, and Jonson himself turned repeatedly to him as the authority for the critical judgments summarized in *Timber* (posthumously published, 1641). Yet none of the conspirators misses a chance to deride his "prodigious rhetoric" (IV.ii.406; cf. also II.136–39; III.i.28; III.iv.23–26; IV.ii.100–102; V.iv.174). It is not altogether clear whether, by putting these remarks into those mouths of "negative" characters, Jonson meant to refute them indirectly;

but the tendency of the modern reader, at least, is to accept them, and it seems that the Jacobean audience did much the same. For his own part, however, Jonson shows no hesitation in displaying the arts of language.[7] He employs the full range of dramatic verse; not only oratory (perhaps the least artificial of them all, because taken over almost directly from his sources: but even here the translation of Latin prose into English verse without injury or loss to either is a major *tour de force*), but also several fine soliloquies, passages of energetic stichomythia, taut and tart dialogue (e.g., II.216–244, III.iii. 94–140), episodes of rhyme (which Dryden, who heavily attacked the language of *Catiline* in his *Defence of the Epilogue* of 1672, nevertheless took as the classical justification of rhyming dramatic verse in his *Essay of Dramatic Poesy* written in 1665), and stanzaic innovation of progressive complexity in the Choruses: in order, iambic tetrameter couplets, iambic tetrameter rhyming abba (the *In Memoriam* stanza), iambic tetrameter rhyming abab, and iambic tetrameter alternating with iambic dimeter on the same rhyme-scheme. Jonson also made use of devices like alliteration ("My stale with whom I stalk," III.iii. 234; "Actions of depth and danger," III.iii.4; "faults, now grown her fate," III.v.52; "more with faith than face," II.377, all expressing a variety of relationships between the items linked by initial sound), puns (see III.ii.47, note), even functional distortions of meaning and structure such as the caustic barbs of Cethegus (V.viii.3). The play offers a showcase of the poet's craft.

Yet language is even more than an item on display in *Catiline*. It is in a sense one of the subjects of the play and in an even greater sense the source of its unifying structure. The remarks of the conspirators about Cicero's rhetoric betray their awareness of their clash with him as a clash in language, of orator against orator, of diction against diction. As Caesar observes (IV.ii.241), it is Cicero's words that defeat Catiline, and Catiline only fulfils the charge laid on him in the Prologue when, in the battle reported in the last scene, he finally goes from exhortation to action and dies in silence. This view of the play sees the orator not only as an "oracle" (V.vi.148; cf. I.530) but as an extension of the poet as Sidney saw him, one whose art shapes society by encouraging good and condemning evil, by giving examples, and by holding a mirror to nature; Cicero exercises

---

[7] This portion of our discussion owes much to G. B. Jackson, *Vision and Judgment in Ben Jonson's Drama* (New Haven, 1968).

the power of creative ordering, and his oratory not only saves civilization from the destructive rhetoric of Catiline, but it embodies the civilization that it saves. Yet if the language of the play, and language in the play, encompassed no more than that, it would mean that dramatic language had taken the place of dramatic action, and be more an explanation of Jonson's failure than a demonstration of his success.

But the view implies the basis of such a demonstration in its observation that the closing lines of the play go back to topics first raised in the Prologue. If, with the Prologue, we take Catiline's soliloquy which follows it, and with the speech of Petreius all of the last scene of the play after the exit of Statilius and Gabinius, we shall see more extended connections: and we shall be justified in doing so by more than these connections, for the Prologue and soliloquy form a single unit of theatrical convention (as Jonson's stage direction at I.15.1 indicates) prior to the "naturalistic" dialogue commencing with the entrance of Aurelia, just as the conventional retrospect of Cato and Cicero and the report of offstage events by the *nuntius* Petreius do after the departure of the conspirators in V.ix.3. The units thus isolated form a roughly symmetrical pair, the first ninety-seven and last ninety-five lines of the play.

Some of the connections are restricted to these two passages, so that the first is a prolepsis of the second unbridged by what goes between. Such is the Ghost's urging that Catiline should "pursue/ . . . The ruin of thy country; thou wert built/ For such a work" (I.43–46), which receives its completion in Petreius' "Catiline came on, not with the face/ Of any man, but of a public ruin" (V.ix.38–39); or the Ghost's "All the names/ Of thy confederates, too, be no less great/ In hell than here, that when we would repeat/ Our strengths in muster, we may name you all" (I.66–69), completed by Petreius' "Fate descended nearer to the earth/ As if she meant to hide the name of . things" (V.ix.31–32); or Catiline's "A spirit within me chides my sluggish hands" (I.81), completed by Petreius' "his hands still mov'd/ As if he labor'd yet to grasp the state/ With those rebellious parts" (V.ix.82–84). In each, the violent optimism of the first Act is ironically ratified by the events of the last, for even in the proud tokens of Catiline's rebellion was the hint either of their extinction or of the reversal of their implications in the very moment of their fulfilment.

The same can be said of other images in the opening and closing lines of the play that are also recurrent in the episodes that span them. They are (in addition to the general preoccupation with slaughter and disorder of nature, instigated by Sylla at the beginning and turned against Catiline in the end) those of day and night, light and dark, waking and sleeping; of rebellion against the gods and the natural order, and of Furies; of the theater and theatrical disguise; and of the whole range of sexual activity from rape to honorable marriage. Sylla urges "Let night grow blacker with thy plots, and day/ . . . start away" (I.61–62); which is what happens when, at the battle ending in Catiline's death, "The sun stood still" (V.ix.56 ff.). Sylla says "be free/ Not heav'n itself from thy impiety" (I.59–60) and Catiline likens himself to one of the rebellious giants, Atlas (I.86); but it is to the defeat of the legendary rebels that Petreius likens him in his moment of death, "as in that rebellion 'gainst the gods" (V.ix.73 ff.). Here too belong the Furies, invoked both literally and figuratively in Sylla's line "And Furies upon you, for Furies, call" (I.70); but when the Furies actually attend Catiline, it is to watch as horrified spectators and tremble "to see men/ Do more than they" (V.ix.52–53). The Furies, indeed, "stood on hills/ Circling the place" (V.ix.51–52), not simply as spectators but specifically as the audience in a classical amphitheater, often an arena in which public contests took place. Sylla's Ghost makes no mention of the theater, but he need not; for, even more than the Chorus, the Prologue was such a distinctively theatrical effect, a character addressing the play as a play with no part in its action, that he constituted in his role the embodiment of theatricality. (The Act IV Chorus alone expresses involvement in the action and web of responsibility in the play, but it does so retrospectively.) Last, Sylla makes repeated reference to Catiline's rape of a Vestal virgin (hence, symbolically, of the integrity of the state) and incest with his daughter and his sister (I.30–36, 42), images which Catiline picks up in his soliloquy and fuses in his impious threat of an incestuous return to the womb of the state (I.92–97). The counterpoise to this is Cato's speech (V.ix.6–12) in which he names Cicero the "Great parent of thy country" and promises him the attention of every generation, from the old men and matrons to the youths and girls and even to their grandchildren, a passage in which the "parent-hood" of the country is seen as the guardianship of its safety; and the family, in its undisturbed generations, is seen as the vehicle for *pietas*, veneration of the state and of its heroes.

The force of these themes and figures in the last scene does not depend wholly on their previous occurrence in the first, but rather on their recapitulation of the many instances of their use throughout the play. When Sylla opens the play with the lines "Dost thou not feel me, Rome? Not yet? Is night/ So heavy on thee, and my weight so light?" (I.1–2) he introduces the concept of night, darkness, and sleep as states of obscured awareness and culpable inactivity. Cicero adopts the same figure (III.ii.5, III.ii.155, III.ii.206, IV.ii.14) of Rome's neglect of the danger of the conspiracy, and the corollary, that of waking as heightened awareness and responsible action (III.v.23; cf. Cato, III.v.44). Cethegus, for his part, uses the same images (I.211, 300) and resigns himself ("Strangle me, I may sleep") at last only in V.viii.11. Cicero and Catiline both see secrecy as a kind of night, that is, an obfuscation (III.ii.198, I.522); each party strives to provide world-wide light, Cicero by defending Rome, "the light of all the earth" (V.iv.158) and Cethegus by supplanting the sun and moon (IV.v.52–55). Nor is the figure continued only in the language of the play: as at Catiline's death in Act V, so in the portents which end Act I "The day goes back" (I.312) and darkness invades the oath-taking; and the confrontation between Cicero and the would-be assassins takes place at dawn, the meeting point of night and day (III.iv and III.v). Language does not subsume the role of action, but action and language both convey the same thematic imagery.

In this process we have noticed, the state, Rome, is from the very first line of the play personified. The Choruses to Acts I and III extend this personification, but it occurs elsewhere as well, especially in the figure of Catiline as an illness in the body politic: he is so described by Sylla's Ghost (I.14), Cicero (III.ii.204 ff., IV.ii.245–247, 301, 363–366 and 387), and Petreius (V.i.47); but Catiline sees his role as that of purging the ailing city (III.i.213). Rome should, of course, be a symbol and a source of soundness, and her liability to the infection, like her sleep, is significant of her weakness. (A further personification of Rome, as mother, is noted below, p. xxii.)

The rebellion of the giant sons of earth against the gods had been Jonson's symbol of Sejanus' assault on Rome (IV.270 ff.). In *Catiline*, he repeated and extended the figure, stressing by implication its impiety, its image of a revolt against legitimate authority, and its ultimate failure, by invoking it directly or by reference to one or another of its participants or consequences. Like the figure of day and night, waking and sleeping, the mythological image is employed by both sides to describe the plot (by the Catilinarians I.74, 143, 348–349, III.i.185, 197–204, III.iii.53, 247, IV.v.45–46, IV.ii.426; by the Ciceronians III.ii.43, IV.ii.294; by the Chorus, I.552, II.369–370,

III.v.47–48). The implication is clear: Catiline, in accepting this description, is guilty at once of both the pride and the obtuseness of the original giants. At times he already foresees the success of the plot by likening himself to the gods (I.112, 181, 221–223); at others later he and Cethegus accept that success would mean, not new occupants in heaven, but a new chaos (III.i.177, 181; III.iii.106). With the failure of the consular plot, Catiline comes to seek the destruction, not the possession, of Rome.

After this change of purpose, he becomes increasingly not super- but sub-human. His failure against Cicero's rhetoric is the consequence of his progressive loss of the uniquely human attribute, language. He himself promises that, if Rome rejects him though he is the greatest of her children, then "If she can lose her nature, I can lose/ My piety, and in her stony entrails/ Dig me a seat where I will live again/ The labor of her womb, and be a burden/ Weightier than all the prodigies and monsters/ That she hath teem'd with" (I.92–97), a concentration of the ideas of sexuality and monstrosity in which Catiline foretells his own degeneration at the same time as he depicts himself as an unwholesome infestation of the body politic. And so it follows: he becomes a monster (III.ii.32, IV.ii.442 and 445; cf. Cethegus, V.iv.175), a prodigy (IV.ii.425), and the plot becomes a Hydra (IV.ii.473, as he predicted at III.i.100). Catiline and the conspirators are, as the Prologue foretold, Furies (III.ii.98, IV.ii.111, 397 and 432, IV.vi.15, V.i.44). Rebels, monsters, Furies, they comprise the principles of disorder in the three firmaments of heaven, earth, and hell: the cosmos. Thus Jonson succeeds in making Rome universal not, as Shakespeare did, through psychological generalization, but by employing the devices of classical mythology in a metaphorical manner congruous with his material. (Compare Jonson's use of mythology for characterization, as when Cethegus, who otherwise almost never refers to myth, employs it lavishly in IV.v.24–32 as a gibe at the self-consciously learned Sempronia.)

We have seen that the theater, or more precisely theatricality, informs the structural significance of the beginning and closing lines of the play, even though Cicero at one time believes that the truth about the plot exceeds "All insolent fictions of the tragic scene" (III.ii.25). Catiline too is dismissive of theatricality ("an Herculean actor in the scene," III.i.99). Cethegus wishes to act instead of remaining like "calm, benumb'd spectators" (I.404), and takes Cicero up on the plot as intending a "spectacle" of carnage as though it were a theatrical spectacle that he meant: "Ay, and it would/ Have been a brave one, Consul. But your part/ Had not then been so long as now it is:/ I should have quite defeated your oration/ . . . I'the first scene" (V.iv.170–175). But theater symbolizes more than a surrogate for reality: it is positively a false reality. Catiline characterizes the changeable disguises of the conspirators as "a visor chang'd,/ Or the scene shifted in our theaters" (I.184–185), a connection Curius also makes when he seeks to "pluck/ The tragic visor off" (II.277–278). "Visor" is usually a disguise in the play ("Where is thy visor," V.iv.102; "Rather a visor than a face," II.63), although for Catiline it is also a protection as well as a disguise ("It is a visor that hath poison'd me," III.i.171). Yet the redeeming detail of Cicero's remark, "insolent *fictions* of the tragic scene," hints that this tragic scene is not a fiction because it is not something feigned or pretended but attends to sober fact, and Jonson's play can contain and even implement such comments by virtue of the strength its very historicity lends it.

Catiline foresees his monstrosity in a passage in which he terms himself one of Rome's "brood" (I.88), and he continues the image of Rome as a mother undergoing gang rape (I.348–349) and painful birth (I.279). Cicero, on the other hand, views "mother Rome" optimistically: "our common mother," "a thankful and a bounteous mother" (III.ii.132 and 197), and even the nervous Chorus sees her worst fate as abandonment (III.v.56). The differing points of view arise from a difference marked by the deviant violence of Catiline's sexuality and the honest fatherhood of Cicero, already noted. Catiline extends his view in offering a range of sexual experience to the conspirators (I.476, 505 ff., 171) and by sharing with Cethegus a view of wives as the instruments of betrayal (III.iii.238, IV.v.19 ff.) instead of loyalty. All of Act II concerns itself with whores as commentators on the state, manipulators of the state, and indeed as alternative symbols of the body politic in just the way that the Act I Chorus would predict (perhaps with a play on "Commonwealth"); and so it is that both Catiline and Cicero share the notion that their ends will be served, though unworthily, by attaching the loyalties of whores. Yet whores are the very types of waywardness, of fragile loyalty: "the whore Fortune" exclaims the thwarted Cethegus (V.viii.9). Throughout the play, sexual imagery and sexual action distinguish the points of view of the disordering conspirators and the creative Ciceronians, and posit Jonson's own view of the relationship of family to state both as a constituent part and as a microcosm.

The four great clusters of images in the play concern four great topics of human activity and decision: darkness and light, sleeping and waking, concern those of perception and responsibility; the rebellion against the gods, those of authority and obedience; theater and disguise, those of appearance and reality; sexual deviation and normality, those of destruction and procreation. That these were also the central issues in the Catilinarian conspiracy, and in historians' views of it, validates the choice of the figures, their interaction with the plot, and Jonson's employment of them and the story to project his own intellectual preoccupations. Moreover, the sets are all, in one way or another, made up of polarities or oppositions. In their organization of the historical materials lie the unequivocated absolutes missing in the natural backdrop and behavioral patterns of the play and in the unstable resolution at the end. The artifact informs the historical fable with the essential visionary (ideal and imagistic) center. Jonson is saying, among many other things, that the poet and his art are necessary to history to prevent its being over-literal and over-particular, limited to the facts of an actual human life; but he is able to hold this outlook without relaxing "truth of argument," and to maintain the precious integrity of both kinds of truth in a single poem.

If the opening and closing lines of the poem define a frame in both form and content, we may ask whether any other formal feature of the play is similarly put to use. Our attention must fall on the Chorus, the only device of theatricality similar to the Prologue and the recital of the *nuntius*; and on the apparent imperfection in the lack of a Chorus to end Act V. Yet even this imperfection disappears, and the structural function of the Chorus becomes clear, if we consider the Choruses as the internal structural transitions just as the Prologue and *nuntius* are the external structural frame. Once again Jonson has taken over a device of the classical drama, for the Senecan drama likewise conventionally omitted the Chorus at the end of the last Act, but its contribution to the structural unity of his play is the consequence of the unique use he has made of it, not of his fidelity to any received theatrical convention.

In the roles of the principal characters, too, there is substantial but incomplete structural symmetry. Catiline and Cicero, oratorical opponents, vie to dominate the fate of Rome. Each has a rash lieutenant in Cethegus and Cato respectively, and these two in turn bear a special enmity toward each other. The whores, one in each party, are also competitors between themselves; each is moreover a trivialized counterfoil to the opposing leader, for Sempronia reckons herself an orator and Greek scholar to compare to Cicero, and Fulvia has Catiline's desire for sex and money, his contempt for the Senate, and competes with him for the loyalty of Curius. In each set the Catilinarian half is the weaker, the more errant, the doomed. Once again, as in the imagery and the five-act structure, this aspect of the play is one wholly of Jonson's creation, and it shows that the alleged defect of the dual plot is in fact a master stroke, part of a greater and perfectly articulated unity.

The moral imperatives, the constant political viewpoint, the purposeful characterization, the significant figurative language, the unity of design that critics have missed in their attention to the handling of tragedy and history in *Catiline*, are present instead in the overall integration of metaphor and action with intellectual concern, in the five-act structure, and in the complementarity of the principal characters, in patterns and processes largely the same in all three categories: that is, language and action, structure, and character all spring from a rigorous intellectual perception of opposites which between them make up totalities. This level of organization in Jonson's play, at once the most fundamental and the highest, is also the most original and expressive of the greatest imaginative power. Yet it goes beyond the expression of this power; it asserts the transcendental unity of the historian's private study with the poet's public stage in the preservation of civilized life.[8]

DATE AND TEXT

The first edition of *Catiline* was the quarto (Q) which bears the date 1611 on its title page, the year which the folio of 1616 (F1) gives as that of the first performance. There is no entry for Q in the Stationers' Register.

In common with many other first quartos by Jonson, Q underwent considerable correction at his hand during the course of printing. By far the largest part of these press corrections is of punctuation and capitalization, and those do not figure in the textual apparatus of the present edition. Herford and Simpson did not make a thorough survey of the press corrections in Q, nor has one been made for this edition; but a new collation of two copies has shown one further substantive

[8] A different view is that of Angela G. Dorenkamp, "Jonson's *Catiline*: History as the Trying Faculty," *Studies in Philology*, LXVII (1970), 210–220.

variant (III.i.214) that was restricted to the original, uncorrected state of Q (Q(o)).

The next edition was that of the 1616 collected *Workes* (F1) of Jonson, also prepared and printed under his supervision. A corrected copy of Q, with further manuscript alterations, was used for the printer's copy. F1 appears to have undergone no authorial press corrections in *Catiline*, although there were many in other plays in the volume, including *Sejanus*. A very few copies have a variant state of 3R3.4^v, i.e., pages 749 and 752; this involved a complete resetting of the forme but resulted in no substantive and very few accidental variants, sure evidence that it was carried out for the printer's convenience, perhaps to remedy some accident to the forme or to provide for the perfection of some overlooked sheets. Even fewer copies have a variant title page, the result of the resetting of 3L3.4. Ten copies of F1 were collated for this edition.

Two years before Jonson's death in 1637 appeared a second quarto set from Q and not from F1, a pirated edition without his authority or supervision, to judge by its many omissions and other blunders; it has no place in the textual transmission and the present edition ignores it. The second folio (F2) of 1640 included *Catiline* in its first volume. It provides almost no improvements over F1: it adds a host of minor misprints, and it shows a "modernity" of spelling that is most un-Jonsonian. Its improvements at I.297, II.57, III.iii.131, IV.v.58, V.iv.225, and perhaps IV.ii.180, are to be seen in the context of its many failures to cope with the text of F1, and particularly to deal with outstanding textual problems or to understand its metrical practices. A new collation of ten copies of F2 for this edition has added a dozen substantive variants from F1 to those traced by Herford and Simpson, and revealed a number of press corrections.

Substantive variants are the only ones recorded in the textual apparatus of this edition, which thus excludes variants of spelling, typography, punctuation, and (except where, as e.g. at I.340, it offers a real alternative reading) word-spacing, as it does also literal errors, turned letters, and failures to print. When Jonson wrote an extra syllable that he wanted actors to retain, he put an apostrophe between any adjacent vowels in consecutive words in that line to prevent elision. We have omitted this mark from our text. In modernizing the spelling, we have made Jonson's *loose* into "loose" or "lose" and his *counsell* into "counsel" or "council" as appropriate and without note.

Jonson's entry stage directions spell out the characters' names in full, but his speech prefixes usually give only the first three letters:

thus if the entry stage direction tells us that two or three of these characters are on stage at once, the speech prefix "CAT." may be ambiguous. Jonson often avoided the problem by using the speech prefixes "CATI.," "CATV.," or "CATO" in these circumstances, but not always. F1 is much more careful about this problem than was Q, and F2 is a slight improvement on F1. We have indicated the presence of the problem only as it arises in F1, without reference to Q or F2, and only when the entry stage directions show that the speech prefix "CAT." is ambiguous. Jonson's lists of characters at the beginning of a scene are not strictly entrances; rather they include everyone who will speak in that scene. Such lists almost always begin with the name of the character who has the first speech, and the name does not introduce the speech itself. We have silently supplied these speech prefixes. (Jonson's spelling of names, while not always strictly classical, has been retained throughout.)

We have broken the acts into scenes as the action requires, although it may be that V.vi–ix were meant to be played continuously; if so that is a theatrical solution to the demands of the action, not an alteration to them, and we have thought it best to let the present somewhat fragmentary arrangement stand rather than to predetermine what a director of the play might wish to make of it. We have also rearranged Jonson's block entries by addition, subtraction, and paraphrase, but in each case the original form of the stage direction is recorded in the textual notes.

In this century *Catiline* has been edited by L. H. Harris (Yale Studies in English, LIII, 1916) and in the Oxford *Ben Jonson*, ed. C. H. Herford and Percy and Evelyn Simpson (vol. V, 1937). Both give very full commentary, including extensive quotations from the sources (in Herford and Simpson, vol. X, 1950). We have made use of these selectively, but the serious student will want to refer to them for himself. We have also taken note of the editions by P. Whalley (London, 1756), W. Gifford (London, 1816), and F. Cunningham (London, 1875).

We have benefited from the help of many colleagues, among whom we should especially wish to name Dr. E. M. Brennan, Professor Johan Gerritsen, Professor D. J. Gordon, and Mr. Paul M. Smith.

W. F. Bolton, *Douglass College, Rutgers University*
Jane F. Gardner, *University of Reading*

CATILINE

To the Great Example of Honor and Virtue, The Most Noble William, Earl of Pembroke, Lord Chamberlain, etc.

MY LORD,

In so thick and dark an ignorance as now almost covers the age, I crave leave to stand near your light and by that to be read. Posterity may pay your benefit the honor and thanks, when it shall know that you dare, in these jig-given times, 5 to countenance a legitimate poem. I must call it so against all noise of opinion, from whose crude and airy reports I appeal to that great and singular faculty of judgment in your Lordship, able to vindicate truth from error. It is the first of this race that ever I dedicated to any person, and had I not 10 thought it the best, it should have been taught a less ambition. Now it approacheth your censure cheerfully and with the same assurance that innocency would appear before a magistrate.

Your Lordship's most faithful honorer, 15

BEN JONSON

Lord Chamberlain] *Ff*; *om. Q.*

William, Earl of Pembroke] Jonson's friend and benefactor, who gave him £20 a year to buy books (*Conversations*, xiii. 312–313) and whom Jonson eulogized in *Epigram* cii, mentioned in *The Gypsies Metamorphosed*, and made the dedicatee of the *Epigrams*.

5. *jig-given*] devoted to light entertainments with songs and dances.

7. *opinion*] majority view.

7. *airy*] insubstantial.

9. *vindicate*] set free.

9. *first*] *Sejanus* (1603), also of the tragic "race," violated the unity of time and lacked a Chorus; nor was there a dedication in the quarto edition.

11. *less*] smaller.

12. *censure*] judgment.

14. *magistrate*] main official with governmental powers over a large political body.

To the Reader in Ordinary

The Muses forbid, that I should restrain your meddling, whom I see already busy with the title, and tricking over the leaves: it is your own, I departed with my right when I let it first abroad. And now so secure an interpreter I am of my chance, that neither praise nor dispraise from you can   5
affect me. Though you commend the two first acts with the people, because they are the worst, and dislike the oration of Cicero, in regard you read some pieces of it at school and understand them not yet, I shall find the way to forgive you. Be anything you will be, at your own charge. Would I had   10
deserv'd but half so well of it in translation as that ought to deserve of you in judgment, if you have any. I know you will pretend (whosoever you are) to have that, and more. But all pretenses are not just claims. The commendation of good things may fall within a many, their approbation but in a   15
few; for the most commend out of affection, self-tickling, an easiness, or imitation, but men judge only out of knowledge. That is the trying faculty. And to those works that will bear a judge, nothing is more dangerous than a foolish praise. You will say I shall not have yours, therefore, but rather the con-   20
trary all vexation of censure. If I were not above such moles-
tations now, I had great cause to think unworthily of my studies, or they had so of me. But I leave you to your exercise. Begin.

0.1–28. To the Reader . . . Jonson]
Q; om. Ff. Following this, Q adds
commendatory verses by Francis Beaumont, John Fletcher and Nathan Field,
*of which the one by Beaumont is re-
printed at the beginning of the 1616 folio
volume (F1) but not in connection with
the text of* Catiline.

2. *title*] title page.
2. *tricking*] flipping.
4–5. *secure . . . chance*] confident a judge of my reward.
8. *in regard*] because.
10. *charge*] responsibility.
11. *that*] i.e., the original oration.
13. *that*] i.e., judgment.
16. *affection*] affectation.
16. *tickling*] pleasing.
18. *trying faculty*] capacity for judgment.
22–23. *I had . . . me*] I would have had . . . or they would have had from me.

To the Reader Extraordinary

You I would understand to be the better man, though places   25
in court go otherwise; to you I submit myself and work.
Farewell.

BEN JONSON

THE PERSONS OF THE PLAY

Ghost [of Lucius Cornelius] Sylla [, *sometime dictator of Rome*]

[Lucius Sergius] Catiline [, *a Senator, the archconspirator*]

[Publius Cornelius] Lentulus [Sura, *a disgraced Senator, in the conspiracy*]

[Caius Cornelius] Cethegus [, *a young Senator, in the conspiracy*]   5

[Quintus] Curius [, *a disgraced Senator, in the conspiracy*]

[Publius] Autronius [Paetus, *a Senator, in the conspiracy*]

[Lucius] Vargunteius [, *a Senator, in the conspiracy*]

[Lucius Cassius] Longinus [, *a Senator, in the conspiracy*]

[Marcus Porcius] Lecca [, *a Senator, in the conspiracy*]   10

[Marcus] Fulvius [Nobilior, *a conspirator of equestrian rank*]

[Lucius Calpurnius] Bestia [, *a Senator, in the conspiracy*]

[Publius] Gabinius [Capito, *a conspirator of equestrian rank*]

[Lucius] Statilius [, *a conspirator of equestrian rank*]

[Marcus] Ceparius [, *a supporter of Catiline*]   15

[Caius] Cornelius [, *a conspirator of equestrian rank*]

[Titus] Volturtius [, *a supporter of Catiline*]

Aurelia [Orestilla, *wife to Catiline*]

Fulvia [, *a woman of rank, mistress to Curius*]

Sempronia [, *a learned noblewoman, in the conspiracy*]   20

Galla [, *a slave-girl, servant to Fulvia*]

[Marcus Tullius] Cicero [, *Consul-elect and later Consul*]

[Caius] Antonius [Hybrida, *Consul with Cicero*]

[Marcus Porcius] Cato [, *a righteous Senator*]

[Quintus Lutatius] Catulus [, *an elderly Senator*]   25

[Marcus Licinius] Crassus [, *a wealthy Senator, associate of Caesar*]

[Caius Julius] Caesar [, *a Praetor-elect*]

Qu[intus Tullius] Cicero [, *brother to M. Tullius Cicero*]

[Decimus Junius] Syllanus [, *Consul-elect*]

[Lucius Valerius] Flaccus [, *Praetor*]   30

[Caius] Pomtinius [, *Praetor*]

[Quintus Fabius] Sanga [, *a Senator, patron of the Allobroges*]

Senators

Allobroges [, *tribesmen from Gaul*]

[Marcus] Petreius [, *an officer*]   35

0.1. THE PERSONS OF THE PLAY] *Ff*; The names of the Actors *Q*.   1. Ghost ... Sylla] *this edn.*; SYLLA'S GHOST *Q, Ff*.

SOLDIERS
[TRIBUNES]
[GUARDS]
PORTER
LICTORS   40
SERVANTS
PAGES
CHORUS

The Scene, *Rome*

44. The Scene, *Rome*] *Ff*; *om. Q*.

Catiline His Conspiracy

—*His non plebecula gaudet,*
Verum equitis quoque jam migravit ab aure voluptas
Omnis ad incertos oculos et gaudia vana.

Horat.

[I]   [*Enter*] Sylla's Ghost.

SYLLA'S GHOST.

Dost thou not feel me, Rome? Not yet? Is night
So heavy on thee, and my weight so light?
Can Sylla's ghost arise within thy walls
Less threat'ning than an earthquake, the quick falls
Of thee and thine? Shake not the frighted heads   5
Of thy steep towers, or shrink to their first beds,
Or, as their ruin the large Tiber fills,
Make that swell up and drown thy seven proud hills?
What sleep is this doth seize thee, so like death
And is not it? Wake, feel her in my breath;   10
Behold, I come, sent from the Stygian sound
As a dire vapor that had cleft the ground
T'engender with the night and blast the day,
Or like a pestilence that should display
Infection through the world, which thus I do.   15

Discovers Catiline *in his study.*

Pluto be at thy counsels, and into
Thy darker bosom enter Sylla's spirit:

15.1. *F1*; *om. Q*; *opp. l. 14, F2*.

His . . . Horat.] "The rabble does not enjoy these, and the whole pleasure
of the gentry has now transferred itself from the ear to transient shows and
empty delight" (Horace *Epist.* 2. 1. 186–188, reading *nam* for *non*). Jonson,
altering his source, refers to the progress up the social scale of the preference
for jigs and similar productions.
   6. *steep*] lofty.
   7. *ruin*] collapse.
   14. *display*] spread.
   15.1. *Discovers*] reveals.

–9–

All that was mine, and bad, thy breast inherit.
Alas, how weak is that for Catiline!
Did I but say—vain voice!—all that was mine?   20
All that the Gracchi, Cinna, Marius would;
What now, had I a body again, I could,
Coming from hell; what fiends would wish should be,
And Hannibal could not have wish'd to see;
Think thou, and practice. Let the long-hid seeds   25
Of treason in thee now shoot forth in deeds
Ranker than horror, and thy former facts
Not fall in mention, but to urge new acts.
Conscience of them provoke thee on to more.
Be still thy incests, murders, rapes before   30
Thy sense: thy forcing first a Vestal nun;
Thy parricide, late, on thine own only son,
After his mother, to make empty way
For thy last wicked nuptials; worse than they
That blaze, that act of thy incestuous life   35
Which got thee at once a daughter and a wife.
I leave the slaughters that thou didst for me
Of Senators, for which I hid for thee
Thy murder of thy brother, being so brib'd,
And writ him in the list of my proscrib'd   40
After thy fact, to save thy little shame;
Thy incest with thy sister, I not name.
These are too light. Fate will have thee pursue
Deeds after which no mischief can be new,

32. thine] *Q, F1*; thy *F2*.   35. blaze] *Ff*; fame *Q*.
32. only] *Ff*; naturall *Q*.

---

25. *practice*] carry out.
27. *facts*] crimes.
28. *fall in mention*] be mentioned (Lat. *in mentionem incidere*).
28. *but*] except.
29. *Conscience*] consciousness.
30–31. *Be . . . sense*] let . . . remain in your awareness.
31. *forcing*] raping.
31. *Vestal nun*] Cicero's wife's sister, according to Asconius 82.
32. *parricide*] murder of a close relative (not necessarily a father).
35. *blaze*] flagrant crime.
37. *leave*] pass over.
38. *Senators*] The ancient sources specify only *equites*, knights.
44. *mischief*] cause of evil.

The ruin of thy country; thou wert built   45
For such a work, and born for no less guilt.
What though defeated once th'hast been, and known,
Tempt it again: that is thy act, or none.
What all the several ills that visit earth,
Brought forth by night with a sinister birth,   50
Plagues, famine, fire could not reach unto,
The sword, nor surfeits, let thy fury do:
Make all past, present, future ill thine own,
And conquer all example in thy one,
Nor let thy thought find any vacant time   55
To hate an old, but still a fresher crime
Drown the remembrance; let not mischief cease
But while it is in punishing, increase.
Conscience and care die in thee, and be free
Not heav'n itself from thy impiety.   60
Let night grow blacker with thy plots, and day,
At showing but thy head forth, start away
From this half-sphere, and leave Rome's blinded walls
T'embrace lusts, hatreds, slaughters, funerals,
And not recover sight till their own flames   65
Do light them to their ruins. All the names
Of thy confederates, too, be no less great
In hell than here, that when we would repeat
Our strengths in muster, we may name you all,
And Furies upon you, for Furies, call;   70
Whilst what you do may strike them into fears,
Or make them grieve and wish your mischief theirs.   [*Exit.*]

CATILINE.

It is decreed. Nor shall thy fate, O Rome,
Resist my vow. Though hills were set on hills
And seas met seas to guard thee, I would through;   75
Ay, plow up rocks steep as the Alps, in dust,

71. may] *Ff*; doth *Q*.   72. S.D.] *Gifford*.

47. *defeated*] in the alleged conspiracy of 66/65 B.C.
47. *known*] discovered.
48. *Tempt*] attempt.
54. *conquer all example*] outdo all similar deeds.
60. *impiety*] lack of dutiful attitude.
73. *decreed*] decided (Lat. *decerno*).
75. *through*] win through.

And lave the Tyrrhene waters into clouds,
But I would reach thy head, thy head, proud city.
The ills that I have done cannot be safe
But by attempting greater, and I feel   80
A spirit within me chides my sluggish hands
And says they have been innocent too long.
Was I a man bred great as Rome herself,
One form'd for all her honors, all her glories,
Equal to all her titles, that could stand   85
Close up with Atlas, and sustain her name
As strong as he doth heav'n? And was I
Of all her brood mark'd out for the repulse
By her no-voice when I stood candidate
To be commander in the Pontic war?   90
I will hereafter call her step-dame ever.
If she can lose her nature, I can lose
My piety, and in her stony entrails
Dig me a seat where I will live again
The labor of her womb, and be a burden   95
Weightier than all the prodigies and monsters
That she hath teem'd with since she first knew Mars.

[Enter] Aurelia.

Who's there?

AURELIA.   'Tis I.

CATILINE.   Aurelia?

AURELIA.   Yes.

CATILINE.   Appear,
And break like day, my beauty, to this circle;
Upbraid thy Phoebus that he is so long   100

87. heav'n] *Q*, *F1*; Heaven *F2*.   98. S.P. CATILINE. Appear] *Ff*;
97.1.] *Gifford*; CATILINE, AV-   AVR. Appeare *Q*.
RELIA *Q*, *Ff*.

---

77. *lave*] dip up.
81. *chides*] that chides (the omission of the relative "that" is very common
in the play).
82. *innocent*] not giving harm.
88. *repulse*] "defeat in an election" (H & S).
89. *no-voice*] rejection.
91. *step-dame*] stepmother, hence not a true mother.
99. *circle*] orb, world.

In mounting to that point which should give thee
Thy proper splendor. Wherefore frowns my sweet?
Have I too long been absent from these lips,
This cheek, these eyes?   *He kisseth them.*
               What is my trespass? Speak.

AURELIA.

    It seems you know, that can accuse yourself.   105

CATILINE.

    I will redeem it.

AURELIA.   Still, you say so. When?

CATILINE.

    When Orestilla, by her bearing well
These my retirements and stol'n times for thought,
Shall give their effects leave to call her queen
Of all the world, in place of humbled Rome.   110

AURELIA.

    You court me now.

CATILINE.   As I would always, love,
By this ambrosiac kiss, and this of nectar,
Wouldst thou but hear as gladly as I speak.
(Could my Aurelia think I meant her less
When, wooing her, I first remov'd a wife   115
And then a son to make my bed and house
Spacious and fit t'embrace her?)These were deeds
Not t'have begun with, but to end with more
And greater: he that, building, stays at one
Floor, or the second, hath erected none.   120
'Twas how to raise thee, I was meditating;
To make some act of mine answer thy love,
That love that, when my state was now quite sunk,
Came with thy wealth and weigh'd it up again,
And made my emergent fortune once more look   125
Above the main, which now shall hit the stars

104. S.D.] *Ff*; *om. Q.*

101. *point*] summit.
113. *Wouldst thou but*] if you would only.
124. *weigh'd*] raised.
125. *emergent*] arising, especially from the sea (opposite of "submerging").
126. *main*] high sea.

And stick my Orestilla there amongst 'em,
If any tempest can but make the billow,
And any billow can but lift her greatness.
But I must pray my love she will put on   130
Like habits with myself. I have to do
With many men and many natures: some
That must be blown and sooth'd, as Lentulus,
Whom I have heav'd with magnifying his blood
And a vain dream out of the sibyl's books   135
That a third man of that great family
Whereof he is descended, the Cornelii,
Should be a king in Rome, which I have hir'd
The flatt'ring augurs to interpret him,
Cinna and Sylla dead; then bold Cethegus,   140
Whose valor I have turn'd into his poison
And prais'd so into daring as he would
Go on upon the gods, kiss lightning, wrest
The engine from the Cyclops, and give fire
At face of a full cloud, and stand his ire   145
When I would bid him move; others there are,
Whom envy to the state draws and puts on
For contumelies receiv'd, and such are sure ones,
As Curius and the forenam'd Lentulus,
Both which have been degraded in the Senate   150
And must have their disgraces still new rub'd
To make 'em smart, and labor of revenge;
Others whom mere ambition fires, and dole
Of provinces abroad which they have feign'd

139. flatt'ring] *Q, F1*; flattering *F2*.

---

134. *magnifying his blood*] exaggerating his noble lineage.
140. *dead*] being dead.
143. *Go on*] make an attack.
144. *engine*] thunderbolt (manufactured by Cyclops for Jove).
144–145. *give . . . of*] discharge a missile straight against.
145. *stand his ire*] withstand its rage.
147. *envy . . . on*] malice (Lat. *invidia*) . . . attracts and incites.
150. *degraded . . . Senate*] expelled from the Senate for immorality; sixty-four members, including these two and Antonius (Consul 63 B.C.), were expelled by the Censors of 70 B.C.
153. *dole*] allotted share.
154. *feign'd*] shaped (Lat. *fingo*).

To their crude hopes, and I as amply promis'd: 155
These, Lecca, Vargunteius, Bestia, Autronius;
Some whom their wants oppress, as th'idle captains
Of Sylla's troops, and divers Roman knights,
The profuse wasters of their patrimonies,
So threaten'd with their debts as they will now   160
Run any desperate fortune for a change.
These for a time we must relieve, Aurelia,
And make our house the safeguard; like for those
That fear the law or stand within her grip
For any act past or to come. Such will   165
From their own crimes be factious, as from ours.
Some more there be, slight airlings, will be won
With dogs and horses or perhaps a whore,
Which must be had; and if they venture lives
For us, Aurelia, we must hazard honors   170
A little. Get thee store and change of women
As I have boys, and give 'em time and place
And all connivance; be thyself too, courtly,
And entertain, and feast, sit up, and revel;
Call all the great, the fair and spirited dames   175
Of Rome about thee, and begin a fashion
Of freedom and community. Some will thank thee
Though the sour Senate frown, whose heads must ache
In fear and feeling too. We must not spare
Or cost or modesty. It can but show   180
Like one of Juno's or of Jove's disguises
In either thee or me, and will as soon
When things succeed be thrown by or let fall

---

160. their] Q, Ff; om. Q(o).   163. the] Ff; their Q.

---

155. *crude*] premature.
161. *Run . . . fortune*] take any risk.
166. *From . . . factious*] be seditious because of their own criminal records.
167. *airlings*] rash youngsters.
171. *store and change*] quantity and variety.
174. *sit up*] stay up late.
177. *community*] social intercourse.
179. *feeling*] presentiment.
180. *Or . . . or*] either . . . or.

As is a veil put off, a visor chang'd,
Or the scene shifted in our theaters— 185

A noise without.

Who's that? It is the voice of Lentulus.
AURELIA.
    Or of Cethegus.
CATILINE.   In, my fair Aurelia,
    And think upon these arts. They must not see
    How far you are trusted with these privacies
    Though on their shoulders, necks, and heads you rise. 190
                                  [*Exit* Aurelia.]

[Enter] Lentulus, Cethegus.

LENTULUS.
    It is, methinks, a morning full of fate!
    It riseth slowly, as her sullen car
    Had all the weights of sleep and death hung at it.
    She is not rosy-finger'd, but swoll'n black.
    Her face is like a water turn'd to blood 195
    And her sick head is bound about with clouds
    As if she threaten'd night ere noon of day.
    It does not look as it would have a hail
    Or health wish'd in it as on other morns.
CETHEGUS.
    Why, all the fitter, Lentulus; our coming 200
    Is not for salutation, we have business.
CATILINE.
    Said nobly, brave Cethegus. Where's Autronius?
CETHEGUS.
    Is he not come?
CATILINE   Not here.
CETHEGUS.   Nor Vargunteius?
CATILINE.
    Neither.

185.1.] *Ff*; *om. Q*.
190. on] *Ff*; by *Q*.
190.1.] *Gifford*.

190.2.] *Gifford*; LENTVLVS, CE-
THEGVS, CATILINE. *Q, Ff*.

184. *visor*] mask.
185. *scene*] place of dramatic action.
188. *arts*] artful plans.
192. *sullen car*] slow chariot.

CETHEGUS.   A fire in their beds and bosoms
    That so will serve their sloth rather than virtue.   205
    They are no Romans, and at such high need
    As now.
LENTULUS.   Both they, Longinus, Lecca, Curius,
    Fulvius, Gabinius, gave me word last night
    By Lucius Bestia, they would all be here,
    And early.
CETHEGUS.   Yes? As you, had I not call'd you.   210
    Come, we all sleep and are mere dormice, flies
    A little less than dead; more dullness hangs
    On us than on the morn. W'are spirit-bound
    In ribs of ice, our whole bloods are one stone,
    And honor cannot thaw us, nor our wants,   215
    Though they burn hot as fevers to our states.
CATILINE.
    I muse they would be tardy at an hour
    Of so great purpose.
CETHEGUS.   If the gods had call'd
    Them to a purpose, they would just have come
    With the same tortoise speed, that are thus slow   220
    To such an action, which the gods will envy
    As asking no less means than all their powers
    Conjoin'd, t'effect. I would have seen Rome burn'd
    By this time, and her ashes in an urn,
    The kingdom of the Senate rent asunder,   225
    And the degenerate talking gown run frighted
    Out of the air of Italy.
CATILINE.   Spirit of men!
    Thou heart of our great enterprise, how much
    I love these voices in thee!

---

204. *A fire*] let a fire be.
205. *virtue*] courage, manliness.
211. *dormice*] small rodents regarded as "sleepy" (French *dormeuse*).
214. *ribs*] bars.
216. *states*] conditions of being.
217. *muse*] wonder.
226. *degenerate . . . gown*] *degenerem . . . togam* (Lucan *Phars.* 1. 365). The toga was the formal dress of Roman citizens. *Talking* may refer to the Senate, or to forensic orators like Cicero (cf. Cicero *Off.* 1. 77, *cedant arma togae, concedat laurea linguae*).
229. *voices*] opinions.

CETHEGUS.   O the days
Of Sylla's sway, when the free sword took leave   230
To act all that it would!
CATILINE.   And was familiar
With entrails as our augurs!
CETHEGUS.   Sons kill'd fathers,
Brothers their brothers.
CATILINE.   And had price and praise.
All hate had license given it, all rage reins.
CETHEGUS.

Slaughter bestrid the streets and stretch'd himself   235
To seem more huge, whilst to his stained thighs
The gore he drew flow'd up and carried down
Whole heaps of limbs and bodies through his arch.
No age was spar'd, no sex.
CATILINE.   Nay, no degree.
CETHEGUS.

Not infants in the porch of life were free.   240
The sick, the old, that could but hope a day
Longer by nature's bounty, not let stay.
Virgins and widows, matrons, pregnant wives
All died.
CATILINE.   'Twas crime enough that they had lives.
To strike but only those that could do hurt   245
Was dull and poor. Some fell to make the number,
As some the prey.
CETHEGUS.   The rugged Charon fainted
And ask'd a navy, rather than a boat,
To ferry over the sad world that came;
The maws and dens of beasts could not receive   250
The bodies that those souls were frighted from,

---

233. *price*] reward.
234. *all rage reins*] all rage (was given) reins, i.e., allowed to run unchecked
(Lat. *dare frena*).
235. *bestrid*] straddled.
238. *arch*] i.e., made of his legs.
239. *degree*] rank in society.
240. *porch*] entrance.
247. *prey*] booty.
249. *sad*] heavy.

And e'en the graves were fill'd with men yet living
Whose flight and fear had mix'd them with the dead.

CATILINE.

    And this shall be again, and more and more,
    Now Lentulus, the third Cornelius,   255
    Is to stand up in Rome.

LENTULUS.   Nay, urge not that
    Is so uncertain.

CATILINE.   How!

LENTULUS.   I mean, not clear'd,
    And therefore not to be reflected on.

CATILINE.

    The Sibyl's leaves uncertain? Or the comments
    Of our grave, deep, divining men not clear?   260

LENTULUS.

    All prophecies, you know, suffer the torture.

CATILINE.

    But this already hath confess'd, without,
    And so been weigh'd, examin'd, and compar'd
    As 'twere malicious ignorance in him,
    Would faint in the belief.

LENTULUS.   Do you believe it?   265

CATILINE.

    Do I love Lentulus? Or pray to see it?

LENTULUS.

    The augurs all are constant, I am meant.

CATILINE.

    They had lost their science else.

LENTULUS.   They count from Cinna.

CATILINE.

    And Sylla next, and so make you the third;
    All that can say the sun is ris'n must think it.   270

LENTULUS.

    Men mark me more of late as I come forth.

---

   256. *stand up*] be eminent.
   257. *clear'd*] proven trustworthy.
   259. *leaves*] of books (anachronistically: Roman books were in rolls), or of trees, used for giving oracular responses.
   261. *suffer the torture*] undergo the test of truth; Roman slave witnesses were regularly tortured to ensure the truth of their evidence.

CATILINE.

 Why, what can they do less? Cinna and Sylla
 Are set and gone, and we must turn our eyes
 On him that is and shines. Noble Cethegus,
 But view him with me here: he looks already   275
 As if he shook a scepter o'er the Senate
 And the aw'd purple drop'd their rods and axes.
 The statues melt again, and household gods
 In groans confess the travail of the city;
 The very walls sweat blood before the change,   280
 And stones start out to ruin ere it comes.

CETHEGUS.

 But he and we and all are idle still.

LENTULUS.

 I am your creature, Sergius; and whate'er
 The great Cornelian name shall win to be,
 It is not augury, nor the Sibyls' books,   285
 But Catiline that makes it.

CATILINE.   I am shadow
 To honor'd Lentulus and Cethegus here,
 Who are the heirs of Mars.

CETHEGUS.   By Mars himself,
 Catiline is more my parent, for whose virtue
 Earth cannot make a shadow great enough,   290
 Though envy should come too. O, there they are.
 Now we shall talk more, though we yet do nothing.

[*Enter*] *to them* Autronius, Vargunteius, Longinus, Curius, Lecca,
Bestia, Fulvius, Gabinius [, Pages and Servants], *etc.*

AUTRONIUS.

 Hail, Lucius Catiline.

VARGUNTEIUS.   Hail, noble Sergius.

279. travail] *Q*, *F1*; travailes *F2*. 292.1. *to them*] *Ff*; *om. Q*.

---

 273. *set*] i.e., like the sun.

 277. *purple . . . axes*] Consuls dropped their symbols of office; rods signified
power to inflict corporal, axes capital, punishment (cf. I.359–360, below).

 278. *statues melt*] i.e., when struck by lightning, usually a bad omen (cf.
Cicero *3 Cat.* 19).

 284. *win to be*] succeed in becoming.

LONGINUS.

    Hail, Publius Lentulus.

CURIUS.   Hail, the third Cornelius.

LECCA.

    Caius Cethegus, hail.

CETHEGUS.   Hail sloth and words,   295
    Instead of men and spirits.

CATILINE.   Nay, dear Caius—

CETHEGUS.

    Are your eyes yet unseel'd? Dare they look day
    In the dull face?

CATILINE.   He's zealous for the affair,
    And blames your tardy coming, gentlemen.

CETHEGUS.

    Unless we had sold ourselves to sleep and ease   300
    And would be our slaves' slaves—

CATILINE.   Pray you forbear.

CETHEGUS.

    The north is not so stark and cold.

CATILINE.   Cethegus—

BESTIA.

    We shall redeem all, if your fire will let us.

CATILINE.

    You are too full of lightning, noble Caius.
    Boy, see all doors be shut, that none approach us   305
    On this part of the house. Go you and bid
    The priest he kill the slave I mark'd last night,
    And bring me of his blood when I shall call him;
    Till then, wait all without.   *[Exeunt Servants.]*

VARGUNTEIUS.   How is't, Autronius?

AUTRONIUS.

    Longinus?

LONGINUS.   Curius?

CURIUS.   Lecca?

VARGUNTEIUS.   Feel you nothing?   310

297. S.P. CETHEGUS] *Q*, *F2*; GET.   297. unseel'd] *Q*; vnsee'ld *Ff*.
F1.   309. S.D.] *Gifford*.

    297–298. *Are . . . face*] Are the stitches yet off your eyes (as of a falcon's
when his early training is over)? Do your eyes dare even so much as to look
at a dull (as opposed to dazzling) day?
    307. *mark'd*] designated.

LONGINUS.

    A strange, unwonted horror doth invade me;
    I know not what it is.

A darkness comes over the place.

LECCA.   The day goes back,
    Or else my senses.

CURIUS.   As at Atreus' feast.

FULVIUS.

    Darkness grows more and more.

LENTULUS.   The Vestal flame,
    I think, be out.

A groan of many people is heard underground.

GABINIUS.   What groan was that?

CETHEGUS.   Our fant'sy's.   315
    Strike fire out of ourselves, and force a day.

Another [groan].

AUTRONIUS.

    Again it sounds.

BESTIA.   As all the city gave it.

CETHEGUS.

    We fear what ourselves feign.

A fiery light appears.

VARGUNTEIUS.   What light is this?

CURIUS.

    Look forth.

LENTULUS.   It still grows greater.

LECCA.   From whence comes it?

312. S.D.] *F1*; *om. Q*; *opp. l. 313,*   316.1.] *F1*; *om. Q*; *opp. l. 318, F2.*
F2.   318. S.D.] *F1*; *om. Q*; *opp. l. 320,*
315. S.D.] *F1*; *om. Q*; *opp. l. 316,*   *F2.*
F2.

316. *Strike ... day*] kindle light from our own fieriness, and provide artificial daylight.
    317. *As*] as if.
    318. *feign*] imagine.
    319. *Look forth*] look out (the window).

LONGINUS.

    A bloody arm it is, that holds a pine   320
    Lighted above the Capitol. And now
    It waves unto us.

CATILINE.   Brave and ominous.

    Our enterprise is seal'd.

CETHEGUS.   In spite of darkness
    That would discountenance it. Look no more;
    We lose time and ourselves. To what we came for,   325
    Speak, Lucius, we attend you.

CATILINE.   Noblest Romans,
    If you were less, or that your faith and virtue
    Did not hold good that title with your blood,
    I should not now unprofitably spend
    Myself in words or catch at empty hopes,   330
    By airy ways, for solid certainties.
    But since in many and the greatest dangers
    I still have known you no less true than valiant,
    And that I taste in you the same affections
    To will or nill, to think things good or bad   335
    Alike with me, which argues your firm friendship,
    I dare the boldlier with you set on foot
    Or lead unto this great and goodliest action.
    What I have thought of it afore, you all
    Have heard apart. I then express'd my zeal   340
    Unto the glory; now, the need inflames me

340. apart] *Q, F1*; a part *F2.*

---

320. *pine*] pinewood torch.

322. *ominous*] full of omen.

323. *seal'd*] confirmed (as if by a seal).

324. *discountenance*] look with disfavor on.

326. *attend*] give attention to.

327–328. *that . . . blood*] if your loyalty and courage did not justify the name (of Romans) as your birth does.

330. *catch*] snatch.

331. *airy ways*] ineffective means.

333. *still*] always.

334. *affections*] propensities.

335. *will or nill*] want or not want.

336. *argues*] testifies to.

337. *set on foot*] investigate.

340. *apart*] individually.

When I forethink the hard conditions
Our states must undergo, except in time
We do redeem ourselves to liberty
And break the iron yoke forg'd for our necks.   345
For what less can we call it, when we see
The Commonwealth engross'd so by a few,
The giants of the state that do, by turns,
Enjoy her and defile her. All the earth,
Her kings and tetrarchs, are their tributaries;   350
People and nations pay them hourly stipends;
The riches of the world flows to their coffers,
And not to Rome's. While—but those few—the rest,
However great we are, honest, and valiant,
Are herded with the vulgar, and so kept   355
As we were only bred to consume corn,
Or wear out wool, to drink the city's water,
Ungrac'd, without authority or mark,
Trembling beneath their rods to whom, if all
Were well in Rome, we should come forth bright axes.   360
All places, honors, offices are theirs,
Or where they will confer 'em. They leave us
The dangers, the repulses, judgments, wants,
Which how long will you bear, most valiant spirits?
Were we not better to fall once with virtue   365
Than draw a wretched and dishonor'd breath,
To lose with shame, when these men's pride will laugh?
I call the faith of gods and men to question:
The power is in our hands; our bodies able;
Our minds as strong; o'th' contrary, in them,   370

357. out] *Q, F1*; our *F2.*

---

342. *forethink*] consider beforehand.
343. *except in time*] unless in due course.
347. *engross'd*] monopolized.
350. *tetrarchs . . . tributaries*] petty rulers (literally, rulers of the fourth part of a country) . . . subject rulers (who pay tribute to another ruler or state).
351. *stipends*] "taxes" (H & S).
355. *vulgar*] common people.
358. *Ungrac'd . . . mark*] unhonored . . . distinction.
361. *honors*] magistracies.
363. *dangers . . . judgments*] liabilities . . . decreed obligations.
368. *call . . . to question*] call . . . as witness.

All things grown aged with their wealth and years:
There wants but only to begin the business,
The issue is certain.
CETHEGUS. LONGINUS.   On, let us go on.
CURIUS. BESTIA.
   Go on, brave Sergius.
CATILINE.   It doth strike my soul
   (And who can 'scape the stroke that hath a soul   375
   Or but the smallest air of man within him?)
   To see them swell with treasure which they pour
   Out i'their riots, eating, drinking, building,
   Ay, i'the sea; planing of hills with valleys,
   And raising valleys above hills, whilst we   380
   Have not to give our bodies necessaries.
   They ha' their change of houses, manors, lordships,
   We scarce a fire or poor household Lar.
   They buy rare Attic statues, Tyrian hangings,
   Ephesian pictures and Corinthian plate,   385
   Attalic garments, and now new-found gems
   Since Pompey went for Asia, which they purchase
   At price of provinces. The river Phasis
   Cannot afford 'em fowl, nor Lucrine lake
   Oysters enow; Circei too is search'd   390
   To please the witty gluttony of a meal.
   Their ancient habitations they neglect
   And set up new; then, if the echo like not
   In such a room, they pluck down those, build newer,
   Alter them too, and by all frantic ways   395
   Vex their wild wealth as they molest the people
   From whom they force it. Yet they cannot tame

383. poor] *Q*, *F1*; a poore *F2*.   390. Circei] *Q*, *F1*; *Circes F2*.

---

383. *issue*] outcome.
376. *air*] breath.
379. *planing*] making level.
381. *Have . . . necessaries*] lack what we need to give the essentials to our
bodies.
390. *enow*] enough.
391. *witty*] ingenious.
393. *like*] please.
396. *Vex*] keep in constant use.

Or overcome their riches; not by making
Baths, orchards, fish-pools, letting in of seas
Here, and then there forcing 'em out again   400
With mountainous heaps for which the earth hath lost
Most of her ribs as entrails, being now
Wounded no less for marble than for gold.
We, all this while, like calm, benumb'd spectators
Sit till our seats do crack, and do not hear   405
The thund'ring ruins; whilst at home our wants,
Abroad our debts do urge us; our states daily
Bending to bad, our hopes to worse; and what
Is left but to be crush'd? Wake, wake, brave friends,
And meet the liberty you oft have wish'd for.   410
Behold renown, riches, and glory court you.
Fortune holds out these to you as rewards.
Methinks though I were dumb, th'affair itself,
The opportunity, your needs and dangers,
With the brave spoil the war brings, should invite you.   415
Use me your general or soldier; neither
My mind nor body shall be wanting to you,
And being Consul, I not doubt t'effect
All that you wish, if trust not flatter me,
And you'd not rather still be slaves than free.   420

CETHEGUS.

Free, free.

LONGINUS.   'Tis freedom.

CURIUS.   Freedom we all stand for.

CATILINE.

Why, these are noble voices. Nothing wants then,
But that we take a solemn sacrament
To strengthen our design.

CETHEGUS.   And so to act it.

Deferring hurts, where powers are so prepar'd.   425

420. you'd not] *Ff*; you had *Q*.   425. so] *Ff*; most *Q*.

---

407. *urge*] subject to pressure (Lat. *urgeo*).
408. *Bending*] tending.
415. *brave*] splendid.
416. *Use . . . soldier*] treat me as (Lat. *imperatore me utimini*) . . . one of the
ordinary rank and file.
423. *sacrament*] oath.

AUTRONIUS.

    Yet ere we enter into open act
    (With favor) 'twere no loss, if 't might be inquir'd
    What the condition of these arms would be?

VARGUNTEIUS.

    Ay, and the means to carry us through?

CATILINE.   How, friends!

    Think you that I would bid you grasp the wind   430
    Or call you to th'embracing of a cloud,
    Put your known valures on so dear a business,
    And have no other second than the danger,
    Nor other garland than the loss? Become
    Your own assurances, and, for the means,   435
    Consider first the stark security
    The Commonwealth is in now: the whole Senate
    Sleepy and dreaming no such violent blow;
    Their forces all abroad, of which the greatest
    That might annoy us most is farthest off   440
    In Asia, under Pompey; those nearhand
    Commanded by our friends, one army in Spain
    By Cneus Piso, th'other in Mauretania
    By Nucerinus, both which I have firm
    And fast unto our plot; myself, then, standing   445
    Now to be Consul with my hop'd colleague
    Caius Antonius, one no less engag'd
    By his wants than we, and whom I have power to melt
    And cast in any mold; beside, some others
    That will not yet be nam'd, both sure and great ones   450
    Who when the time comes shall declare themselves
    Strong for our party, so that no resistance
    In nature can be thought. For our reward, then,

---

427. *favor*] permission.

431. *embracing . . . cloud*] possibly an allusion to the story of Ixion, whose attempted seduction of Hera was baffled by the substitution of a cloud in her form.

432. *Put . . . on*] incite (as in a duel) your recognized worth in.

435. *assurances*] guarantees.

436. *stark security*] absolute lack of anxiety.

441. *nearhand*] nearby.

447. *engag'd*] committed.

453. *In nature*] anywhere.

First, all our debts are paid; dangers of law,
Actions, decrees, judgments against us quitted;   455
The rich men, as in Sylla's times, proscrib'd
And publication made of all their goods:
That house is yours; that land is his; those waters,
Orchards and walks a third's; he has that honor
And he that office; such a province falls   460
To Vargunteius; this to Autronius; that
To bold Cethegus; Rome to Lentulus.
You share the world, her magistracies, priesthoods,
Wealth and felicity amongst you, friends;
And Catiline your servant. Would you, Curius,   465
Revenge the contumely stuck upon you
In being removed from the Senate? Now,
Now is your time. Would Publius Lentulus
Strike for the like disgrace? Now is his time.
Would stout Longinus walk the streets of Rome   470
Facing the Praetor? Now has he a time
To spurn and tread the fasces into dirt
Made of the usurers' and the Lictors' brains.
Is there a beauty here in Rome you love,
An enemy you would kill? What head's not yours?   475
Whose wife, which boy, whose daughter, of what race,
That th' husband or glad parents shall not bring you
And boasting of the office? Only spare
Yourselves and you have all the earth beside,
A field to exercise your longings in.   480
I see you rais'd, and read your forward minds
High in your faces. Bring the wine and blood
You have prepar'd there.

[*Enter Servants with a bowl*]

LONGINUS.   How!

CATILINE.   I have kill'd a slave

482. in] *Ff*; i' *Q*.   483. S.D.] *Gifford*.

---

457. *publication*] "confiscation (Lat. *publicatio*)" (H & S).
470. *stout*] brave (but perhaps also with a play on "portly": *Cassii adipes*,
Cicero *3 Cat.* 7).
478. *office*] service.
481. *rais'd*] aroused.
482. *High*] eager.

⌈ And of his blood caus'd to be mix'd with wine.
  Fill every man his bowl. There cannot be   485
  A fitter drink to make this sanction in.
  Here I begin the sacrament to all. ⌉
  O for a clap of thunder now, as loud
  As to be heard throughout the universe
  To tell the world the fact and to applaud it.   490
  Be firm, my hand; not shed a drop, but pour
  Fierceness into me with it, and fell thirst
  Of more and more, till Rome be left as bloodless
  As ever her fears made her, or the sword.
  And when I leave to wish this to thee, stepdame,   495
  Or stop to effect it, with my powers fainting,
  So may my blood be drawn and so drunk up
  As is this slave's.
LONGINUS.   And so be mine.
LENTULUS.   And mine.

They drink.

AUTRONIUS.
  And mine.
VARGUNTEIUS. And mine.
CETHEGUS.   Swell me my bowl yet fuller.
  Here I do drink this as I would do Cato's,   500
  Or the new fellow Cicero's, with that vow
  Which Catiline hath given.
CURIUS.   So do I.
LECCA.
  And I.
BESTIA.   And I.
FULVIUS.   And I.
GABINIUS.   And all of us.

498.1.] *F1*; *om. Q*; *opp. l. 499, F2.*   499. Swell] *Ff*; Crowne *Q*.

---

486. *sanction*] oath.
492. *fell*] cruel.
499. *Swell*] fill.
501. *new fellow*] *novus homo*, the first of his family to attain to the senior
magistracies at Rome.

CATILINE.

Why, now's the business safe, and each man strengthen'd.

He spies one of his boys not answer.

Sirrah, what ail you?

PAGE.   Nothing.

BESTIA.   Somewhat modest.   505

CATILINE.

Slave, I will strike your soul out with my foot,

Let me but find you again with such a face,

You whelp—

BESTIA.   Nay, Lucius.

CATILINE.   Are you coying it

When I command you to be free and general

To all?

BESTIA.   You'll be observ'd.

CATILINE.   Arise, and show   510

But any least aversion i'your look

To him that boards you next, and your throat opens.

Noble confederates, thus far is perfect.

Only your suffrages I will expect

At the assembly for the choosing Consuls   515

And all the voices you can make by friends

To my election. Then let me work out

Your fortunes and mine own. Meanwhile, all rest

Seal'd up and silent as when rigid frosts

Have bound up brooks and rivers, forc'd wild beasts   520

Unto their caves and birds into the woods,

Clowns to their houses, and the country sleeps;

That when the sudden thaw comes, we may break

504.1.] *om. Q; opp. l. 508, F1; opp. l.
504, F2.*

---

504. *strengthen'd*] made sure of (Lat. *confirmatus*).
509. *general*] open.   512. *boards*] accosts.
513. *confederates*] allies.
515. *choosing*] choosing of.
516. *voices . . . by*] votes . . . from.
517. *work out*] achieve by resolving difficulties.
518. *all*] let all.
519. *rigid*] hard.
522. *Clowns*] countrymen.

Upon 'em like a deluge, bearing down
Half Rome before us, and invade the rest   525
With cries and noise able to wake the urns
Of those are dead, and make their ashes fear.
The horrors that do strike the world should come
Loud and unlook'd for: till they strike, be dumb.

CETHEGUS.

    Oraculous Sergius!

LENTULUS.   God-like Catiline!   [*Exeunt.*] 530

CHORUS.

        Can nothing great and at the height
        Remain so long, but its own weight
        Will ruin it? Or is't blind chance
        That still desires new states t'advance
        And quit the old? Else why must Rome   535
        Be by itself now overcome?
        Hath she not foes enow of those
        Whom she hath made such, and enclose
        Her round about? Or are they none
        Except she first become her own?   540
        O wretchedness of greatest states
        To be obnoxious to these fates,
        That cannot keep what they do gain,
        And what they raise so ill sustain!
        Rome now is mistress of the whole   545
        World, sea and land, to either pole,
        And even that fortune will destroy
        The power that made it: she doth joy
        So much in plenty, wealth, and ease,
        As now th'excess is her disease.   550
           She builds in gold, and to the stars,
        As if she threaten'd heav'n with wars,
        And seeks for hell in quarries deep
        Giving the fiends that there do keep

530. S.D.] *Gifford.*

---

524. *bearing*] thrusting.
530. *Oraculous*] oracular.
534. *new states t'advance*] to advance new states.
542. *obnoxious*] subjected.
554. *keep*] dwell.

A hope of day. Her women wear   555
The spoils of nations in an ear
Chang'd for the treasure of a shell,
And in their loose attires do swell
More light than sails when all winds play;
Yet are the men more loose than they,   560
More kemb'd and bath'd and rub'd and trim'd,
More sleek'd, more soft, and slacker limb'd,
As prostitute; so much that kind
May seek itself there and not find.
They eat on beds of silk and gold,   565
At ivory tables, or wood sold
Dearer than it, and leaving plate
Do drink in stone of higher rate.
They hunt all grounds and draw all seas,
Fowl every brook and bush to please   570
Their wanton tastes, and in request
Have new and rare things—not the best.
    Hence comes that wild and vast expense
That hath enforc'd Rome's virtue thence
Which simple poverty first made,   575
And now ambition doth invade
Her state with eating avarice,
Riot, and every other vice.
Decrees are bought and laws are sold,
Honors and offices for gold,   580
The people's voices; and the free
Tongues in the Senate bribed be.

---

557. *Chang'd*] exchanged.
558. *swell*] puff up.
560. *loose*] vain.
561. *kemb'd*] "combed" (H & S).
562. *sleek'd*] "smoothed" (H & S).
563. *kind*] nature.
566. *wood*] The wood of the *citrus* (North African cedar) was very expensive; particularly prized were tables with tops made from a single slice.
567–568. *leaving . . . rate*] setting aside cups of precious metal, use those more expensive ones made of jewels.
569. *draw*] fish in (with a net).
570. *Fowl*] hunt fowl.
571–572. *in request/ Have*] seek after (Lat. *requiro*; cf. French *recherché*).
574. *enforc'd*] compelled.

Such ruin of her manners Rome
Doth suffer now as she's become—
Without the gods it soon gainsay—   585
Both her own spoiler and own prey.
　So, Asia, art thou cru'lly even
With us for all the blows thee given,
When we whose virtue conquer'd thee
Thus by thy vices ruin'd be.   590

[II]　　　　　　　　[*Enter*] Fulvia, Galla, Servant.

FULVIA.

Those rooms do smell extremely. Bring my glass
And table hither. Galla.

GALLA.　　　　　　　　Madam.

FULVIA.　　　　　　　　　　　Look

Within i' my blue cabinet for the pearl
I had sent me last, and bring it.

GALLA.　　　　　　　　　　That from Clodius?

FULVIA.

From Caius Caesar. You are for Clodius still,   5
Or Curius.　　　　　　　　　　[*Exit* Galla.]

　　　　Sirrah, if Quintus Curius come,
I am not in fit mood, I keep my chamber;
Give warning so without.　　　　[*Exit* Servant.]

[*Re-enter* Galla.]

GALLA.　　　　　　　Is this it, madam?

FULVIA.

Yes, help to hang it in mine ear.

GALLA.　　　　　　　　　　Believe me,

It is a rich one, madam.

6, 8. S.D.] *Gifford.*　　　　　6. Sirrah] *F1*; Sitha *Q*; Sirrha *F2*.

583. *manners*] customs.
584. *now as*] now that.
585. *Without*] unless.
586. *spoiler*] despoiler.
[II]
　1. *glass*] mirror.
　8. *without*] outside.

FULVIA.   I hope so;   10
     It should not be worn there else. Make an end
     And bind my hair up.

GALLA.   As 'twas yesterday?

FULVIA.
     No, nor the t'other day. When knew you me
     Appear two days together in one dressing?

GALLA.
     Will you ha't i'the globe or spire?

FULVIA.   How thou wilt,   15
     Any way, so thou wilt do it, good impertinence.
     Thy company, if I slept not very well
     O' nights, would make me an arrant fool with questions.

GALLA.
     Alas, madam—

FULVIA.   Nay, gentle half o'the dialogue, cease.

GALLA.
     I do it indeed but for your exercise,   20
     As your physician bids me.

FULVIA.   How! Does he bid you
     To anger me for exercise?

GALLA.   Not to anger you,
     But stir your blood a little; there's difference
     Between lukewarm and boiling, madam.

FULVIA.   Jove!
     She means to cook me, I think. Pray you, ha' done.   25

GALLA.
     I mean to dress you, madam.

FULVIA.   O my Juno,
     Be friend to me! Off'ring at wit, too? Why, Galla,
     Where hast thou been?

GALLA.   Why, madam?

FULVIA.   What hast thou done
     With thy poor innocent self?

GALLA.   Wherefore, sweet madam?

---

11. *else*] otherwise.

15. *globe or spire*] "the hair plaited in circles and pinned behind the head
... a coil on top of the head" (H & S).

FULVIA.

    Thus to come forth so suddenly a wit-worm?   30

GALLA.

    It pleases you to flout one. I did dream

    Of lady Sempronia—

FULVIA.   O, the wonder is out.

    That did infect thee? Well, and how?

GALLA.   Methought

    She did discourse the best—

FULVIA.   That ever thou heard'st?

GALLA.

    Yes.

1755965

FULVIA. I'thy sleep? Of what was her discourse?   35

GALLA.

    O'the Republic, madam, and the state,

    And how she was in debt, and where she meant

    To raise fresh sums. She's a great stateswoman.

FULVIA.

    Thou dream'st all this?

GALLA.   No, but you know she is, madam,

    And both a mistress of the Latin tongue   40

    And of the Greek.

FULVIA.   Ay, but I never dream'd it, Galla,

    As thou hast done, and therefore you must pardon me.

GALLA.

    Indeed you mock me, madam.

FULVIA.   Indeed no.

    Forth with your learned lady. She has a wit, too?

GALLA.

    A very masculine one.

FULVIA.   A she-critic, Galla,   45

    And can compose in verse, and make quick jests,

    Modest or otherwise?

GALLA.   Yes, madam.

---

30. *wit-worm*] an emergent wit (like a caterpillar from the egg).

33. *Methought*] it seemed to me.

40–41. *And . . ./And*] both . . . and (here redundant).

44. *Forth with*] Say more about.

45. *masculine . . . she-critic*] vigorous . . . female judge of literature.

FULVIA.   She can sing, too,
      And play on instruments?
GALLA.   Of all kinds, they say.
FULVIA.
      And doth dance rarely?
GALLA.   Excellent! So well,
      As a bald Senator made a jest and said   50
      'Twas better than an honest woman need.
FULVIA.
      Tut, she may bear that. Few wise women's honesties
      Will do their courtship hurt.
GALLA.   She's liberal too, madam.
FULVIA.
      What, of her money or her honor, pray thee?
GALLA.
      Of both; you know not which she doth spare least.   55
FULVIA.
      A comely commendation.
GALLA.   Troth, 'tis pity
      She is in years.
FULVIA.   Why, Galla?
GALLA.   For it is.
FULVIA.
      O, is that all? I thought thou hadst had a reason.
GALLA.
      Why so I have. She has been a fine lady,
      And yet she dresses herself, except you, madam,   60
      One o' the best in Rome, and paints and hides
      Her decays very well.
FULVIA.   They say it is
      Rather a visor than a face she wears.
GALLA.
      They wrong her verily, madam, she does sleek
      With crumbs of bread and milk, and lies o' nights   65

54. pray] *Q, F1*; pr'y *F2*.   57. S.P. GALLA. For] *F2*; GAI. For
                                       Q; For *F1*.

---

49. *rarely*] excellently.
51. *honest*] chaste.
57. *in years*] aged.

In as neat gloves; but she is fain of late
To seek more than she's sought to, the fame is,
And so spends that way.

FULVIA.   Thou know'st all! But, Galla,
What say you to Catiline's lady, Orestilla?
There is the gallant!

GALLA.   She does well. She has   70
Very good suits and very rich, but then
She cannot put 'em on. She knows not how
To wear a garment. You shall have her all
Jewels and gold sometimes, so that her self
Appears the least part of herself. No, in troth,   75
As I live, madam, you put 'em all down
With your mere strength of judgment, and do draw, too,
The world of Rome to follow you; you attire
Yourself so diversly, and with that spirit,
Still to the noblest humors. They could make   80
Love to your dress although your face were away, they say.

FULVIA.
And body too, and ha' the better match on't,
Say they not so too, Galla?

                    [*Re-enter* Servant.]

                         Now, what news
Travails your count'nance with?

SERVANT.   If 't please you, madam,
The lady Sempronia is lighted at the gate.   85

GALLA.
Castor, my dream, my dream.

SERVANT.   And comes to see you.

78. follow you] *Q, F1*; follow *F2*.   83, 87. S.D.] *Gifford*.

---

66. *as*] very, "ever such."

67. *fame*] rumor (Lat. *fama*).

69. *to*] about.

76. *put . . . down*] excel.

77. *mere*] absolute.

80. *Still . . . humors*] always aiming to attract men of the most discriminating taste.

82. *match on't*] counterpart thereby.

GALLA.

    For Venus' sake, good madam, see her.   [*Exit* Servant.]

FULVIA.   Peace,

    The fool is wild, I think.

GALLA.   And hear her talk,

    Sweet madam, of state-matters and the Senate.

[Enter] Sempronia.

SEMPRONIA.

    Fulvia, good wench, how dost thou?

FULVIA.   Well, Sempronia.   90

    Whither are you thus early address'd?

SEMPRONIA.   To see

    Aurelia Orestilla. She sent for me.

    I came to call thee with me; wilt thou go?

FULVIA.

      I cannot now, in troth, I have some letters

      To write and send away.

SEMPRONIA.   Alas, I pity thee.   95

      I ha' been writing all this night (and am

      So very weary) unto all the tribes

      And centuries for their voices to help Catiline

      In his election. We shall make him Consul,

      I hope, amongst us. Crassus, I, and Caesar   100

      Will carry it for him.

FULVIA.   Does he stand for't?

SEMPRONIA.

    H'is the chief candidate.

FULVIA.   Who stands beside?—

    [*To* Galla.]   Give me some wine and powder for my teeth.

89.1.] *Gifford*; SEMPRONIA, FVL-
VIA, GALLA. *Q, Ff.*

---

    87. *Peace*] Be quiet.

    88. *wild*] out of her wits.

    90. *wench*] young woman (note the alternation of the polite "you" and familiar "thee" and "thou" in the following lines).

    91. *address'd*] taking yourself.

    93. *call thee with*] invite you to come with.

    94. *troth*] truth.

    101. *carry*] gain.

SEMPRONIA.

    Here's a good pearl, in troth.

FULVIA.   A pretty one.

SEMPRONIA.

    A very orient one. There are competitors: 105
    Caius Antonius, Publius Galba, Lucius
    Cassius Longinus, Quintus Cornificius,
    Caius Licinius, and that talker Cicero.
    But Catiline and Antonius will be chosen,
    For four o'the other, Licinius, Longinus,   110
    Galba, and Cornificius, will give way,
    And Cicero they will not choose.

FULVIA.   No? Why?

SEMPRONIA.

    It will be cross'd by the nobility.

GALLA [aside].

    How she does understand the common business!

SEMPRONIA.

    Nor were it fit. He is but a new fellow,   115
    An inmate here in Rome, as Catiline calls him,
    And the Patricians should do very ill
    To let the Consulship be so defil'd
    As 'twould be if he obtain'd it, a mere upstart
    That has no pedigree, no house, no coat,   120
    No ensigns of a family.

FULVIA.   He has virtue.

SEMPRONIA.

    Hang virtue, where there is no blood; 'tis vice,
    And, in him, sauciness. Why should he presume
    To be more learned or more eloquent
    Than the nobility, or boast any quality   125
    Worthy a noble man, himself not noble?

---

110. o'] *Ff*; of *Q*.   114. S.D.] *Gifford*.

  105. *orient*] lustrous.
  105. *competitors*] fellow candidates for office (*not* opponents).
  113. *cross'd*] opposed, thwarted.
  114. *common*] public.
  116. *inmate*] lodger; hence, not indigenous (Sallust 31, *inquilinus civis Romanus*, "a foreign-born Roman citizen," of Cicero).
  120. *house . . . coat*] family . . . coat of arms (an anachronism).
  121. *ensigns*] insignia.

FULVIA.

'Twas virtue only, at first, made all men noble.

SEMPRONIA.

I yield you it might, at first, in Rome's poor age
When both her kings and Consuls held the plow
Or garden'd well; but now we ha' no need   130
To dig or lose our sweat for't. We have wealth,
Fortune, and ease, and then their stock to spend on
Of name for virtue, which will bear us out
'Gainst all newcomers, and can never fail us
While the succession stays; and we must glorify   135
A mushroom, one of yesterday, a fine speaker,
'Cause he has suck'd at Athens, and advance him
To our own loss? No, Fulvia. There are they
Can speak Greek too, if need were. Caesar and I
Have sat upon him, so hath Crassus too,   140
And others. We have all decreed his rest
For rising farther.

GALLA.   Excellent rare lady!

FULVIA.

Sempronia, you are beholden to my woman here,
She does admire you.

SEMPRONIA.   O good Galla, how dost thou?

GALLA.

The better for your learned ladyship.   145

SEMPRONIA.

Is this gray powder a good dentifrice?

---

128. *yield*] grant.

129. *kings . . . plow*] Lucius Quinctius Cincinnatus, allegedly appointed
dictator in 458 B.C. during a military crisis, was a small farmer and according
to tradition was actually plowing when the senatorial mission arrived with
news of his appointment.

132–133. *then . . . out*] therefore their accumulated reputation of virtue
to draw on, which will sustain us.

135. *succession*] i.e., the continued securing of high office for members of
certain noble families by the influence of their connections.

136. *mushroom*] upstart.

137. *suck'd*] nourished himself (on rhetoric).

140. *sat upon*] deliberated.

141–142. *decreed . . .| For*] ordered him to stop.

FULVIA.

 You see I use it.

SEMPRONIA.   I have one is whiter.

FULVIA.

 It may be so.

SEMPRONIA.   Yet this smells well.

GALLA.   And cleanses

 Very well, madam, and resists the crudities.

SEMPRONIA.

 Fulvia, I pray thee, who comes to thee now?   150

 Which of our great Patricians?

FULVIA.   Faith, I keep

 No catalogue of 'em. Sometimes I have one,

 Sometimes another, as the toy takes their bloods.

SEMPRONIA.

 Thou hast them all. Faith, when was Quintus Curius,

 Thy special servant, here?

FULVIA.   My special servant?   155

SEMPRONIA.

 Yes, thy idolater, I call him.

FULVIA.   He may be yours

 If you do like him.

SEMPRONIA.   How!

FULVIA.   He comes not here,

 I have forbid him hence.

SEMPRONIA.   Venus forbid!

FULVIA.

 Why?

SEMPRONIA. Your so constant lover.

FULVIA.   So much the rather.

 I would have change. So would you too, I am sure; 160

 And now you may have him.

SEMPRONIA.   He's fresh yet, Fulvia;

 Beware how you do tempt me.

---

 149. *crudities*] undigested matter; ?halitosis.

 153. *toy . . . bloods*] desire excites them.

 155. *servant*] lover.

 159. *the rather*] with more reason.

 161. *fresh*] in good condition (but later with a play on "lacking preservative such as salt").

FULVIA.   Faith, for me
　　He is somewhat too fresh indeed. The salt is gone
　　That gave him season. His good gifts are done.
　　He does not yield the crop that he was wont.   165
　　And for the act, I can have secret fellows
　　With backs worth ten of him, and shall please me,
　　Now that the land is fled, a myriad better.
SEMPRONIA.
　　And those one may command.
FULVIA.   'Tis true; these lordings,
　　Your noble fauns, they are so imperious, saucy,   170
　　Rude, and as boist'rous as centaurs, leaping
　　A lady at first sight.
SEMPRONIA.   And must be borne
　　Both with and out, they think.
FULVIA.   Tut, I'll observe
　　None of 'em all, nor humor 'em a jot
　　Longer than they come laden in the hand   175
　　And say, here's t'one for th' t'other.
SEMPRONIA.   Does Caesar give well?
FULVIA.
　　They shall all give and pay well that come here
　　If they will have it, and that jewels, pearl,
　　Plate, or round sums, to buy these. I am not taken
　　With a cob-swan or a high-mounting bull   180
　　As foolish Leda and Europa were,
　　But the bright gold, with Danae. For such price
　　I would endure a rough, harsh Jupiter
　　Or ten such thund'ring gamesters, and refrain
　　To laugh at 'em till they are gone, with my much suff'ring. 185

163. He is] *Q, F1*; Hee's *F2*.   169. lordings] *Q, F1*; Lordlings *F2*.

---

　　164. *season*] flavor.
　　166. *act*] sexual act.
　　168. *Now . . . fled*] now that he has sold his property and spent the proceeds.
　　172–173. *borne . . . out*] both tolerated and encouraged.
　　173. *observe*] defer to the wishes of.
　　179. *these*] these favors.
　　180. *cob-swan*] "male swan" (H & S).
　　185. *suff'ring*] toleration.

SEMPRONIA.

    Th'art a most happy wench, that thus canst make
    Use of thy youth and freshness in the season,
    And hast it to make use of.

FULVIA [*aside*].   Which is the happiness.

SEMPRONIA.

    I am now fain to give to them, and keep
    Music and a continual table to invite 'em.   190

FULVIA [*aside*].

    Yes, and they study your kitchen more than you.

SEMPRONIA.

    Eat myself out with usury, and my lord, too,
    And all my officers and friends beside,
    To procure moneys for the needful charge
    I must be at to have 'em; and yet scarce   195
    Can I achieve 'em so.

FULVIA.   Why, that's because
    You affect young faces only, and smooth chins,
    Sempronia. If you'd love beards and bristles,
    One with another, as others do, or wrinkles—

               [*Knocking within.*]

    Who's that? Look, Galla.

GALLA.   'Tis the party, madam.   200

FULVIA.

    What party? Has he no name?

GALLA.   'Tis Quintus Curius.

FULVIA.

    Did I not bid 'em say I kept my chamber?

GALLA.

    Why, so they do.

SEMPRONIA.   I'll leave you, Fulvia.

FULVIA.

    Nay, good Sempronia, stay.

SEMPRONIA.   In faith, I will not.

FULVIA.

    By Juno, I would not see him.

199.1, 214. S.D.] *Gifford.*

___

   193. *officers*] domestic servants.
   196. *achieve*] get.

SEMPRONIA.   I'll not hinder you.   205
GALLA.

  You know, he will not be kept out, madam.
SEMPRONIA.   No,

  Nor shall not, careful Galla, by my means.
FULVIA.

  As I do live, Sempronia—
SEMPRONIA.   What needs this?
FULVIA.

  Go, say I am asleep and ill at ease.
SEMPRONIA.

  By Castor no, I'll tell him you are awake   210
  And very well. Stay, Galla; farewell, Fulvia;
  I know my manners. Why do you labor thus
  With action against purpose? Quintus Curius,
  She is, i'faith, here and in disposition.   [*Exit.*]
FULVIA.

  Spite with your courtesy. How shall I be tortured!   215

                [*Enter*] Curius.

CURIUS.

  Where are you, fair one, that conceal yourself
  And keep your beauty within locks and bars here
  Like a fool's treasure?
FULVIA.   True, she was a fool
  When first she show'd it to a thief.
CURIUS.   How, pretty sullenness,
  So harsh and short?
FULVIA.   The fool's artillery, sir.   220
CURIUS.

  Then take my gown off for th'encounter.
FULVIA.   Stay, sir.

  I am not in the mood.
CURIUS.   I'll put you into't.

215.1.] *Gifford*; CVRIVS, FVLVIA,   221. th'encounter] *Ff*; the'encoun-
GALLA. *Q*, *Ff*.   ter *Q*.

---

  207. *means*] intervention.
  213. *With . . . purpose*] acting against your real wishes.
  214. *in disposition*] "in health" (H & S).

FULVIA.

    Best put yourself i'your case again, and keep

    Your furious appetitite warm against you have place for't.

CURIUS.

    What! Do you coy it?

FULVIA.   No, sir. I am not proud.   225

CURIUS.

    I would you were. You think this state becomes you?

    By Hercules, it does not. Look i'your glass, now,

    And see how scurvily that countenance shows;

    You would be loath to own it.

FULVIA.   I shall not change it.

CURIUS.

    Faith, but you must, and slack this bended brow   230

    And shoot less scorn; there is a fortune coming

    Towards you, dainty, that will take thee thus

    And set thee aloft to tread upon the head

    Of her own statue here in Rome.

FULVIA.   I wonder

    Who let this promiser in. Did you, good diligence?   235

    Give him his bribe again. Or if you had none,

    Pray you demand him why he is so vent'rous

    To press thus to my chamber, being forbidden

    Both by myself and servants?

CURIUS.   How! This's handsome

    And somewhat a new strain.

FULVIA.   'Tis not strain'd, sir,   240

    'Tis very natural.

CURIUS.   I have known it otherwise

    Between the parties, though.

FULVIA.   For your foreknowledge

    Thank that which made it. It will not be so

    Hereafter, I assure you.

CURIUS.   No, my mistress?

---

223. *case*] cover.

224. *against*] until.

230. *slack*] relax.

231. *shoot*] i.e., from your eyes.

234. *her own statue*] i.e., of Fortuna as a goddess.

237. *vent'rous*] bold.

FULVIA.

 No, though you bring the same materials.

CURIUS.   Hear me,   245

 You overact when you should underdo.
 A little call yourself again and think.
 If you do this to practice on me, or find
 At what forc'd distance you can hold your servant,
 That it be an artificial trick to inflame   250
 And fire me more, fearing my love may need it
 As heretofore you ha' done, why, proceed.

FULVIA.

 As I ha' done heretofore?

CURIUS.   Yes, when you'd feign
 Your husband's jealousy, your servants' watches,
 Speak softly, and run often to the door   255
 Or to the windore, form strange fears that were not,
 As if the pleasure were less acceptable
 That were secure.

FULVIA.   You are an impudent fellow.

CURIUS.

 And when you might better have done it at the gate,
 To take me in at the casement.

FULVIA.   I take you in?   260

CURIUS.

 Yes, you, my lady. And then, being abed with you,
 To have your well-taught waiter here come running
 And cry "her lord!" and hide me without cause
 Crush'd in a chest or thrust up in a chimney
 When he, tame crow, was winking at his farm   265
 Or, had he been here and present, would have kept
 Both eyes and beak seal'd up for six sesterces.

FULVIA.

 You have a slanderous, beastly, unwash'd tongue

---

 246. *overact . . . underdo*] go too far in action when you should show restraint.
 247. *call yourself*] remember who you are.
 248. *practice on*] trick.
 254. *watches*] keeping guard.
 256. *windore*] window.
 262. *waiter*] someone on the look-out.
 267. *sesterces*] Roman coins of low denomination.

I'your rude mouth, and savoring yourself,
Unmanner'd lord.
CURIUS.   How now!
FULVIA.   It is your title, sir,   270
Who, since you ha' lost your own good name and know not
What to lose more, care not whose honor you wound
Or fame you poison with it. You should go
And vent yourself i'the region where you live
Among the suburb-brothels, bawds, and brokers,   275
Whither your broken fortunes have design'd you.
CURIUS.
Nay, then I must stop your fury, I see, and pluck
The tragic visor off. Come, lady Cypris,
Know your own virtues quickly. I'll not be
Put to the wooing of you thus, afresh   280
At every turn, for all the Venus in you.
Yield and be pliant, or by Pollux—

He offers to force her, and she draws her knife.

How now?

Will Lais turn a Lucrece?
FULVIA.   No, but by Castor,
Hold off your ravisher's hands; I pierce your heart, else.
I'll not be put to kill myself as she did   285
For you, sweet Tarquin. What? Do you fall off?
Nay, it becomes you graciously! Put not up.
You'll sooner draw your weapon on me, I think it,
Than on the Senate, who have cast you forth
Disgracefully to be the common tale   290
Of the whole city; base, infamous man!
For were you other, you would there employ
Your desperate dagger.
CURIUS.   Fulvia, you do know
The strengths you have upon me; do not use

282. S.D.] *om. Q; opp. l. 278, Ff.*

---

269. *savoring*] tasting like.
275. *suburb-brothels . . . brokers*] brothels in the parts of town outside the wall . . . pimps.
276. *design'd*] consigned.
286. *fall off*] withdraw.
287. *Put not up*] Do not sheathe your sword.

Your power too like a tyrant; I can bear   295
Almost until you break me.
FULVIA.   I do know, sir,
So does the Senate, too, know you can bear.
CURIUS.
    By all the gods, that Senate will smart deep
    For your upbraidings. I should be right sorry
    To have the means so to be veng'd on you   300
    (At least, the will) as I shall shortly on them.
    But go you on still, fare you well, dear lady;
    You could not still be fair unless you were proud.
    You will repent these moods, and ere't be long, too.
    I shall ha' you come about again.
FULVIA.   Do you think so?   305
CURIUS.
    Yes, and I know so.
FULVIA.   By what augury?
CURIUS.
    By the fair entrails of the matrons' chests,
    Gold, pearl, and jewels, here in Rome, which Fulvia
    Will then, but late, say that she might have shar'd,
    And, grieving, miss.
FULVIA.   Tut, all your promis'd mountains   310
    And seas, I am so stalely acquainted with—
CURIUS.
    But when you see the universal flood
    Run by your coffers; that my lords the Senators
    Are sold for slaves, their wives for bondwomen,
    Their houses and fine gardens given away,   315
    And all their goods under the spear at outcry,
    And you have none of this but are still Fulvia,

298. that] *Q*, *F1*; the *F2*.

---

300. *veng'd*] avenged.

302. *go you on*] continue.

305. *come about*] change direction.

307. *entrails*] One form of divination in Rome was by the inspection of the entrails of sacrificial beasts.

311. *stalely*] tediously (from familiarity).

316. *under . . . outcry*] confiscated and put up for sale at auction under the spear, a traditional sign when the proceeds were for the public treasury.

Or perhaps less while you are thinking of it,
You will advise then, coyness, with your cushion,
And look o'your fingers, say how you were wish'd,   320
And so he left you.   [*Exit.*]
FULVIA.   Call him again, Galla.   [*Exit* Galla.]
This is not usual. Something hangs on this
That I must win out of him.

[*Re-enter* Curius.]

CURIUS.   How now, melt you?
FULVIA.
Come, you will laugh now at my easiness.
But 'tis no miracle: doves, they say, will bill   325
After their pecking and their murmuring.
CURIUS.   Yes,
And then 'tis kindly. I would have my love
Angry, sometimes, to sweeten off the rest
Of her behavior.
FULVIA.   You do see I study
How I may please you, then. But you think, Curius,   330
'Tis covetise hath wrought me; if you love me,
Change that unkind conceit.
CURIUS.   But my lov'd soul,
I love thee like to it, and 'tis my study
More than mine own revenge to make thee happy.
FULVIA.
And 'tis that just revenge doth make me happy   335
To hear you prosecute, and which indeed
Hath won me to you more than all the hope
Of what can else be promis'd. I love valor

321, 323. S.D.] *Gifford.*

---

319. *You . . . cushion*] You will talk alone to your pillow.
320. *wish'd*] "invited" (H & S). The passage imitates *Othello*, V.ii.347–352.
322. *hangs on*] is left unresolved in.
323. *win out of*] obtain by effort from.
327. *kindly*] natural.
328. *sweeten off*] make more sweet by contrast.
331. *covetise*] covetousness.
332. *conceit*] thought.
336. *prosecute*] strive after (Lat. *prosequor*).

Better than any lady loves her face
Or dressing, than myself does. Let me grow   340
Still where I do embrace. But what good means
Ha' you t'effect it? Shall I know your project?

CURIUS.

Thou shalt, if thou'lt be gracious.

FULVIA.   As I can be.

CURIUS.

And wilt thou kiss me, then?

FULVIA.   As close as shells
Of cockles meet.

CURIUS.   And print 'em deep?

FULVIA.   Quite through   345
Our subtle lips.

CURIUS.   And often?

FULVIA.   I will sow 'em
Faster than you can reap. What is your plot?

CURIUS.

Why, now my Fulvia looks like her bright name
And is herself.

FULVIA.   Nay, answer me, your plot;
I pray thee tell me, Quintus.

CURIUS.   Ay, these sounds   350
Become a mistress. Here is harmony.

She kisses and flatters him along still.

When you are harsh, I see the way to bend you
Is not with violence, but service. Cruel,
A lady is a fire; gentle, a light.

FULVIA.

Will you not tell me what I ask you?

CURIUS.   All   355
That I can think, sweet love, or my breast holds,
I'll pour into thee.

350. pray thee] *Q, F1*; pr'ythee *F2*.   351.1.] *F1*; *om. Q*; *after l. 352, F2.*

340. *grow*] become rooted.
343. *gracious*] giving favors.
346. *subtle*] delicate.
348. *bright name*] i.e., Fulvia. Jonson implies derivation from *fulvus*, "deep yellow, tawny, gold-colored."
353. *service*] compliance.

FULVIA.   What is your design, then?

CURIUS.

I'll tell thee: Catiline shall now be Consul;
But you will hear more, shortly.

FULVIA.   Nay, dear love—

CURIUS.

I'll speak it in thine arms; let us go in.   360
Rome will be sack'd, her wealth will be our prize;
By public ruin, private spirits must rise.   [*Exeunt.*]

CHORUS.

Great father Mars, and greater Jove,
    By whose high auspice Rome hath stood
    So long, and first was built in blood   365
Of your great nephew, that then strove
Not with his brother, but your rites;
    Be present to her now as then,
    And let not proud and factious men
Against your wills oppose their mights.   370
Our Consuls now are to be made;
    O put it in the public voice
    To make a free and worthy choice
Excluding such as would invade
The Commonwealth. Let whom we name   375
    Have wisdom, foresight, fortitude,
    Be more with faith than face endu'd,
And study conscience above fame;
Such as not seek to get the start
    In state by power, parts, or bribes,   380
    Ambition's bawds, but move the tribes
By virtue, modesty, desert;

---

362. S.D.] *Gifford.*

362. *spirits*] men of courage (Lat. *animi*).
364. *auspice*] divine protection (indicated by signs).
366. *nephew*] descendant, here "grandson" (*nepos*), namely Remus (as a son of Mars, who was son of Jupiter and Juno).
366–367. *strove . . . rites*] Romulus and Remus took auspices to decide which should found the new city; Romulus received the better signs, so Remus quarreled with him and was killed.
377. *face*] pretense.
379. *get the start*] gain the advantage.
380. *parts*] factions (Lat. *partes*).

Such as to justice will adhere,
    Whatever great one it offend,
    And from the embraced truth not bend   385
For envy, hatred, gifts or fear,
That by their deeds will make it known
    Whose dignity they do sustain,
    And life, state, glory, all they gain
Count the Republic's, not their own.   390
Such the old Bruti, Decii were,
    The Cipi, Curtii, who did give
    Themselves for Rome, and would not live
As men good only for a year.
Such were the great Camilli too,   395
    The Fabii, Scipios, that still thought
    No work at price enough was bought
That for their country they could do,
And to her honor so did knit
    As all their acts were understood   400
    The sinews of the public good
And they themselves one soul with it.
These men were truly magistrates;
    These neither practic'd force nor forms,
    Nor did they leave the helm in storms;   405
And such they are make happy states.

[III.i]

[*Enter*] Cicero, Cato, Catulus, Antonius, Crassus, Caesar, Chorus, *Lictors.*

CICERO.

    Great honors are great burdens, but on whom
    They are cast with envy, he doth bear two loads.
    His cares must still be double to his joys
    In any dignity, where if he err

III.i.] *Scene divisions in this Act follow Gifford.*

---

397. *price enough*] too high a cost.
399. *knit*] grow together.
404. *forms*] manipulation of formal procedures, "playing the rule-book."
[III.i]
2. *envy*] odium.

He finds no pardon, and for doing well   5
A most small praise, and that wrung out by force.
I speak this, Romans, knowing what the weight
Of the high charge you have trusted to me is.
Not that thereby I would with art decline
The good or greatness of your benefit,   10
For I ascribe it to your singular grace
And vow to owe it to no title else,
Except the gods, that Cicero is your Consul.
I have no urns, no dusty monuments,
No broken images of ancestors   15
Wanting an ear or nose, no forged tables
Of long descents to boast false honors from
Or be my undertakers to your trust,
But a new man, as I am styl'd in Rome,
Whom you have dignified, and more, in whom   20
Yo'have cut a way and left it ope for virtue
Hereafter to that place which our great men
Held shut up with all ramparts for themselves.
Nor have but few of them in time been made
Your Consuls so; new men before me, none;   25
At my first suit, in my just year, prefer'd
To all competitors, and some the noblest—

CRASSUS [*aside to* Caesar].
    Now the vein swells.
CAESAR.   Up glory.
CICERO.   And to have
    Your loud consents from your own utter'd voices,

23. ramparts] *Ff*; rampires *Q*.   28. S.D.] *Gifford*.

---

8. *charge*] thing committed to another.
9. *with art decline*] pretend to undervalue.
11. *your singular grace*] the favor (Lat. *gratia*) of you alone.
12. *title*] entitlement.
16–17. *tables . . . descents*] lists of forefathers.
18. *undertakers*] sureties.
21. *ope*] open.
26. *suit*] quest.
26. *just year*] forty-third, the earliest at which he could be elected Consul.
28. *vein*] line of thought.

Not silent books nor from the meaner tribes   30
But first and last the universal concourse:
This is my joy, my gladness. But my care,
My industry and vigilance now must work
That still your counsels of me be approv'd
Both by yourselves and those to whom you have   35
With grudge prefer'd me; two things I must labor,
That neither they upbraid nor you repent you,
For every lapse of mine will now be call'd
Your error, if I make such. But my hope is
So to bear through and out the Consulship   40
As spite shall ne'er wound you, though it may me,
And for myself I have prepar'd this strength
To do so well, as, if there happen ill
Unto me, it shall make the gods to blush
And be their crime, not mine, that I am envied.   45

CAESAR [aside].

O confidence, more new than is the man!

CICERO.

I know well in what terms I do receive
The Commonwealth, how vexed, how perplex'd,
In which there's not that mischief or ill fate
That good men fear not, wicked men expect not.   50
I know, beside, some turbulent practices
Already on foot, and rumors of moe dangers—

CRASSUS [aside].

Or you will make them, if there be none.

CICERO.   Last,

34. counsels] *Ff*; counsell *Q*.   53. S.D.] *Gifford*.

---

30. *books . . . tribes*] The books are voting tablets, used in the secret ballot.
Jonson's source (Cicero 2 *leg. agr.* 4) speaks of "the last division of the votes."
Voting proceeded in descending order of the economic classes; *the meaner
tribes* were those centuries of each tribe which came from the poorest classes
and were announced last.

31. *universal concourse*] unanimity of all classes of society (Lat. *concursus*).

34. *of me*] about me.

36. *With grudge*] so as to raise their enmity (Lat. *invidia*).

40. *bear . . . out*] sustain to the end and complete (Lat. *perferre et efferre*).

43. *do so well*] act so righteously.

51. *practices*] conspiracies.

52. *moe*] more.

I know 'twas this which made the envy and pride
Of the great Roman blood 'bate and give way   55
To my election.

CATO.   Marcus Tullius, true;
Our need made thee our Consul, and thy virtue.

CAESAR.
Cato, you will undo him with your praise.

CATO.
Caesar will hurt himself with his own envy.

CHORUS.
The voice of Cato is the voice of Rome.   60

CATO.
The voice of Rome is the consent of heaven,
And that hath plac'd thee, Cicero, at the helm
Where thou must render, now, thyself a man
And master of thy art. Each petty hand
Can steer a ship becalm'd, but he that will   65
Govern and carry her to her ends must know
His tides, his currents, how to shift his sails,
What she will bear in foul, what in fair weathers,
Where her springs are, her leaks, and how to stop 'em,
What sands, what shelves, what rocks do threaten her,   70
The forces and the natures of all winds,
Gusts, storms, and tempests, when her keel plows hell
And deck knocks heaven; then to manage her
Becomes the name and office of a pilot.

CICERO.
Which I'll perform with all the diligence   75
And fortitude I have, not for my year
But for my life, except my life be less
And that my year conclude it; if it must,

56, 59. S.P. CATO] *Whalley*; CAT.
Q, Ff.

---

55. *'bate*] abate.
63. *render*] cause to become.
65. *becalm'd*] in calm weather.
66. *Govern . . . ends*] steer (Lat. *guberno*) . . . destinations.
69. *springs*] "breaches through the splitting of a plank" (H & S).
70. *shelves*] ledges of rock.

Your will, lov'd gods. This heart shall yet employ
A day, an hour is left me, so for Rome   80
As it shall spring a life out of my death
To shine forever glorious in my facts.
The vicious count their years, virtuous their acts.

CHORUS.

Most noble Consul! Let us wait him home.

> [*Exeunt* Cato, Cicero, *Lictors, and* Chorus.]

CAESAR.

Most popular Consul he is grown, methinks.   85

CRASSUS.

How the rout cling to him.

CAESAR.   And Cato leads 'em.

CRASSUS.

You, his colleague, Antonius, are not look'd on.

ANTONIUS.

Not I, nor do I care.

CAESAR.   He enjoys rest
And ease the while. Let th'other's spirit toil
And wake it out that was inspir'd for turmoil.   90

CATULUS.

If all reports be true, yet, Caius Caesar,
The time hath need of such a watch and spirit.

CAESAR.

Reports? Do you believe 'em, Catulus?
Why, he does make and breed 'em for the people
T'endear his service to 'em. Do you not taste   95
An art that is so common? Popular men,
They must create strange monsters and then quell 'em

84.1.] *Gifford.*

---

79. *Your will*] let it be according to your will.
82. *facts*] deeds.
84. *wait*] escort.
85. *popular*] demagogic (Lat. *popularis*).
86. *rout*] throng, mob.
87. *look'd on*] paid regard to.
90. *wake it out*] remain awake.
90. *inspir'd*] created.
95. *taste*] perceive.
96. *art*] trick.

To make their arts seem something. Would you have
Such an Herculean actor in the scene,
And not his Hydra? They must sweat no less   100
To fit their properties than t'express their parts.

CRASSUS.

Treasons and guilty men are made in states
Too oft to dignify the magistrates.

CATULUS.

Those states be wretched that are forc'd to buy
Their rulers' fame with their own infamy.   105

CRASSUS.

We therefore should provide that ours do not.

CAESAR.

That will Antonius make his care.

ANTONIUS.   I shall.

CAESAR.

And watch the watcher.

CATULUS.   Here comes Catiline.
How does he brook his late repulse?

CAESAR.   I know not,
But hardly, sure.

CATULUS.   Longinus too did stand?   110

CAESAR.

At first, but he gave way unto his friend.

CATULUS.

Who's that come? Lentulus?

CAESAR.   Yes. He is again
Taken into the Senate.

ANTONIUS.   And made Praetor.

CATULUS.

I know't. He had my suffrage, next the Consul's.

110. S.P. CATULUS] *Whalley*; CAT.   114. S.P. CATULUS] *F2*; CAT. *Q*,
Q, *Ff*.   *F1*.
112. that] *Q*, *F1*; that's *F2*.

---

101. *fit their properties*] supply their theatrical props.
106. *provide*] take precautions.
109. *brook . . . repulse*] endure his recent defeat in the election.
110. *hardly*] painfully.
114. *suffrage, next*] vote, immediately following.

CAESAR.

    True, you were there prince of the Senate, then.   115

          [*Enter*] Catiline, Longinus, Lentulus.

CATILINE.

    Hail, noblest Romans. The most worthy Consul,
    I 'gratulate your honor.

ANTONIUS.   I could wish

    It had been happier by your fellowship,
    Most noble Sergius, had it pleas'd the people.

CATILINE.

    It did not please the gods who instruct the people,   120
    And their unquestion'd pleasures must be serv'd.
    They know what's fitter for us than ourselves,
    And 'twere impiety to think against them.

CATULUS.

    You bear it rightly, Lucius, and it glads me
    To find your thoughts so even.

CATILINE.   I shall still   125

    Study to make them such to Rome and heaven.—
    [*Aside to* Caesar.]   I would withdraw with you a little, Julius.

CAESAR [*aside to* Catiline].

    I'll come home to you; Crassus would not ha' you
    To speak to him, 'fore Quintus Catulus.

CATILINE.

    I apprehend you.   [*To them.*]   No, when they shall judge   130
    Honors convenient for me, I shall have 'em
    With a full hand; I know it. In meantime

115.1.] *Gifford*; CATILINE, AN-   CRASSVS, LONGINVS, LEN-
TONIVS, CATVLVS, CÆSAR,   TVLVS. *Q*, *Ff*.
                              127, 128. S.D.] *Gifford*.

---

    115. *prince of the Senate*] senior Senator, "father of the house" (Lat. *princeps Senatus*).

    117. *'gratulate*] congratulate.

    124. *bear*] endure.

    125. *even*] calm (Lat. *aequus*).

    126. *to make . . . heaven*] to make them even (equal) to Rome and heaven; cf. Lat. *se aequare caelo*, to rival the gods.

    130. *apprehend*] understand.

    131. *convenient*] suitable.

    132. *With a full hand*] bountifully (Lat. *plena manu*).

They are no less part of the Commonwealth
That do obey, than those that do command.

CATULUS.

 O let me kiss your forehead, Lucius.   135
 How are you wrong'd!

CATILINE.   By whom?

CATULUS.   Public report,
 That gives you out to stomach your repulse
 And brook it deadly.

CATILINE.   Sir, she brooks not me.
 Believe me rather, and yourself, now, of me;
 It is a kind of slander to trust rumor.   140

CATULUS.

 I know it, and I could be angry with it.

CATILINE.

 So may not I. Where it concerns himself,
 Who's angry at a slander makes it true.

CATULUS.

 Most noble Sergius! This your temper melts me.

CRASSUS.

 Will you do office to the Consul, Quintus?   145

CAESAR.

 Which Cato and the rout have done the other?

CATULUS.

 I wait when he will go. Be still yourself.
 He wants no state or honors, that hath virtue.
      [*Exeunt* Catulus, Antonius, Caesar, Crassus.]

CATILINE [*aside*].

 Did I appear so tame, as this man thinks me?
 Look'd I so poor, so dead, so like that nothing   150
 Which he calls virtuous? O my breast, break quickly
 And show my friends my in-parts, lest they think
 I have betray'd 'em.

LONGINUS.   Where's Gabinius?

LENTULUS.   Gone.

146. Which] *Ff*; That *Q*.   148.1.] *Gifford*.

---

137. *stomach*] take offense at (Lat. *stomachor*).
144. *temper*] equanimity.
145. *do office*] render observance.

LONGINUS.

    And Vargunteius?

LENTULUS.   Slip'd away, all shrunk

    Now that he miss'd the Consulship.

CATILINE [aside].   I am   155

    The scorn of bondmen, who are next to beasts.

    What can I worse pronounce myself, that's fitter?

    The owl of Rome whom boys and girls will hoot,

    That, were I set up for that wooden god

    That keeps our gardens, could not fright the crows   160

    Or the least bird from muting on my head.

LONGINUS.

    'Tis strange how he should miss it.

LENTULUS.   Is't not stranger

    The upstart Cicero should carry it so

    By all consents from men so much his masters?

LONGINUS.

    'Tis true.

CATILINE [aside]. To what a shadow am I melted!   165

LONGINUS.

    Antonius won it but by some few voices.

CATILINE [aside].

    Struck through like air, and feel it not. My wounds

    Close faster than they're made.

LENTULUS.   The whole design

    And enterprise is lost by't. All hands quit it

    Upon his fail.

CATILINE [aside].   I grow mad at my patience.   170

    It is a visor that hath poison'd me.

155, 165, 167, 170 S.D.] *Gifford.*

---

157. *pronounce*] declare.

159. *that wooden god*] Priapus, of whom wooden statues were sometimes set up in gardens (cf. Horace, *Satires* 1. 8).

161. *muting*] excreting.

170. *fail*] failure.

171. *visor*] i.e., mask; but perhaps also helmet, one that both blinds and protects him; for the poisoned helmet, cf. Webster, *White Devil*, V.ii–iii (completed between 1609 and 1612).

Would it had burn'd me up and I died inward,
My heart first turn'd to ashes.

LONGINUS.   Here's Cethegus yet.

[*Enter*] Cethegus.

CATILINE [*aside*].

Repulse upon repulse? An inmate Consul?
That I could reach the axle where the pins are   175
Which bolt this frame, that I might pull 'em out
And pluck all into chaos with myself.

CETHEGUS.

What, are we wishing now?

CATILINE.   Yes, my Cethegus.
Who would not fall with all the world about him?

CETHEGUS.

Not I, that would stand on it when it falls   180
And force new nature out to make another.
These wishings taste of woman, not of Roman.
Let us seek other arms.

CATILINE.   What should we do?

CETHEGUS.

Do, and not wish, something that wishes take not;
So sudden as the gods should not prevent   185
Nor scarce have time to fear.

CATILINE.   O noble Caius.

CETHEGUS.

It likes me better that you are not Consul.
I would not go through open doors, but break 'em;
Swim to my ends through blood; or build a bridge
Of carcasses; make on upon the heads   190
Of men struck down like piles, to reach the lives

173.1.] *Gifford*; CATILINE, CE-   INVS, CATO. *Q, Ff.*
THEGVS, LENTVLVS, LONG-   174. S.D.] *Gifford*.

---

182. *woman . . . Roman*] The words rhymed in Jonson's day.
184. *take*] grasp.
185. *prevent*] anticipate.
190. *make on*] proceed.

Of those remain, and stand; then is't a prey
When danger stops and ruin makes the way.

CATILINE.

How thou dost utter me, brave soul, that may not
At all times show such as I am, but bend   195
Unto occasion. Lentulus, this man
If all our fire were out would fetch down new
Out of the hand of Jove, and rivet him
To Caucasus, should he but frown, and let
His own gaunt eagle fly at him, to tire.   200

LENTULUS.

Peace, here comes Cato.

CATILINE.   Let him come and hear.
I will no more dissemble. Quit us, all;
I and my lov'd Cethegus here alone
Will undertake this giants' war, and carry it.

[*Re-enter* Cato.]

LENTULUS.

What needs this, Lucius?

LONGINUS.   Sergius, be more wary.   205

CATILINE.

Now, Marcus Cato, our new Consul's spy,
What is your sour austerity sent t'explore?

CATO.

Nothing in thee, licentious Catiline;
Halters and racks cannot express from thee
More than thy deeds. 'Tis only judgment waits thee.   210

CATILINE.

Whose? Cato's? Shall he judge me?

196. Unto] *Q*, *F1*; Upon *F2*.   204.1.] *Gifford*.
201. S.P. CATILINE] *Ff*; CAT. *Q*.   211. S.P. CATO] *Ff*; CAT. *Q*.

192–193. *then . . . way*] It is a booty worth having, when danger obstructs
the seeker, and devastation removes the obstruction.

194. *utter me*] give voice to my feelings.

195–196. *show . . . occasion*] be what I am capable of, but who sometimes
surrenders to cares of the moment.

197–200. *If . . . at him*] See *Titan* in Glossary (Appendix A).

200. *tire*] as a hawk tugging meat with its beak.

205. *What needs this*] why is this necessary?

209. *Halters . . . express*] instruments of torture cannot wring.

CATO.   No, the gods
   Who ever follow those they go not with,
   And Senate who with fire must purge sick Rome
   Of noisome citizens, whereof thou art one.
   Be gone, or else let me. 'Tis bane to draw   215
   The same air with thee.
CETHEGUS.   Strike him.
LENTULUS.   Hold, good Caius.
CETHEGUS.
   Fear'st thou not, Cato?
CATO.   Rash Cethegus, no.
   'Twere wrong with Rome, when Catiline and thou
   Do threat, if Cato fear'd.
CATILINE.   The fire you speak of,
   If any flame of it approach my fortunes   220
   I'll quench it, not with water, but with ruin.
CATO.
   You hear this, Romans.   [*Exit.*]
CATILINE.   Bear it to the Consul.
CETHEGUS.
   I would have sent away his soul before him.
   You are too heavy, Lentulus, and remiss;
   It is for you we labor, and the kingdom   225
   Promis'd you by the Sibyls.
CATILINE.   Which his Praetorship
   And some small flattery of the Senate more
   Will make him to forget.
LENTULUS.   You wrong me, Lucius.
LONGINUS.
   He will not need these spurs.
CETHEGUS.   The action needs 'em.
   These things, when they proceed not, they go backward.   230

214. thou art] *Q, Ff*; thou'rt *Q(o)*.   222. S.D.] *Gifford*
220. flame] *Q, F1*; flames *F2*.

---

  212. *follow . . . with*] pursue those whom they do not accompany (as benefactors).
  214. *noisome*] unwholesome.
  224. *heavy*] sluggish.
  229. *spurs*] goads to action.

LENTULUS.

    Let us consult then.

CETHEGUS.   Let us first take arms.

    They that deny us just things now will give

    All that we ask, if once they see our swords.

CATILINE.

    Our objects must be sought with wounds, not words.   [*Exeunt.*]

[III.ii]   [*Enter*] Cicero, Fulvia.

CICERO.

    Is there a heaven, and gods, and can it be
    They should so slowly hear, so slowly see?
    Hath Jove no thunder, or is Jove become
    Stupid as thou art, O near-wretched Rome,
    When both thy Senate and thy gods do sleep   5
    And neither thine nor their own states do keep?
    What will awake thee, heaven, what can excite
    Thine anger if this practice be too light?
    His former drifts partake of former times,
    But this last plot was only Catiline's.   10
    O that it were his last, but he before
    Hath safely done so much, he'll still dare more.
    Ambition, like a torrent, ne'er looks back,
    And is a swelling and the last affection
    A high mind can put off, being both a rebel   15
    Unto the soul and reason, and enforceth
    All laws, all conscience, treads upon religion
    And offereth violence to nature's self.
    But here is that transcends it: a black purpose
    To confound nature and to ruin that   20

---

234. S.P. CATILINE] *this edn.*; CAT. .   234. S.D.] *Gifford.*
Q, *Ff.*

233–234. *swords . . . words*] The words rhymed in Jonson's day.
[III.ii]
    4. *Stupid*] torpid.
    8. *light*] trivial.
    9. *drifts*] plots.
    9. *partake*] have the qualities.
    14. *swelling*] increasing.
    16. *enforceth*] overcomes by force.
    20. *confound*] cast into confusion.

Which never age nor mankind can repair.
Sit down, good lady; Cicero is lost
In this your fable, for to think it true
Tempteth my reason, it so far exceeds
All insolent fictions of the tragic scene:　　　　　　25
The Commonwealth yet panting underneath
The stripes and wounds of a late civil war,
Gasping for life, and scarce restor'd to hope;
To seek t'oppress her with new cruelty
And utterly extinguish her long name　　　　　　30
With so prodigious and unheard-of fierceness!
What sink of monsters, wretches of lost minds
Mad after change and desp'rate in their states,
Wearied and gall'd with their necessities,
For all this I allow them, durst have thought it?　　35
Would not the barbarous deeds have been believ'd
Of Marius and Sylla by our children
Without this fact had rise forth greater for them?
All that they did was piety to this:
They yet but murder'd kinsfolk, brothers, parents,　　40
Ravish'd the virgins and, perhaps, some matrons.
They left the city standing, and the temples;
The gods and majesty of Rome were safe yet.
These purpose to fire it, to despoil them,
Beyond the other evils, and lay waste　　　　　　45
The far-triumphed world, for unto whom
Rome is too little, what can be enough?

33. desp'rate] *Q, F1*; desperate *F2*.

---

21. *age*] time.　23. *fable*] narrative.
24. *Tempteth*] tests.
25. *insolent . . . tragic scene*] unusual (Lat. *insolens*) . . . stage tragedies.
27. *stripes*] strokes.
30. *long*] ancient.
32. *sink*] place where vice collects.
34. *gall'd*] chafed.
38. *Without . . . them*] unless the even greater atrocity had appeared to confirm the lesser.
39. *to*] compared with.
46. *far-triumphed*] over which victories had been won far and wide, and celebrated with triumphs at Rome.
47. *Rome*] "There is a pun on 'Rome' and 'room' similarly pronounced . . . *Julius Caesar*, I.ii.157–8" (H & S).

FULVIA.

    'Tis true, my lord, I had the same discourse.

CICERO.

    (And then to take a horrid sacrament
    In human blood for execution   50
    Of this their dire design, which might be call'd
    The height of wickedness, but that that was higher
    For which they did it.)

FULVIA.   I assure your lordship
    The extreme horror of it almost turn'd me
    To air when first I heard it. I was all   55
    A vapor when 'twas told me, and I long'd
    To vent it anywhere. T'was such a secret
    I thought it would have burn'd me up.

CICERO.   Good Fulvia,
    Fear not your act, and less repent you of it.

FULVIA.

    I do not, my good lord. I know to whom   60
    I have utter'd it.

CICERO.   You have discharg'd it safely.
    Should Rome, for whom you have done the happy service,
    Turn most ingrate, yet were your virtue paid
    In conscience of the fact; so much good deeds
    Reward themselves.

FULVIA.   My lord, I did it not   65
    To any other aim but for itself,
    To no ambition.)

CICERO.   You have learn'd the difference
    Of doing office to the public weal
    And private friendship, and have shown it, lady.
    Be still yourself. I have sent for Quintus Curius,   70
    And for your virtuous sake, if I can win him
    Yet to the Commonwealth, he shall be safe too.

---

52. height] *Q, F1*; heigh *F2(o)*;
heighth *F2.*

---

48. *discourse*] reasoning.
63. *ingrate*] ungrateful.

FULVIA.

    I'll undertake, my lord, he shall be won.

CICERO.

    Pray you join with me, then, and help to work him.

[Enter a] Lictor.

    How now? Is he come?

LICTOR.   He is here, my lord.

CICERO.   Go presently,   75

    Pray my colleague Antonius I may speak with him

    About some present business of the state

    And as you go call on my brother Quintus

    And pray him, with the Tribunes, to come to me.

    Bid Curius enter. Fulvia, you will aid me?   *[Exit* Lictor.]   80

FULVIA.

    It is my duty.

[Enter Curius.]

CICERO.   O my noble lord,

    I have to chide you, i'faith. Give me your hand.

    Nay, be not troubled; 't shall be gently, Curius.

    You look upon this lady? What, do you guess

    My business yet? Come, if you frown, I thunder;   85

    Therefore put on your better looks and thoughts.

    There's nought but fair and good intended to you,

    And I would make those your complexion.

    Would you of whom the Senate had that hope

    As on my knowledge it was in their purpose   90

    Next sitting to restore you, as they ha' done

    The stupid and ungrateful Lentulus

    (Excuse me that I name you thus together,

    For yet you are not such), would you, I say,

    A person both of blood and honor, stock'd   95

    In a long race of virtuous ancestors,

---

73. shall]*Ff*; will *Q*.   FVLVIA, CVRIVS. *Q*, *Ff*.
74.1.] *Gifford*; CICERO, LICTOR,   80. S.D., 81. S.D.] *Gifford*.

    74. *work*] persuade.
    75. *presently*] at once.
    88. *complexion*] "habit of mind" (H & S).
    94. *yet . . . such*] you are as yet not like him.
    95–96. *stock'd/In*] coming from the stock or family of.

    Embark yourself for such a hellish action
    With parricides and traitors, men turn'd Furies
    Out of the waste and ruin of their fortunes
    (For 'tis despair that is the mother of madness),   100
    Such as want that which all conspirators,
    But they, have first, mere color for their mischief?
    O, I must blush with you. Come, you shall not labor
    To extenuate your guilt, but quit it clean;
    Bad men excuse their faults, good men will leave 'em.   105
    He acts the third crime that defends the first.
    Here is a lady that hath got the start,
    In piety, of us all, and for whose virtue
    I could almost turn lover again, but that
    Terentia would be jealous. What an honor   110
    Hath she achieved to herself; what voices,
    Titles, and loud applauses will pursue her
    Through every street; what windores will be fill'd
    To shoot eyes at her; what envy and grief in matrons
    They are not she; when this her act shall seem   115
    Worthier a chariot than if Pompey came
    With Asia chain'd. All this is, while she lives;
    But dead, her very name will be a statue,
    Not wrought for time, but rooted in the minds
    Of all posterity when brass and marble,   120
    Ay, and the Capitol itself is dust.

FULVIA.

    Your honor thinks too highly of me.

CICERO.   No,

118. a] *Q, F1; om. F2.*

---

102. *color*] pretext.

106. *third*] the first, the deed itself; the second, the failure to repent; the third, self-justification.

111. *achieved to*] gained for.

114. *shoot eyes at*] gaze on (Lat. *oculos adicere*).

116–117. *chariot . . . chain'd*] as in the triumph awarded to Roman generals after notable victories. The conqueror drove to the temple of Jupiter Optimus Maximus in a chariot, attended by a long procession of captives in chains, attendants carrying booty, and tableaux or pictures illustrating his campaign. Thus *Asia chain'd* might mean prisoners from that region, or refer to a picture of Asia, personified, in chains.

I cannot think enough, and I would have
Him emulate you. 'Tis no shame to follow
The better precedent. She shows you, Curius,   125
What claim your country lays to you, and what duty
You owe to it; be not afraid to break
With murderers and traitors for the saving
A life so near and necessary to you
As is your country's. Think but on her right.   130
No child can be too natural to his parent.
She is our common mother and doth challenge
The prime part of us; do not stop, but give it.
He that is void of fear may soon be just,
And no religion binds men to be traitors.   135

FULVIA.

My lord, he understands it, and will follow
Your saving counsel, but his shame yet stays him.
I know that he is coming.

CURIUS.   Do you know it?

FULVIA.

Yes, let me speak with you.

CURIUS.   O you are—

FULVIA.   What am I?

CURIUS.

Speak not so loud.

FULVIA.   I am what you should be.   140
Come, do you think I'd walk in any plot
Where madam Sempronia should take place of me
And Fulvia come i'the rear or o'the by,
That I would be her second in a business

143. o'] Ff; on Q.

---

131. *natural*] given to feelings of natural affection or gratitude.

132. *challenge*] demand as of right.

133. *prime*] best.

135. *religion binds*] with a pun on Lat. *ligare*, "bind"; Lat. *religio* can mean simply "sense of obligation," "scruples."

138. *coming*] "giving way to your wishes" (Gifford).

141. *walk*] associate.

142. *take place of*] take precedence over.

143. *o'the by*] in a place of secondary importance.

Though it might 'vantage me all the sun sees?   145
It was a silly fant'sy of yours. Apply
Yourself to me and the Consul, and be wise;
Follow the fortune I ha' put you into;
You may be something this way, and with safety.

CICERO.

Nay, I must tolerate no whisperings, lady.   150

FULVIA.

Sir, you may hear. I tell him in the way
Wherein he was, how hazardous his course was.

CICERO.

How hazardous? How certain to all ruin.
Did he, or do yet any of them, imagine
The gods would sleep to such a Stygian practice   155
Against that Commonwealth which they have founded
With so much labor, and like care have kept
Now near seven hundred years? It is a madness
Wherewith heaven blinds 'em when it would confound 'em
That they should think it. Come, my Curius,   160
I see your nature's right, you shall no more
Be mention'd with them; I will call you mine
And trouble this good shame no farther. Stand
Firm for your country, and become a man
Honor'd and lov'd. It were a noble life   165
To be found dead, embracing her. Know you
What thanks, what titles, what rewards the Senate
Will heap upon you, certain, for your service?
Let not a desperate action more engage you

---

146. silly] *Ff*; seely *Q*.   164. your] *Q*, *F1*; you *F2*.

---

145. *'vantage . . . sees*] give me a whole world of profit.

146. *Apply*] attach (Lat. *applico*).

155. *sleep*] pay no attention.

158. *seven hundred years*] The traditional date of the foundation of Rome was 753 B.C.

158–160. *It is . . . think it*] "Whom the god will destroy, he first makes mad" was an old Latin proverb; see *Ate* in Glossary (Appendix A).

163–166. *Stand . . . her*] Cf. ll. 173–174, and Horace *Carm.* 3. 2. 13, "It is a sweet and becoming thing to die for one's country," *dulce et decorum est pro patria mori.*

Than safety should, and wicked friendship force   170
What honesty and virtue cannot work.

FULVIA.

He tells you right, sweet friend; 'tis saving counsel.

CURIUS.

Most noble Consul, I am yours and hers,
I mean my country's; you have form'd me new,
Inspiring me with what I should be truly,   175
And I entreat my faith may not seem cheaper
For springing out of penitence.

CICERO.   Good Curius,
It shall be dearer rather, and because
I'd make it such, hear how I trust you more.
Keep still your former face, and mix again   180
With these lost spirits. Run all their mazes with 'em,
For such are treasons. Find their windings out
And subtle turnings, watch their snaky ways
Through brakes and hedges into woods of darkness
Where they are fain to creep upon their breasts   185
In paths ne'er trod by men, but wolves and panthers.
Learn, beside Catiline, Lentulus, and those
Whose names I have, what new ones they draw in;
Who else are likely; what those great ones are
They do not name; what ways they mean to take;   190
And whither their hopes point, to war or ruin
By some surprise. Explore all their intents,
And what you find may profit the Republic.
Acquaint me with it either by yourself
Or this your virtuous friend, on whom I lay   195
The care of urging you. I'll see that Rome
Shall prove a thankful and a bounteous mother.
Be secret as the night.

CURIUS.   And constant, sir.

---

178. *dearer*] of greater price.
180. *face*] outward appearance.
184. *brakes*] rough, overgrown land.
188. *draw*] entice.
189. *likely*] probable.
195. *lay*] impose.

CICERO.

I do not doubt it, though the time cut off
All vows. The dignity of truth is lost   200
With much protesting. Who is there?

[Enter a Servant.]

                This way,
Lest you be seen and met. And when you come,
Be this your token to this fellow.

He whispers with him.

                 Light 'em.

[Exit Servant, Curius, Fulvia.]

O Rome, in what a sickness art thou fall'n,
How dangerous and deadly, when thy head   205
Is drown'd in sleep, and all thy body fev'ry.
No noise, no pulling, no vexation wakes thee,
Thy lethargy is such; or if by chance
Thou heav'st thy eyelids up, thou dost forget
Sooner than thou wert told thy proper danger.   210
I did unreverendly to blame the gods
Who wake for thee, though thou snore to thyself.
Is it not strange thou shouldst be so diseas'd
And so secure? But more that the first symptoms
Of such a malady should not rise out   215
From any worthy member, but a base
And common strumpet, worthless to be nam'd
A hair or part of thee? Think, think, hereafter,
What thy needs were when thou must use such means,
And lay it to thy breast how much the gods   220
Upbraid thy foul neglect of them by making
So vile a thing the author of thy safety.
They could have wrought by nobler ways, have struck

---

201. S.D.] *Gifford.*   *F2.*
203. S.D.] *F1; om. Q; opp. l. 202,*   203.1.] *Gifford.*

---

199. *time cut off*] lack of time may prevent.
201. *Who is there*] i.e., to attend Curius to the door.
203. *Light 'em*] Provide torchlight for them.
210. *proper*] own (Lat. *proprius*).
220. *lay . . . breast*] remember (Lat. *pectus,* the breast as the seat of reason).

Thy foes with forked lightning or ram'd thunder,
Thrown hills upon 'em in the act, have sent   225
Death like a damp to all their families,
Or caus'd their consciences to burst 'em; but
When they will show thee what thou art, and make
A scornful difference 'twixt their power and thee,
They help thee by such aids as geese and harlots.   230

[*Re-enter* Lictor.]

How now? What answer? Is he come?
LICTOR.   Your brother
Will straight be here, and your colleague Antonius
Said coldly he would follow me.   [*Exit.*]
CICERO.   Ay, that
Troubles me somewhat, and is worth my fear.
He is a man 'gainst whom I must provide   235
That, as he'll do no good, he do no harm.
He, though he be not of the plot, will like it
And wish it should proceed, for unto men
Press'd with their wants, all change is ever welcome.
I must with offices and patience win him,   240
Make him by art that which he is not born,
A friend unto the public, and bestow
The province on him which is by the Senate
Decreed to me; that benefit will bind him.
'Tis well if some men will do well for price;   245
So few are virtuous when the reward's away.
Nor must I be unmindful of my private,
For which I have call'd my brother and the Tribunes,

230.1, 233. S.D.] *Gifford.*

---

224. *ram'd*] "driven home" (H & S).
226. *damp*] noxious gas.
230. *geese*] i.e., in 390 B.C., when the cackling of the sacred geese on the
Capitol gave warning that the Gauls were about to make their way into the
citadel.
232. *straight*] immediately.
243. *The province*] "Macedonia" (H & S).
247. *private*] "own interests" (H & S).

My kinsfolk, and my clients to be near me:
He that stands up 'gainst traitors and their ends   250
Shall need a double guard, of law, and friends,
Especially in such an envious state
That sooner will accuse the magistrate
Than the delinquent, and will rather grieve
The treason is not acted, than believe.   [*Exit.*] 255

[III.iii]   [*Enter*] Caesar, Catiline.

CAESAR.

The night grows on, and you are for your meeting;
I'll therefore end in few. Be resolute
And put your enterprise in act. The more
Actions of depth and danger are consider'd,
The less assuredly they are perform'd,   5
And thence it happ'neth that the bravest plots,
Not executed straight, have been discover'd.
Say you are constant, or another, a third,
Or more; there may be yet one wretched spirit
With whom the fear of punishment shall work   10
'Bove all the thoughts of honor and revenge.
You are not now to think what's best to do
As in beginnings, but what must be done
Being thus enter'd, and slip no advantage
That may secure you. Let 'em call it mischief;   15

---

255. S.D.] *Gifford.*

249. *clients*] persons of humbler status, to whom a noble Roman was patron. The reciprocal relationship of services and duties was in some respects afforded legal recognition. Foreign states and tribes, such as the Allobroges, could also secure a Roman family or individual as patron, and the relationship was usually regarded as hereditary on both sides.
[III.iii.] Gifford placed this scene in Catiline's house; but see IV.ii.205 and M. J. Warren, "The Location of Jonson's *Catiline* III.490–754," *Philological Quarterly*, XLVIII (1969), 561–565, for its location in Lecca's.

1. *grows on*] grows later.
1. *are for*] are on your way to.
2. *few*] few words.
3. *put . . . act*] put your plans in action.
4. *depth*] gravity.
14. *enter'd*] begun.
14. *slip*] let escape.

When it is past and prosper'd, 'twill be virtue.
Th'are petty crimes are punish'd, great rewarded.
Nor must you think of peril, since attempts
Begun with danger still do end with glory,
And when need spurs, despair will be call'd wisdom.   20
Less ought the care of men or fame to fright you,
For they that win do seldom receive shame
Of victory, howe'er it be achiev'd,
And vengeance least, for who besieg'd with wants
Would stop at death or anything beyond it?   25
Come, there was never any great thing yet
Aspired, but by violence or fraud,
And he that sticks for folly of a conscience
To reach it—

CATILINE.   Is a good religious fool.

CAESAR.

A superstitious slave, and will die beast.   30
Good night. You know what Crassus thinks, and I,
By this: prepare you wings as large as sails
To cut through air and leave no print behind you.
A serpent, ere he comes to be a dragon,
Does eat a bat, and so must you a Consul   35
That watches. What you do, do quickly, Sergius.
You shall not stir for me.

CATILINE.   Excuse me, lights there.

CAESAR.

By no means.

---

17. *Th'are ... punish'd*] The crimes that are punished are small ones.
21. *the care of*] anxiety about.
28. *sticks*] balks.
29. *religious*] superstitious.
33. *print*] impression.
34–35. *A serpent ... bat*] a commonplace proverb from classical times to
Jonson's own day in the form ". . . must eat another serpent," i.e., to prosper, one must benefit from others' failings; but Fletcher et al., *Honest Man's
Fortune* (1613?), III.iii. 27–30, "The snake that would be a dragon, and
have wings, must eat a spider . . . he that would have the suit of wealth,
must not care whom he feeds on," suggests a meaning closer to Jonson's.
37. *stir for me*] leave your seat because I am going.
37. *Excuse ... there*] On the contrary; bring torches!

CATILINE.   Stay then. All good thoughts to Caesar,
  And like to Crassus.
CAESAR.   Mind but your friends' counsels.   [*Exit.*]
CATILINE.
  Or I will bear no mind.

                    [*Enter*] Aurelia.

                    How now, Aurelia?   40
  Are your confederates come, the ladies?
AURELIA.   Yes.
CATILINE.
  And is Sempronia there?
AURELIA.   She is.
CATILINE.   That's well.
  She has a sulphurous spirit, and will take
  Light at a spark. Break with them, gentle love,
  About the drawing as many of their husbands   45
  Into the plot as can; if not, to rid 'em.
  That'll be the easier practice unto some
  Who have been tir'd with 'em long. Solicit
  Their aids for money, and their servants' help
  In firing of the city at the time   50
  Shall be design'd. Promise 'em states and empires
  And men for lovers made of better clay
  Than ever the old potter Titan knew.
  Who's that?

                    [*Enter* Lecca.]

                    O, Porcius Lecca. Are they met?
LECCA.
  They are all here.
CATILINE.   Love, you have your instructions: 55

39. S.D.] *Gifford.*   53. potter] *Q, F1*; porter *F2.*
40. S.D.] *Gifford*; CATILINE, AV-   54, 57. S.D., 58.1.] *Gifford.*
RELIA, LECCA *after l. 39, Q, Ff.*

---

  38. *Stay then*] (to the servants).
  40. *bear no mind*] have no courage (Lat. *animum gero*).
  44. *Break with*] broach the subject to.

I'll trust you with the stuff you have to work on.
You'll form it? [*Exit* Aurelia.]
        Porcius, fetch the silver eagle
I ga' you in charge, and pray 'em they will enter.
                          [*Exit* Lecca.]
[*Enter*] Cethegus, Curius, Lentulus, Vargunteius, Longinus, Gabin-
ius, Ceparius, Autronius, *etc.*

    O friends, your faces glad me. This will be
    Our last, I hope, of consultation. 60
CETHEGUS.
    So it had need.
CURIUS.   We lose occasion daily.
CATILINE.
    Ay, and our means, whereof one wounds me most
    That was the fairest: Piso is dead in Spain.
CETHEGUS.
    As we are here.
LONGINUS.   And, as it is thought, by envy
    Of Pompey's followers.
LENTULUS.   He too's coming back 65
    Now out of Asia.
CATILINE.   Therefore what we intend
    We must be swift in. Take your seats and hear.
    I have already sent Septimius
    Into the Picene territory, and Julius
    To raise force for us in Apulia; 70
    Manlius at Fesulae is by this time up
    With the old needy troops that follow'd Sylla;
    And all do but expect when we will give
    The blow at home.

58.2. Cethegus] *Gifford*; CATI- 61. S.P. CETHEGUS] *Ff*; CAT. *Q.*
LINE, CETHEGVS *Q*, . . . *Ff*.

56. *stuff*] material of which something is made.
57. *form*] give form to.
58. *ga' you in charge*] gave into your keeping.
61. *occasion*] opportunity.
70. *raise force*] gather an army.
71. *up*] ready.
73. *expect when*] wait until (Lat. *expecto*).

[Re-enter Lecca *with the eagle.]*

Behold this silver eagle:
'Twas Marius' standard in the Cimbrian war,   75
Fatal to Rome and, as our augurs tell me,
Shall still be so, for which one ominous cause
I have kept it safe and done it sacred rites
As to a godhead, in a chapel built
Of purpose to it. Pledge then all your hands   80
To follow it with vows of death and ruin
Struck silently and home. So waters speak
When they run deepest. Now's the time, this year,
The twenti'th from the firing of the Capitol,
As fatal too, to Rome, by all predictions,   85
And in which honor'd Lentulus must rise
A king, if he pursue it.

CURIUS.   If he do not,
He is not worthy the great destiny.

LENTULUS.
It is too great for me, but what the gods
And their great loves decree me, I must not   90
Seem careless of.

CATILINE.   No, nor we envious.
We have enough beside, all Gallia, Belgia,
Greece, Spain, and Afric.

CURIUS.   Ay, and Asia too,
Now Pompey is returning.

CATILINE.   Noblest Romans,
Methinks our looks are not so quick and high   95
As they were wont.

CURIUS.   No? Whose is not?

CATILINE.   We have
No anger in our eyes, no storm, no lightning;
Our hate is spent and fum'd away in vapor

---

74. S.D.] *Gifford.*   75. 'Twas] *Ff*; Was *Q.*

76. *Fatal to*] influencing the fate of.
80. *Of purpose*] expressly.
80. *Pledge . . . hands*] clasp your hands as a pledge.
91. *careless*] negligent.
95. *quick and high*] fiery and noble.

Before our hands be at work. I can accuse
Not any one, but all of slackness.

CETHEGUS.   Yes,   100
And be yourself such, while you do it.

CATILINE.   Ha?
'Tis sharply answer'd, Caius.

CETHEGUS.   Truly, truly.

LENTULUS.
Come, let us each one know his part to do,
And then be accus'd. Leave these untimely quarrels.

CURIUS.
I would there were more Romes than one to ruin.   105

CETHEGUS.
More Romes? More worlds.

CURIUS.   Nay then, more gods and natures,
If they took part.

LENTULUS.   When shall the time be, first?

CATILINE.
I think the Saturnals.

CETHEGUS.   'Twill be too long.

CATILINE.
They are not now far off, 'tis not a month.

CETHEGUS.
A week, a day, an hour is too far off;   110
Now were the fittest time.

CATILINE.   We ha' not laid
All things so safe and ready.

CETHEGUS.   While we are laying,
We shall all lie and grow to earth. Would I
Were nothing in it, if not now. These things,
They should be done ere thought.

CATILINE.   Nay, now your reason   115
Forsakes you, Caius. Think but what commodity
That time will minister, the city's custom
Of being then in mirth and feast—

_____

108. *long*] far off.
114. *Were . . . it*] had no part in the plot.
116. *commodity*] convenience.
117. *minister*] furnish.

−79−

LENTULUS.   Loos'd whole
    In pleasure and security—
AUTRONIUS.   Each house
    Resolv'd in freedom—
CURIUS.   Every slave a master—   120
LONGINUS.
    And they too no mean aids—
CURIUS.   Made from their hope
    Of liberty—
LENTULUS.   Or hate unto their lords.
VARGUNTEIUS.
    'Tis sure there cannot be a time found out
    More apt and natural.
LENTULUS.   Nay, good Cethegus,
    Why do your passions now disturb our hopes?   125
CETHEGUS.
    Why do your hopes delude your certainties?
CATILINE.
    You must lend him his way. Think for the order
    And process of it.
LONGINUS.   Yes.
LENTULUS.   I like not fire;
    'Twill too much waste my city.
CATILINE.   Were it embers,
    There will be wealth enough rak'd out of them   130
    To spring anew. It must be fire or nothing.
LONGINUS.
    What else should fright or terrify 'em?
VARGUNTEIUS.   True.
    In that confusion must be the chief slaughter.
CURIUS.
    Then we shall kill 'em bravest.
CEPARIUS.   And in heaps.

126. your certainties] *Q*, *F1*; our   131. anew] *F2*; a new *Q*, *F1*.
certainties *F2*.

---

  118. *Loos'd whole*] entirely relaxed.
  120. *Resolv'd*] "relaxed (Lat. *resolutus*)" (H & S).
  127. *lend*] let have.
  127–128. *Think . . . process*] Consider the arrangement and method.
  134. *bravest*] most splendidly.

AUTRONIUS.

    Strew sacrifices.

CURIUS.   Make the earth an altar.   135

LONGINUS.

    And Rome the fire.

LECCA.   'Twill be a noble night.

VARGUNTEIUS.

    And worth all Sylla's days.

CURIUS.   When husbands, wives,

    Grandsires and nephews, servants and their lords,

    Virgins and priests, the infant and the nurse

    Go all to hell together in a fleet.   140

CATILINE.

    I would have you, Longinus and Statilius,

    To take the charge o'the firing, which must be

    At a sign given with a trumpet, done

    In twelve chief places of the city at once.

    The flax and sulphur are already laid   145

    In at Cethegus' house. So are the weapons.

    Gabinius, you with other force shall stop

    The pipes and conduits, and kill those that come

    For water.

CURIUS.   What shall I do?

CATILINE.   All will have

    Employment, fear not; ply the execution.   150

CURIUS.

    For that, trust me and Cethegus.

CATILINE.   I will be

    At hand with the army, to meet those that 'scape.

    And Lentulus, begirt you Pompey's house

    To seize his sons alive, for they are they

    Must make our peace with him. All else cut off   155

    As Tarquin did the poppy heads, or mowers

    A field of thistles, or else up, as plows

    Do barren lands; and strike together flints

145–146. *laid/ In*] stored.

150. *ply the execution*] carry out the plan.

153. *begirt*] surround.

157. *up*] i.e., cut up.

And clods, th'ungrateful Senate and the people,
Till no rage gone before or coming after   160
May weigh with yours, though horror leap'd herself
Into the scale, but in your violent acts
The fall of torrents and the noise of tempests,
The boiling of Charybdis, the sea's wildness,
The eating force of flames and wings of winds,   165
Be all outwrought by your transcendent furies.
It had been done ere this, had I been Consul;
We had had no stop, no let.

LENTULUS.   How find you Antonius?

CATILINE.

The other has won him, lost; that Cicero
Was born to be my opposition,   170
And stands in all our ways.

CURIUS.   Remove him first.

CETHEGUS.

May that yet be done sooner?

CATILINE.   Would it were done.

CURIUS. VARGUNTEIUS.

I'll do't.

CETHEGUS.   It is my province; none usurp it.

LENTULUS.

What are your means?
CETHEGUS.   Inquire not. He shall die.
"Shall" was too slowly said. He is dying. That   175
Is yet too slow. He is dead.

CATILINE.   Brave, only Roman,
Whose soul might be the world's soul, were that dying,
Refuse not yet the aids of these your friends.

LENTULUS.

Here's Vargunteius holds good quarter with him.

175–176. He is ... He is] *Q*, *F1*;
He's ... He's *F2*.

---

159. *ungrateful*] displeasing.
161. *weigh with*] be equal in weight to.
168. *let*] hindrance.
173. S.P. *Curius. Vargunteius*] so Q, Ff; but cf. III.v.0.1 ("[*Enter*] Vargunteius, Cornelius"), which has the warrant of Sallust 28.
179. *quarter*] relations.

CATILINE.

  And under the pretext of clientele   180
  And visitation with the morning "hail"
  Will be admitted.

CETHEGUS.   What is that to me?

VARGUNTEIUS.

  Yes, we may kill him in his bed, and safely.

CETHEGUS.

  Safe is your way, then; take it. Mine's mine own.   [*Exit.*]

CATILINE.

  Follow him, Vargunteius, and persuade   185
  The morning is the fittest time.

LONGINUS.   The night
  Will turn all into tumult.

LENTULUS.   And perhaps
  Miss of him too.

CATILINE.   Entreat and conjure him,
  In all our names—

LENTULUS.   By all our vows and friendships.
                                    [*Exit* Vargunteius.]

        [*Enter*] *to them* Sempronia, Aurelia, Fulvia.

SEMPRONIA.

  What, is our council broke up first?

AURELIA.   You say   190
  Women are greatest talkers.

SEMPRONIA.   We ha' done
  And are now fit for action.

LONGINUS.   Which is passion:

184. S.D., 189.1.] *Gifford.*   189.2.] *F1*; SEMPRONIA ...
                                           FVLVIA, *To them* Q, *F2.*

---

180. *clientele*] "attendance on a patron (Lat. *clientela*)" (H & S).
188. *Miss of*] fail to hit.
188. *conjure*] plead with.
192. *action . . . passion*] with a play on *agere* and *pati*, "to do" and "to undergo," the Latin words from which the English derive: they were held, from Roman times to Jonson's own, to be the opposite or complementary states which between them included all human physical and moral experience. In the philosophical sense, then, Longinus' words are a paradox; in the common sense, a slur; and in both an insult to Sempronia, who thought herself an intellectual but had a reputation for licentiousness.

There's your best activity, lady.

SEMPRONIA.   How

Knows your wise fatness that?

LONGINUS.   Your mother's daughter

Did teach me, madam.

CATILINE.   Come, Sempronia, leave him;   195

He is a giber, and our present business

Is of more serious consequence. Aurelia

Tells me you have done most masculinely within,

And play'd the orator.

SEMPRONIA.   But we must hasten

To our design as well, and execute;   200

Not hang still in the fever of an accident.

CATILINE.

You say well, lady.

SEMPRONIA.   I do like our plot

Exceeding well; 'tis sure, and we shall leave

Little to fortune in it.

CATILINE.   Your banquet stays.

Aurelia, take her in. Where's Fulvia?   205

SEMPRONIA.

O, the two lovers are coupling.

CURIUS.   In good faith,

She's very ill with sitting up.

SEMPRONIA.   You'd have her

Laugh and lie down?

FULVIA.   No, faith, Sempronia,

I am not well. I'll take my leave, it draws

Toward the morning. Curius shall stay with you.   210

Madam, I pray you pardon me, my health

I must respect.

195. S.P. CATILINE] *Whalley*; CET.   199. play'd] *Q, F1*; play *F2.*
Q, Ff.

---

197. *consequence*] importance.
201. *hang . . . accident*] remain motionless in anxiety over the unforeseen.
204. *stays*] awaits.
206. *coupling*] making love.
208. *Laugh . . . down*] "the name of an obsolete card-game" (H & S).
209–210. *it . . . morning*] it is almost morning.
212. *respect*] pay attention to.

AURELIA.   Farewell, good Fulvia.

CURIUS (*whispers this to* Fulvia).

    Make haste and bid him get his guards about him,
    For Vargunteius and Cornelius
    Have underta'en it, should Cethegus miss;   215
    Their reason, that they think his open rashness
    Will suffer easier discovery
    Than their attempt, so veiled under friendship.
    I'll bring you to your coach. Tell him beside
    Of Caesar's coming forth here.

CATILINE.   My sweet madam,   220
    Will you be gone?

FULVIA.   I am, my lord, in truth
    In some indisposition.

CATILINE.   I do wish
    You had all your health, sweet lady; Lentulus,
    You'll do her service.

LENTULUS.   To her coach, and duty.

                      [*Exeunt all but* Catiline.]

CATILINE.

    What ministers men must for practice use!   225
    The rash, th'ambitious, needy, desperate,
    Foolish and wretched, ev'n the dregs of mankind,
    To whores and women. Still, it must be so.
    Each have their proper place and in their rooms
    They are the best. Grooms fittest kindle fires,   230
    Slaves carry burdens, butchers are for slaughters,
    Apothecaries, butlers, cooks for poisons,
    As these for me: dull, stupid Lentulus,
    My stale with whom I stalk; the rash Cethegus,
    My executioner; and fat Longinus,   235

213. S.D.] *om. Q*; *"Curius whispers* 224.1.] *Gifford.*
this to Fulvia" Ff.

---

217. *suffer*] permit.
224. *duty*] (to her) service.
225. *ministers*] agents.
229. *rooms*] posts.
230. *Grooms*] menservants.
232. *butlers*] servants in charge of wines.
234. *stale*] "decoy" (H & S).

Statilius, Curius, Ceparius, Cimber,
My laborers, pioneers, and incendiaries;
With these domestic traitors, bosom thieves
Whom custom hath call'd wives, the readiest helps
To betray heady husbands, rob the easy,   240
And lend the moneys on returns of lust.
Shall Catiline not do now with these aids
So sought, so sorted, something shall be call'd
Their labor but his profit, and make Caesar
Repent his vent'ring counsels to a spirit   245
So much his lord in mischief, when all these
Shall like the brethren sprung of dragons' teeth
Ruin each other and he fall amongst 'em
With Crassus, Pompey, or who else appears
But like or near a great one? May my brain   250
Resolve to water and my blood turn phlegm,
My hands drop off unworthy of my sword,
And that be inspired of itself to rip
My breast for my lost entrails, when I leave
A soul that will not serve; and who will, are   255
The same with slaves, such clay I dare not fear.
The cruelty I mean to act I wish
Should be call'd mine and tarry in my name,
Whilst after-ages do toil out themselves
In thinking for the like, but do it less,   260

---

240. betray heady] *Ff*; strangle   253. be inspired] *Gifford*; b'inspired
head-strong *Q*.   *Q*, *Ff*.

---

237. *pioneers*] foot soldiers who dig trenches, clear land, etc.
240. *heady*] impetuous.
240. *easy*] those at ease.
241. *returns*] proceeds.
243. *So sought, so sorted*] so carefully recruited and given assignments.
247. *brethren . . . teeth*] In the myth of Jason and the golden fleece, and also in that of Cadmus and the founding of Thebes, the hero slays a dragon and sows its teeth in the earth, and from them spring warriors who then fight each other to the death.
250. *But . . . one*] even similar to or near a great person.
251. *Resolve*] decompose.
258. *tarry*] remain.
259. *toil out themselves*] work themselves out.
260. *thinking for*] attempting to invent.

And were the power of all the fiends let loose
With fate to boot, it should be still example
When what the Gaul or Moor could not effect,
Nor emulous Carthage with their length of spite,
Shall be the work of one, and that my night.   [*Exit.*] 265

[III.iv]   [*Enter*] Cicero, Fulvia[, *Servant*].

CICERO.

I thank your vigilance. Where's my brother, Quintus?
Call all my servants up.   [*Exit Servant.*]
                Tell noble Curius
And say it to yourself, you are my savers;
But that's too little for you, you are Rome's.
What could I then hope less?

                [*Enter* Quintus.]

                O brother, now   5
The engineers I told you of are working.
The machine 'gins to move. Where are your weapons?
Arm all my household presently, and charge
The porter he let no man in till day.

QUINTUS.

Not clients, and your friends?

CICERO.   They wear those names   10
That come to murder me. Yet send for Cato
And Quintus Catulus; those I dare trust,
And Flaccus and Pomtinius, the Praetors,
By the back way.

265. S.D.] *Gifford.*   2, 5.S.D.] *Gifford.*
[III.iv]   6. engineers] *Whalley*; engines *Q*,
0.1.] *Gifford*; CICERO, FVLVIA,   *Ff.*
QVINTVS. *Q, Ff.*

262. *fate to boot*] destruction as well.
262. *example*] the outstanding instance.
264. *length of spite*] long history of malice.
[III.iv]
2. *Call . . . up*] summon.
5. *What . . . less*] and as you are Rome's salvation, I may hope that you
will be no less than mine.
6–7. *engineers . . . machine*] plotters . . . machinations; the metaphor is
from siege engines.

QUINTUS.   Take care, good brother Marcus,
　　Your fears be not form'd greater than they should,   15
　　And make your friends grieve while your enemies laugh.
CICERO.
　　'Tis brother's counsel, and worth thanks. But do
　　As I entreat you. I provide, not fear.   [*Exit* Quintus.]
　　Was Caesar there, say you?
FULVIA.   Curius says he met him
　　Coming from thence.
CICERO.   O, so. And had you a council   20
　　Of ladies too? Who was your speaker, madam?
FULVIA.
　　She that would be, had there been forty more,
　　Sempronia, who had both her Greek and figures,
　　And ever and anon would ask us if
　　The witty Consul could have mended that,   25
　　Or orator Cicero could have said it better?
CICERO.
　　She's my gentle enemy. Would Cethegus
　　Had no more danger in him. But my guards
　　Are you, great powers, and th'unbated strengths
　　Of a firm conscience, which shall arm each step   30
　　Ta'en for the state, and teach me slack no pace
　　For fear of malice.

　　　　　　　　[*Re-enter* Quintus.]

　　　　　　　　How now, brother?
QUINTUS.   Cato
　　And Quintus Catulus were coming to you,
　　And Crassus with 'em. I have let 'em in
　　By th' garden.
CICERO.   What would Crassus have?
QUINTUS.   I hear   35
　　Some whispering 'bout the gate, and making doubt

18, 32. S.D.] *Gifford*.

18. *not*] do not.
23. *figures*] rhetorical turns of speech.
24. *ever and anon*] time and again.
25. *mended*] improved on.
29. *unbated*] unabated.
36. *making doubt*] wondering.

Whether it be not yet too early, or no;
But I do think they are your friends and clients,
Are fearful to disturb you.

CICERO.   You will change
To another thought anon. Ha' you giv'n the porter   40
The charge I will'd you?

QUINTUS.   Yes.

CICERO.   Withdraw and hearken. [*Exeunt.*]

[III.v]   [*Enter*] Vargunteius, Cornelius.

VARGUNTEIUS.
   The door's not open yet.

CORNELIUS.   You were best to knock.

VARGUNTEIUS.
   Let them stand close, then, and when we are in,
   Rush after us.

CORNELIUS.   But where's Cethegus?

VARGUNTEIUS.   He
   Has left it, since he might not do't his way.

PORTER [*within*].
   Who's there?

VARGUNTEIUS.   A friend, or more.

PORTER.   I may not let   5
   Any man in till day.

VARGUNTEIUS.   No? Why?

CORNELIUS.   Thy reason?

PORTER.
   I am commanded so.

VARGUNTEIUS.   By whom?

CORNELIUS.   I hope
   We are not discover'd.

VARGUNTEIUS.   Yes, by revelation.

41. S.P. CICERO] *Q, F1*; *om. F2.*   LIVS, PORTER, CICERO, CAT-
41. S.D.] *Gifford.*   VLVS, CRASSVS. *Q, Ff.*
[III.v]   5. S.D.] *Gifford.*
0.1.] VARGVNTEIVS, CORNE-

---

   2. *them*] i.e., the other assassins with them.
   4. *left it*] quit the assassination attempt.
   5. *more*] more than one.
   8. *revelation*] betrayal.

Pray thee, good slave, who has commanded thee?

PORTER.

He that may best, the Consul.

VARGUNTEIUS.   We are his friends.   10

PORTER.

All's one.

CORNELIUS.   Best give your name.

VARGUNTEIUS.   Dost thou hear, fellow?

I have some instant business with the Consul.

My name is Vargunteius.

Cicero *speaks to them from above* [, *with* Cato, Catulus, *and Crassus*].

CICERO.   True, he knows it,

And for what friendly office you are sent.

Cornelius too is there?

VARGUNTEIUS.   We are betray'd.   15

CICERO.

And desperate Cethegus, is he not?

VARGUNTEIUS.

Speak you, he knows my voice.

CICERO.   What say you to't?

CORNELIUS.

You are deceiv'd, sir.

CICERO.   No, 'tis you are so,

Poor, misled men. Your states are yet worth pity,

If you would hear and change your savage minds.   20

Leave to be mad, forsake your purposes

Of treason, rapine, murder, fire, and horror.

The Commonwealth hath eyes that wake as sharply

Over her life as yours do for her ruin.

Be not deceiv'd to think her lenity   25

Will be perpetual, or if men be wanting,

---

9. Pray] *Q, F1*; Pr'y *F2*.   13. S.D. *with . . .* Crassus] *Gifford*.
13. S.D. *Cicero . . . above*] *Ff*; om. *Q*

---

11. *All's one*] It's all the same.
12. *instant*] urgent (Lat. *instans*).
21. *to be*] being.
23. *wake as sharply*] keep watch as vigilantly.

The gods will be, to such a calling cause.
Consider your attempts, and while there's time
Repent you of 'em. It doth make me tremble
There should those spirits yet breathe that when they
    cannot 30
Live honestly, would rather perish basely.

CATO.

You talk too much to 'em, Marcus, they are lost.
Go forth and apprehend 'em.

CATULUS.   If you prove
This practice, what should let the Commonwealth
To take due vengeance?

VARGUNTEIUS.   Let us shift away. 35
The darkness hath conceal'd us yet. We'll say
Some have abus'd our names.

CORNELIUS.   Deny it all.
                [*Exeunt* Vargunteius, Cornelius.]

CATO.

Quintus, what guards ha' you? Call the Tribunes' aid
And raise the city. Consul, you are too mild.
The foulness of some facts takes thence all mercy; 40
Report it to the Senate.

It thunders and lightens violently on the sudden.

                Hear, the gods
Grow angry with your patience. 'Tis their care
And must be yours, that guilty men escape not.
As crimes do grow, justice should rouse itself.   [*Exeunt.*]

CHORUS.

What is it, heavens, you prepare 45
    With so much swiftness and so sudden rising?
There are no sons of earth that dare

37.1, 44. S.D.] *Gifford.*

---

27. *calling cause*] i.e., the cause is seen as a plaintiff summoning (*advocans*)
the gods to act as its advocate.
28. *attempts*] assaults.
33. *prove*] approve (Lat. *probo*).
34. *let*] hinder.
35. *shift away*] slip away.
37. *abus'd*] used wrongly.
47. *sons of earth*] "Giants and Titans" (H & S).

Again rebellion, or the gods' surprising?
The world doth shake and nature fears,
    Yet is the tumult and the horror greater   50
Within our minds than in our ears,
    So much Rome's faults, now grown her fate, do threat her.
The priests and people run about,
    Each order, age, and sex amaz'd at other,
And at the ports all thronging out   55
    As if their safety were to quit their mother;
Yet find they the same dangers there
    From which they make such haste to be preserved,
For guilty states do ever bear
    The plagues about them which they have deserved,   60
And till those plagues do get above
    The mountain of our faults, and there do sit,
We see 'em not. Thus still we love
    The evil we do until we suffer it.
But, most, ambition, that near vice   65
    To virtue, hath the fate of Rome provoked,
And made that now Rome's self's no price
    To free her from the death wherewith she's yoked,
That restless ill that still doth build
    Upon success, and ends not in aspiring,   70
But there begins, and ne'er is fill'd
    While aught remains that seems but worth desiring,
Wherein the thought, unlike the eye
    To which things far seem smaller than they are,

---

53. priests] *Q, F1*; Priest *F2*.   67. self's] *Gifford*; selfe *Q, Ff*.
62. mountain] *Q, F1*; mountaines
F2.

---

52. *threat*] threaten.   54. *order*] class.
55. *ports*] "gates (Lat. *porta*)" (H & S).
56. *mother*] i.e. Rome.
60. *plagues*] calamities.
61. *get above*] rise above.
64. *suffer*] suffer for or from.
65–66. *near . . . virtue*] vice near to virtue.
66. *provoked*] occasioned.
67. *made . . . price*] caused Rome herself to be too small a ransom.
71. *fill'd*] satiated.
72. *but*] even.

Deems all contentment plac'd on high,   75
  And thinks there's nothing great but what is far.
O that in time, Rome did not cast
  Her errors up, this fortune to prevent,
T'have seen her crimes ere they were past
  And felt her faults before her punishment.   80

[IV.i]

[*Enter*] Allobroges. *Divers Senators pass by, quaking and trembling.*

ALLOBROX.

  Can these men fear, who are not only ours
  But the world's masters? Then I see the gods
  Upbraid our suff'rings, or would humble them,
  By sending these affrights while we are here,
  That we might laugh at their ridiculous fear   5
  Whose names we trembled at beyond the Alps.
  Of all that pass, I do not see a face
  Worthy a man that dares look up and stand
  One thunder out, but downward all like beasts
  Running away from every flash is made.   10
  The falling world could not deserve such baseness.
  Are we employ'd here by our miseries
  Like superstitious fools, or rather slaves,
  To plain our griefs, wrongs, and oppressions
  To a mere clothed Senate whom our folly   15
  Hath made and still intends to keep our tyrants?
  It is our base petitionary breath
  That blows 'em to this greatness, which this prick
  Would soon let out if we were bold and wretched.

IV.i.] *Scene divisions in this Act follow*   0.1. *Divers . . . trembling.*] *Ff*; *om. Q*.
Gifford.

77–78. *cast . . . up*] calculate her errors.
[IV.i]
  8–9. *stand . . . out*] endure . . . to the end.
  11. *The . . . baseness*] Even if the world were collapsing, such timidity
would not be justified.
  14. *plain*] complain.
  15. *clothed*] taking authority from garb only.
  18. *blows*] inflates.
  18. *prick*] sword.

When they have taken all we have, our goods,   20
Crop, lands, and houses, they will leave us this;
A weapon and an arm will still be found,
Though naked left, and lower than the ground.

[*Enter*] Cato, Catulus, Cicero.

CATO.

Do, urge thine anger still, good heaven, and just;
Tell guilty men what powers are above them.   25
In such a confidence of wickedness
'Twas time they should know something fit to fear.

CATULUS.

I never saw a morn more full of horror.

CATO.

To Catiline and his, but to just men,
Though heaven should speak with all his wrath at once   30
That with his breath the hinges of the world
Did crack, we should stand upright and unfear'd.

CICERO.

Why, so we do, good Cato. Who be these?

CATULUS.

Ambassadors from the Allobroges
I take 'em, by their habits.

ALLOBROX.   Ay, these men   35
Seem of another race; let's sue to these,
There's hope of justice with their fortitude.

CICERO.

Friends of the Senate and of Rome, today
We pray you to forbear us; on the morrow
What suit you have, let us by Fabius Sanga,   40
Whose patronage your state doth use, but know it

23.1.] *Q*; CATO, CATVLVS,
CICERO, ALLOBROGES. *Ff.*

---

24. *urge*] present.
26. *confidence of*] self-confidence arising from.
32. *unfear'd*] unafraid.
35. *habits*] clothing.
36. *sue to*] seek justice from.
39. *forbear*] leave alone.
41. *patronage*] See III.ii.249, n.

And, on the Consul's word, you shall receive
Dispatch, or else an answer worth your patience.

ALLOBROX.

We could not hope for more, most worthy Consul.

                 [*Exeunt* Cato, Catulus, Cicero.]

This magistrate hath struck an awe into me   45
And by his sweetness won a more regard
Unto his place than all the boist'rous moods
That ignorant greatness practiceth to fill
The large, unfit authority it wears.
How easy is a noble spirit discern'd   50
From harsh and sulphurous matter that flies out
In contumelies, makes a noise, and stinks.
May we find good and great men that know how
To stoop to wants and meet necessities,
And will not turn from any equal suits.   55
Such men, they do not succor more the cause
They undertake with favor and success,
Than by it their own judgments they do raise
In turning just men's needs into their praise.   [*Exeunt.*]

[IV.ii]

[*Enter* Cicero, Antonius, Cato, Catulus, Caesar, Crassus, Flaccus, *other members of*] *the Senate.*

FLACCUS.

Room for the Consuls. Fathers, take your places.
Here in the house of Jupiter the Stayer
By edict from the Consul, Marcus Tullius,
You are met, a frequent Senate. Hear him speak.

44.1, 59. S.D.] *Gifford.*   1. S.P. FLACCUS] *this edn.* ; PRAE.
[IV.ii]   *Q, Ff.*

---

43. *Dispatch*] speedy reply.
47. *place*] status.
48. *practiceth*] employs.
54. *stoop to*] condescend to apply their thoughts to.
55. *equal*] fair (Lat. *aequus*).
58. *their own judgments*] judgments of them by others.
[IV.ii]
4. *frequent*] well-attended (Lat. *frequens*).

CICERO.

What may be happy and auspicious still   5
To Rome and hers. Honor'd and Conscript Fathers,
If I were silent and that all the dangers
Threat'ning the state and you were yet so hid
In night or darkness thicker in their breasts
That are the black contrivers, so that no   10
Beam of the light could pierce 'em, yet the voice
Of heav'n this morning hath spoke loud enough
T'instruct you with a feeling of the horror
And wake you from a sleep as stark as death.
I have of late spoke often in this Senate   15
Touching this argument, but still have wanted
Either your ears or faith, so incredible
Their plots have seem'd, or I so vain to make
These things for mine own glory and false greatness,
As hath been given out. But be it so.   20
When they break forth and shall declare themselves
By their too foul effects, then, then, the envy
Of my just cares will find another name.
For me, I am but one, and this poor life
So lately aim'd at, not an hour yet since,   25
They cannot with more eagerness pursue
Than I with gladness would lay down and lose
To buy Rome's peace, if that would purchase it.
But when I see they'd make it but the step
To more and greater, unto yours, Rome's, all,   30
I would with those preserve it, or then fall.

5. What] *Ff*; Which *Q*.   25. yet since] *Q*, *Ff*; sithence *Q*(*o*).
14. stark] *Ff*; dead *Q*.

---

5. *What . . . auspicious*] i.e., I wish . . . (Lat. *quod felix faustumque sit*).
7. *that*] if.
13. *instruct*] provide (Lat. *instruo*).
14. *stark*] rigid.
16. *Touching this argument*] concerning this subject.
16. *wanted*] lacked.
20. *given out*] declared.
22. *effects*] results.
22. *envy*] unpopularity.

CAESAR [*aside to* Crassus].

    Ay, ay, let you alone, cunning artificer!

    See how his gorget 'pears above his gown

    To tell the people in what danger he was.

    It was absurdly done of Vargunteius   35

    To name himself before he was got in.

CRASSUS.

    It matters not, so they deny it all

    And can but carry the lie constantly.

    Will Catiline be here?

CAESAR.   I have sent for him.

CRASSUS.

    And ha' you bid him to be confident?   40

CAESAR.

    To that his own necessity will prompt him.

CRASSUS.

    Seem to believe nothing at all that Cicero

    Relates us.

CAESAR.   It will mad him.

CRASSUS.   O, and help

    The other party.

        Quintus Cicero *brings in the Tribunes and Guards.*

              Who is that, his brother?

    What new intelligence has he brought him now?   45

CAESAR.

    Some cautions from his wife, how to behave him.

CICERO.

    Place some of them without and some bring in.

    Thank their kind loves. It is a comfort yet

    That all depart not from their country's cause.

32. S.D.] *Gifford.*   44. S.D.] *om. Q; opp. l. 45, F1; opp. l. 43, F2.*

---

32. *artificer*] trickster.

33. *gorget*] throat-armor.

37. *so*] provided that.

38. *constantly*] steadfastly.

43. *mad*] madden.

44. *party*] those taking one side in a dispute.

45. *intelligence*] news.

CAESAR.

    How now, what means this muster, Consul Antonius?   50

ANTONIUS.

    I do not know; ask my colleague, he'll tell you.
    There is some reason in state that I must yield to,
    And I have promis'd him; indeed he has bought it
    With giving me the province.

CICERO.   I profess

    It grieves me, Fathers, that I am compell'd   55
    To draw these arms and aids for your defense,
    And more against a citizen of Rome
    Born here amongst you, a Patrician,
    A man, I must confess, of no mean house
    Nor no small virtue, if he had employ'd   60
    Those excellent gifts of fortune and of nature
    Unto the good, not ruin of the state;
    But being bred in's father's needy fortunes,
    Brought up in's sister's prostitution,
    Confirm'd in civil slaughter, ent'ring first   65
    The Commonwealth with murder of the gentry;
    Since, both by study and custom, conversant
    With all licentiousness; what could be hop'd
    In such a field of riot, but a course
    Extreme pernicious? Though, I must protest   70
    I found his mischiefs sooner with mine eyes
    Than with my thought, and with these hands of mine
    Before they touch'd at my suspicion.

CAESAR.

    What are his mischiefs, Consul? You declaim
    Against his manners, and corrupt your own.   75
    No wise man should for hate of guilty men
    Lose his own innocence.

---

59. *house*] family.
63. *in's*] in his.
65–66. *ent'ring . . . Commonwealth*] making his entry into political life.
67. *study and custom*] inclination and habit.
67. *conversant*] familiar.
69. *field of riot*] expanse of debauchery.
70. *protest*] avow.
75. *his manners*] Catiline's behavior (Lat. *mores*).

CICERO.   The noble Caesar
   Speaks godlike truth; but when he hears I can
   Convince him by his manners of his mischiefs,
   He might be silent, and not cast away   80
   His sentences in vain, where they scarce look
   Toward his subject.
CATO.   Here he comes himself.

        Catiline *sits down, and* Cato *rises from him.*

   If he be worthy any good man's voice,
   That good man sit down by him; Cato will not.
CATULUS.
   If Cato leave him, I'll not keep aside.   85
CATILINE.
   What face is this the Senate here puts on
   Against me, Fathers? Give my modesty
   Leave to demand the cause of so much strangeness.
CAESAR.
   It is reported here you are the head
   To a strange faction, Lucius.
CICERO.   Ay, and will   90
   Be prov'd against him.
CATILINE.   Let it be. Why, Consul,
   If in the Commonwealth there be two bodies,
   One lean, weak, rotten, and that hath a head;
   The other strong and healthful, but hath none;
   If I do give it one, do I offend?   95
   Restore yourselves unto your temper, Fathers,
   And without perturbation hear me speak.
   Remember who I am, and of what place,
   What petty fellow this is that opposes:

82. S.P. CATO] *Ff*; CAT. *Q*.   91. S.P. CATILINE] *Ff*; CAT. *Q*.
82.1.] *F1*; *om. Q*; *opp. l. 84, F2*.

   79. *Convince*] convict (Lat. *convinco*).
   81. *sentences*] maxims.
   81–82. *look/ Toward*] have regard to (Lat. *spectare ad*).
   85. *keep aside*] remain at Catiline's side.
   86. *face . . . puts on*] aspect . . . assumes.
   87. *modesty*] sense of honor (Lat. *modestia*).
   88. *strangeness*] estrangement.
   90. *strange*] hostile.

One that hath exercis'd his eloquence   100
Still to the bane of the nobility,
A boasting, insolent tongue-man.

CATO.   Peace, lewd traitor,
Or wash thy mouth. He is an honest man
And loves his country; would thou didst so too.

CATILINE.
Cato, you are too zealous for him.

CATO.   No,   105
Thou art too impudent.

CATULUS.   Catiline, be silent.

CATILINE.
Nay, then I easily fear my just defense
Will come too late to so much prejudice.

CAESAR [*aside*].
Will he sit down?

CATILINE.   Yet let the world forsake me,
My innocence must not.

CATO.   Thou innocent?   110
So are the Furies.

CICERO.   Yes, and Ate too.
Dost thou not blush, pernicious Catiline?
Or hath the paleness of thy guilt drunk up
Thy blood and drawn thy veins as dry of that
As is thy heart of truth, thy breast of virtue?   115
Whither at length wilt thou abuse our patience?
Still shall thy fury mock us? To what license
Dares thy unbridled boldness run itself?
Do all the nightly guards kept on the palace,
The city's watches, with the people's fears,   120
The concourse of all good men, this so strong
And fortified seat here of the Senate,

109. S.D.] *Gifford*.

---

102. *lewd*] evil.

113. *paleness . . . guilt*] paleness caused by a sense of guilt.

116. *Whither at length*] How long, then (Lat. *quo usque tandem*)? See "Jonson's Use of Classical Sources" in Appendix B.

117. *license*] licentiousness.

119. *palace*] "a misleading translation of *Palatium*, the Palatine Hill" (H & S).

The present looks upon thee, strike thee nothing?
Dost thou not feel thy counsels all laid open,
And see thy wild conspiracy bound in   125
With each man's knowledge? Which of all this order
Canst thou think ignorant, if they'll but utter
Their conscience to the right, of what thou didst
Last night, what on the former, where thou wert,
Whom thou didst call together, what your plots were?   130
O age and manners! This the Consul sees,
The Senate understands, yet this man lives.
Lives? Ay, and comes here into council with us,
Partakes the public cares, and with his eye
Marks and points out each man of us to slaughter,   135
And we good men do satisfy the state
If we can shun but this man's sword and madness.
There was that virtue once in Rome when good men
Would with more sharp coercion have restrain'd
A wicked citizen than the deadliest foe.   140
We have that law still, Catiline, for thee;
An act as grave as sharp. The state's not wanting,
Nor the authority of this Senate; we,
We that are Consuls only fail ourselves.
This twenty days the edge of that decree   145
We have let dull and rust, kept it shut up
As in a sheath which drawn should take thy head.
Yet still thou liv'st, and liv'st not to lay by
Thy wicked confidence, but to confirm it.

---

123. *strike thee nothing*] impress you not at all.
125. *bound in*] restrained (Lat. *constrictam*).
128. *conscience*] inward knowledge.
128. *to the right*] correctly.
134. *Partakes . . . cares*] takes part in the deliberations of government.
135. *Marks . . . out*] designates.
136. *satisfy the state*] do our full duty.
139. *coercion*] limitation (Lat. *coerceo*, restrain).
142. *grave*] authoritative.
142. *state's not wanting*] authority of the people is not lacking.
148. *by*] aside.
149. *confidence*] see IV.i.26, n. (Lat. source has *audaciam*).

I could desire, Fathers, to be found   150
Still merciful, to seem in these main perils
Grasping the state a man remiss and slack;
But then I should condemn myself of sloth
And treachery. Their camp's in Italy,
Pitch'd in the jaws here of Hetruria;   155
Their numbers daily increasing, and their general
Within our walls, nay, in our council, plotting
Hourly some fatal mischief to the public.
If, Catiline, I should command thee now,
Here, to be taken, kill'd, I make just doubt   160
Whether all good men would not think it done
Rather too late, than any man too cruel.

CATO.

Except he were of the same meal and batch.

CICERO.

But that which ought to have been done long since
I will, and for good reason, yet forbear.   165
Then will I take thee, when no man is found
So lost, so wicked, nay, so like thyself,
But shall profess 'tis done of need and right.
While there is one that dares defend thee, live;
Thou shalt have leave, but so as now thou liv'st,   170
Watch'd at a hand, besieged and oppress'd
From working least commotion to the state.
I have those eyes and ears shall still keep guard
And spial on thee as they have ever done
And thou not feel it. What then canst thou hope?   175
If neither night can with her darkness hide
Thy wicked meetings, nor a private house

150. Fathers] *Q, F1*; grave Fathers
F2.

---

150. *desire*] "a trisyllable" (H & S).
151. *seem*] The Latin original has "*not* to seem."
151. *main*] great.   155. *Pitch'd*] set up.
155. *jaws here of*] approaches to (Lat. *fauces*).
160. *make just doubt*] justifiably wonder.
163. *meal and batch*] type of flour and batch of loaves.
171. *at a hand*] near by.
171. *oppress'd*] suppressed.
172. *commotion*] civil unrest.   174. *spial*] spying.

Can in her walls contain the guilty whispers
Of thy conspiracy; if all break out,
All be discovered, change thy mind at last   180
And lose thy thoughts of ruin, flame, and slaughter.
Remember how I told here to the Senate
That such a day thy Lictor Caius Manlius
Would be in arms. Was I deceived, Catiline,
Or in the fact or in the time, the hour?   185
I told too in this Senate that thy purpose
Was on the fifth, the kalends of November,
T'have slaughter'd this whole order, which my caution
Made many leave the city. Canst thou here
Deny but this thy black design was hinder'd   190
That very day by me, thyself clos'd in
Within my strengths so that thou couldst not move
Against a public reed, when thou wert heard
To say upon the parting of the rest,
Thou wouldst content thee with the murder of us   195
That did remain. Hadst thou not hope beside
By a surprise by night to take Praeneste,
Where when thou cam'st, didst thou not find the place
Made good against thee with my aids, my watches?
My garrisons fortified it. Thou dost nothing, Sergius,   200
Thou canst endeavor nothing, nay not think
But I both see and hear it and am with thee,
By and before, about and in thee too.
Call but to mind thy last night's business. Come,
I'll use no circumstance: at Lecca's house,   205
The shop and mint of your conspiracy,

180. discovered] *Q, F1*; discover'd   198. Where] *Q, Ff*; And *Q(o)*.
F2.

---

187. *fifth . . . November*] October 27, expressed in Roman style, *ante diem quintum Kalendas Novembres*.
188. *which my caution*] which caution of mine.
190. *but*] that.
192. *strengths*] military garrisons.
193. *reed*] "decree" (H & S).
199. *Made good*] fortified.
205. *circumstance*] "circumlocution" (H & S).
206. *shop and mint*] workshop and foundry.

Among your sword-men, where so many associates
Both of thy mischief and thy madness met.
Dar'st thou deny this? Wherefore art thou silent?
Speak, and this shall convince thee: here they are,   210
I see 'em in this Senate that were with thee.
O you immortal gods, in what clime are we,
What region do we live in, in what air,
What Commonwealth or state is this we have?
Here, here amongst us, our own number, Fathers,   215
In this most holy council of the world,
They are that seek the spoil of me, of you,
Of ours, of all; what I can name's too narrow:
Follow the sun and find not their ambition.
These I behold, being Consul; nay, I ask   220
Their counsels of the state, as from good patriots,
Whom it were fit the axe should hew in pieces,
I not so much as wound, yet, with my voice.
Thou wast last night with Lecca, Catiline,
Your shares of Italy you there divided;   225
Appointed who and whither each should go,
What men should stay behind in Rome were chosen,
Your offices set down, the parts mark'd out
And places of the city for the fire,
Thyself, thou affirm'd'st, wast ready to depart,   230
Only a little let there was that stay'd thee,
That I yet liv'd. Upon the word step'd forth
Three of thy crew to rid thee of that care;
Two undertook this morning before day
To kill me in my bed. All this I knew,   235
Your convent scarce dismiss'd, arm'd all my servants,

---

207. *Among your sword-men*] "mistranslation of '*inter falcarios*' which means 'in the street of the scythemakers'" (H & S).
212. *clime*] part of the earth.
217. *spoil*] spoliation.
218. *name's too narrow*] specify is too limited.
221. *as*] as though.
228. *offices*] tasks.
228–229. *parts . . . city*] parts and places of the city marked out.
231. *stay'd*] held back.
236. *convent*] "meeting (Lat. *conventus*)" (H & S).

Call'd both my brother and friends, shut out your clients
You sent to visit me, whose names I told
To some there, of good place, before they came.

CATO.

Yes, I and Quintus Catulus can affirm it.   240

CAESAR [*aside*].

He's lost and gone. His spirits have forsook him.

CICERO.

If this be so, why, Catiline, dost thou stay?
Go where thou mean'st. The ports are open; forth.
The camp abroad wants thee, their chief, too long.
Lead with thee all thy troops out. Purge the city.   245
Draw dry that noisome and pernicious sink,
Which left behind thee would infect the world.
Thou wilt free me of all my fears at once
To see a wall between us. Dost thou stop
To do that now, commanded, which before   250
Of thine own choice thou'rt prone to? Go: the Consul
Bids thee, an enemy, to depart the city.
Whither, thou'lt ask, to exile? I not bid
Thee that; but ask my counsel, I persuade it.
What is there here in Rome that can delight thee,   255
Where not a soul without thine own foul knot
But fears and hates thee. What domestic note
Of private filthiness but is burn'd in
Into thy life? What close and secret shame
But is grown one with thy known infamy?   260
What lust was ever absent from thine eyes,
What lewd fact from thy hands, what wickedness
From thy whole body? Where's that youth drawn in
Within thy nets or catch'd up with thy baits

241. S.D.] *Gifford.*

---

239. *good place*] high rank
251. *thou'rt*] thou wert.
254. *persuade*] advise (Lat. *suadeo*).
256. *without . . . knot*] outside . . . cluster.
257. *note*] "brand (Lat. *nota*)" (H & S).
259. *close*] hidden.
260. *grown one with*] become part of.

Before whose rage thou hast not borne a sword   265
And to whose lusts thou hast not held a torch?
Thy latter nuptials I let pass in silence
Where sins incredible on sins were heap'd,
Which I not name lest in a civil state
So monstrous facts should either appear to be,   270
Or not to be reveng'd. Thy fortunes too
I glance not at, which hang but till next Ides.
I come to that which is more known, more public:
The life and safety of us all, by thee
Threaten'd and sought. Stood'st thou not in the field   275
When Lepidus and Tullus were our Consuls
Upon the day of choice, arm'd and with forces
To take their lives and our chief citizens',
When not thy fear nor conscience chang'd thy mind
But the mere fortune of the Commonwealth   280
Withstood thy active malice? Speak but right.
How often hast thou made attempt on me?
How many of thy assaults have I declin'd
With shifting but my body, as we'd say,
Wrested thy dagger from thy hand, how oft?   285
How often hath it fall'n or slipp'd by chance?
Yet can thy side not want it, which how vow'd
Or with what rites 'tis sacred of thee I know not,
That still thou mak'st it a necessity
To fix it in the body of a Consul.   290

265–266. *Before ... torch*] whose violence you have not advanced as though by offering a sword, or lusts as though by a torch to light the way.

270–271. *either ... reveng'd*] either be seen to have taken place, or not to have been punished.

271. *fortunes*] ruined finances.

272. *hang*] survive (as he would be ruined when payment fell due on the fixed date for collection).

275–277. *field ... choice*] Cicero says in the *comitium*, which was an open space adjoining the Forum and the Senate-house, used for some voting assemblies. By *field* Jonson means the Campus Martius, a site used for tribal elective assemblies, and *day of choice* is a misunderstanding of *comitium*; on the last day of December, 66 B.C., no elections were held.

283. *declin'd*] avoided (Lat. *declinatione effugi*).

287. *can ... it*] does the sheath at your side not want your dagger back again.

But let me lose this way and speak to thee
Not as one mov'd with hatred, which I ought,
But pity, of which none is owing thee.

CATO.

No more than unto Tantalus or Tityus.

CICERO.

Thou cam'st erewhile into this Senate. Who 295
Of such a frequency, so many friends
And kindred thou hast here, saluted thee?
Were not the seats made bare upon thy entrance?
Riss not the consular men, and left their places
So soon as thou sat'st down, and fled thy side 300
Like to a plague or ruin, knowing how oft
They had been by thee mark'd out for the shambles?
How dost thou bear this? Surely if my slaves
At home fear'd me with half th'affright and horror
That here thy fellow-citizens do thee, 305
I should soon quit my house and think it need too.
Yet thou dar'st tarry here? Go forth at last,
Condemn thyself to flight and solitude.
Discharge the Commonwealth of her deep fear.
Go, into banishment, if thou wait'st the word. 310
Why dost thou look? They all consent unto it.
Dost thou expect th'authority of their voices
Whose silent wills condemn thee? While they sit
They approve it; while they suffer it they decree it;
And while they are silent to it they proclaim it. 315
Prove thou there honest, I'll endure the envy.
But there's no thought thou shouldst be ever he
Whom either shame should call from filthiness,

294. S.P. CATO] *Whalley*; CAT. *Q*,   303. bear] *Q, F1*; heare *F2*.
Ff.

---

291. *lose this way*] drop this manner of speech.
295. *erewhile*] a little while ago.
296. *frequency*] throng (Lat. *frequentia*).
299. *Riss*] rose.
299. *consular men*] ex-Consuls (and therefore the most senior Senators).
302. *shambles*] slaughterhouse.
306. *need*] necessary.
314. *suffer*] allow.
316. *Prove thou*] if you prove.

Terror from danger, or discourse from fury.
Go, I entreat thee; yet why do I so,   320
When I already know they are sent afore
That tarry for thee in arms and do expect thee
On the Aurelian Way. I know the day
Set down 'twixt thee and Manlius, unto whom
The silver eagle too is sent before,   325
Which I do hope shall prove to thee as baneful
As thou conceiv'st it to the Commonwealth.
But may this wise and sacred Senate say,
"What mean'st thou, Marcus Tullius? If thou know'st
That Catiline be look'd for to be chief   330
Of an intestine war, that he is the author
Of such a wickedness, the caller-out
Of men of mark in mischief to an action
Of so much horror, prince of such a treason,
Why dost thou send him forth, why let him 'scape?   335
This is to give him liberty and power;
Rather thou shouldst lay hold upon him, send him
To deserv'd death and a just punishment,"
To these so holy voices thus I answer:
If I did think it timely, Conscript Fathers,   340
To punish him with death, I would not give
The fencer use of one short hour to breathe,
But when there are in this grave order some
Who with soft censures still do nurse his hopes,
Some that with not believing have confirm'd   345
His designs more, and whose authority
The weaker, as the worst men, too, have follow'd,
I would now send him where they all should see

---

321. they are] *Q, F1*; they're *F2*.   323. On the] *Q*; On th' *Ff*.

324. *Set down*] agreed.
327. *conceiv'st*] imagine.
330. *look'd for*] awaited (Lat. *exspectari*).
331. *intestine*] internal.
332. *caller-out*] summoner (Lat. *evocatorem*).
333. *men . . . mischief*] men noted for mischief.
342. *fencer*] Lat. *gladiator*, here used abusively, as the occupation was regarded as very low-class at this period.
344. *soft censures*] "weak judgements" (H & S).
347. *weaker . . . men*] weaker men, as well as the worst.

Clear as the light his heart shine, where no man
Could be so wickedly or fondly stupid,   350
But should cry out he saw, touch'd, felt, and grasp'd it.
Then when he hath run out himself, led forth
His desp'rate party with him, blown together
Aids of all kinds, both shipwreck'd minds and fortunes,
Not only the grown evil that now is sprung   355
And sprouted forth would be pluck'd up and weeded,
But the stock, root, and seed of all the mischiefs
Choking the Commonwealth; where, should we take
Of such a swarm of traitors only him,
Our cares and fears might seem awhile reliev'd,   360
But the main peril would bide still enclos'd
Deep in the veins and bowels of the state,
As human bodies laboring with fevers,
While they are toss'd with heat, if they do take
Cold water, seem for that short space much eas'd   365
But afterward are ten times more afflicted.
Wherefore I say let all this wicked crew
Depart, divide themselves from good men, gather
Their forces to one head; as I said oft,
Let 'em be sever'd from us with a wall,   370
Let 'em leave off attempts upon the Consul
In his own house, to circle in the Praetor,
To girt the court with weapons, to prepare
Fire and balls, swords, torches, sulphur, brands;
In short, let it be writ in each man's forehead   375
What thoughts he bears the public. I here promise,
Fathers Conscript, to you and to myself,
That diligence in us Consuls, for my honor'd
Colleague abroad and for myself at home;
So great authority in you; so much   380

360. awhile] *F2*; a while *Q, F1*.

_____

350. *fondly*] foolishly.
353. *blown together*] collected.
358. *where*] "whereas" (H & S).
364. *toss'd*] caused to toss and turn.
372. *circle in*] surround (Lat. *circumstare*).
373. *girt*] surround.

Virtue in these, the gentlemen of Rome,
Whom I could scarce restrain today in zeal
From seeking out the parricide to slaughter;
So much consent in all good men and minds
As, on the going out of this one Catiline,   385
All shall be clear, made plain, oppress'd, reveng'd.
And with this omen, go, pernicious plague,
Out of the city to the wish'd destruction
Of thee and those that, to the ruin of her,
Have ta'en that bloody and black sacrament.   390
Thou Jupiter, whom we do call the Stayer
Both of this city and this empire, wilt,
With the same auspice thou didst raise it first,
Drive from thy altars and all other temples
And buildings of this city, from our walls,   395
Lives, states, and fortunes of our citizens,
This fiend, this Fury, with his complices,
And all the offense of good men, these known traitors
Unto their country, thieves of Italy,
Join'd in so damn'd a league of mischief, thou   400
Wilt with perpetual plagues, alive and dead
Punish for Rome, and save her innocent head.

CATILINE.

If an oration or high language, Fathers,
Could make me guilty, here is one hath done it;
H'has strove to emulate this morning's thunder   405
With his prodigious rhetoric. But I hope
This Senate is more grave than to give credit

398. the offense] *Q*, *F1*; th'offence
F2.

---

381. *gentlemen*] the *equites*, the moneyed, non-Senatorial Romans; together with the members of the Senate, they formed the upper classes.

384. *consent*] unanimity (Lat. *consensionem*).

385. *this one Catiline*] Catiline alone.

387. *omen*] portent of the future, good or bad. Cicero refers to what he has just said: in Roman belief, to declare something an omen was tantamount to making it one.

397. *complices*] associates.

403. *high*] highly wrought, in the most elaborate of the three main styles of oratory.

407. *grave*] serious.

Rashly to all he vomits 'gainst a man
Of your own order, a Patrician,
And one whose ancestors have more deserv'd   410
Of Rome than this man's eloquence could utter
Turn'd the best way, as still it is the worst.

CATO.

His eloquence hath more deserv'd today
Speaking thy ill, than all thy ancestors
Did in their good, and that the state will find   415
Which he hath sav'd.

CATILINE.   How, he? Were I that enemy
That he would make me, I'd not wish the state
More wretched than to need his preservation.
What do you make him, Cato, such a Hercules,
An Atlas? A poor petty inmate!

CATO.   Traitor.   420

CATILINE.

He save the state, a burgess' son of Arpinum?
The gods would rather twenty Romes should perish
Than have that contumely stuck upon 'em
That he should share with them in the preserving
A shed or signpost.

CATO.   Peace, thou prodigy.   425

CATILINE.

They would be forc'd themselves again, and lost
In the first rude and indigested heap
Ere such a wretched name as Cicero
Should sound with theirs.

CATULUS.   Away, thou impudent head.

CATILINE.

Do you all back him? Are you silent too?   430

426. forc'd] *Ff*; runne *Q*.

---

421. *burgess*'] Lat. *municeps*, continuing the *inmate* taunt; Cicero's family
was not only not senatorial, it was domiciled in an Italian township, not in
Rome (cf. English "provincial").
    425. *prodigy*] monster.
    426. *forc'd*] attacked.
    427. *rude . . . heap*] the primal chaos, without arrangement or order (Ovid
Met. 1. 7, *rudis indigestaque moles*).
    429. *head*] person (Lat. *caput*).

Well, I will leave you, Fathers; I will go.
But, my fine dainty speaker—

He turns suddenly on Cicero.

CICERO.   What now, Fury,
Wilt thou assault me here?
SENATORS.   Help, aid the Consul.
CATILINE.
    See, Fathers, laugh you not? Who threaten'd him?
    In vain thou dost conceive, ambitious orator,   435
    Hope of so brave a death as by this hand.
CATO.
    Out of the court with the pernicious traitor.
CATILINE.
    There is no title that this flattering Senate,
    Nor honor the base multitude can give thee,
    Shall make thee worthy Catiline's anger.
CATO.   Stop,   440
    Stop that portentous mouth.
CATILINE.   Or when it shall,
    I'll look thee dead.
CATO.   Will none restrain the monster?
CATULUS.
    Parricide.
QUINTUS.   Butcher, traitor, leave the Senate.
CATILINE.
    I am gone to banishment to please you, Fathers,
    Thrust headlong forth.
CATO.   Still dost thou murmur, monster?   445
CATILINE.
    Since I am thus put out and made a—
CICERO.   What?
CATULUS.
    Not guiltier than thou art.
CATILINE.   I will not burn
    Without my funeral pile.

432. S.D.] *Ff*; *om. Q.*   433. S.P. SENATORS] *this edn.*; CHO.
                                                        Q, F1; CHOR. *F2.*

441. *portentous*] monstrous.
442. *look thee dead*] kill you with a glance.
448. *pile*] pyre.

CATO.   What says the fiend?

CATILINE.

    I will have matter, timber.

CATO.   Sing out, screech owl.

CATILINE.

    It shall be in—

CATULUS.   Speak thy imperfect thoughts.   450

CATILINE.

    The common fire rather than mine own,

    For fall I will with all ere fall alone.   [*Exit.*]

CRASSUS [*aside to* Caesar].

    H'is lost, there is no hope of him.

CAESAR.   Unless

    He presently take arms and give a blow

    Before the Consul's forces can be levied.   455

CICERO.

    What is your pleasure, Fathers, shall be done?

CATULUS.

    See that the Commonwealth receive no loss.

CATO.

    Commit the care thereof unto the Consuls.

CRASSUS.

    'Tis time.

CAESAR.   And need.

CICERO.   Thanks to this frequent Senate.

    But what decree they unto Curius   460

    And Fulvia?

CATULUS.   What the Consul shall think meet.

CICERO.

    They must receive reward, though't be not known,

    Lest when a state needs ministers, they ha' none.

452, 453. S.D.] *Gifford.*   453. H'is] *Q, F1*; He's *F2.*

---

449. *matter, timber*] material to build a pyre; Lat. *materies* also means "timber."

449. *screech owl*] bird of ill-omen.

450. *imperfect*] incomplete.

457–458. *See . . . Consuls*] part of the formal wording of the emergency decree, *consules videant ne quid detrimenti res publica capiat.*

462–463. *known . . . none*] The words sounded alike.

CATO [*aside to* Cicero].

> Yet, Marcus Tullius, do not I believe
> But Crassus and this Caesar here ring hollow.   465

CICERO.

> And would appear so, if that we durst prove 'em.

CATO.

> Why dare we not? What honest act is that,
> The Roman Senate should not dare and do?

CICERO.

> Not an unprofitable, dangerous act,
> To stir too many serpents up at once.   470
> Caesar and Crassus, if they be ill men,
> Are mighty ones, and we must so provide
> That while we take one head from this foul Hydra
> There spring not twenty more.

CATO.   I 'prove your counsel.

CICERO.

> They shall be watch'd and look'd too. Till they do   475
> Declare themselves, I will not put 'em out
> By any question. There they stand. I'll make
> Myself no enemies, nor the state no traitors.   [*Exeunt.*]

[IV.iii]

[*Enter*] Catiline, Lentulus, Cethegus, Curius, Gabinius, Longinus, Statilius.

CATILINE.

> False to ourselves? All our designs discover'd
> To this state-cat?

CETHEGUS.   Ay; had I had my way,

478. S.D.] *Gifford.*

464–465. *do not . . . But*] I believe that.
465. *ring hollow*] are false.
466. *prove*] put to the proof.
475. *look'd too*] examined also; but perhaps "look'd to," i.e., minded.
476–477. *put . . . question*] expel them by any inquiry.
[IV.iii]
1. *discover'd*] made known.
2. *state-cat*] interfering busybody (as a cat watching for mice) on behalf of the state.

He had mew'd in flames at home, not i'the Senate.
I had sing'd his furs by this time.

CATILINE.   Well, there's now
No time of calling back or standing still.   5
Friends, be yourselves; keep the same Roman hearts
And ready minds you had yesternight. Prepare
To execute what we resolv'd, and let not
Labor or danger or discovery fright you.
I'll to the army; you, the while, mature   10
Things here at home. Draw to you any aids
That you think fit, of men of all conditions
Or any fortunes that may help a war.
I'll bleed a life or win an empire for you.
Within these few days look to see my ensigns   15
Here at the walls: be you but firm within.
Meantime, to draw an envy on the Consul
And give a less suspicion of our course,
Let it be given out here in the city
That I am gone, an innocent man, to exile   20
Into Massilia, willing to give way
To fortune and the times, being unable
To stand so great a faction without troubling
The Commonwealth, whose peace I rather seek
Than all the glory of contention   25
Or the support of mine own innocence.
Farewell the noble Lentulus, Longinus,
Curius, the rest, and thou, my better genius,
The brave Cethegus; when we meet again
We'll sacrifice to liberty.

CETHEGUS.   And revenge,   30
That we may praise our hands once.

13. Or] *Q, F1*; Of *F2*.

---

5. *calling back*] retracting.
10. *I'll to*] I'll go to.
17. *draw an envy on*] cause dislike of.
23. *stand*] remain firm in the face of.
25. *contention*] a struggle.
28. *genius*] attendant spirit.

LENTULUS.   O you Fates,
　　Give Fortune now her eyes to see with whom
　　She goes along, that she may ne'er forsake him.
CURIUS.
　　He needs not her nor them. Go but on, Sergius.
　　A valiant man is his own fate and fortune.   35
LONGINUS.
　　The fate and fortune of us all go with him.
GABINIUS. STATILIUS.
　　And ever guard him.
CATILINE.   I am all your creature.   [*Exit.*]
LENTULUS.
　　Now friends, 'tis left with us. I have already
　　Dealt by Umbrenus with the Allobroges
　　Here resiant in Rome, whose state, I hear,   40
　　Is discontent with the great usuries
　　They are oppress'd with, and have made complaints
　　Divers unto the Senate, but all vain.
　　These men I have thought both for their own oppressions,
　　As also that by nature they are a people   45
　　Warlike and fierce, still watching after change
　　And now in present hatred with our state,
　　The fittest and the easiest to be drawn
　　To our society and to aid the war;
　　The rather for their seat, being next bord'rers   50
　　On Italy, and that they abound with horse
　　Of which one want our camp doth only labor;
　　And I have found 'em coming. They will meet
　　Soon at Sempronia's house, where I would pray you

---

37. S.D.] *Gifford*.   46. Warlike] *Q, F1*; Warlick *F2*.

32. *eyes*] Fortune was traditionally represented as blind and hence un-
discriminating in the bestowal of her favors.
　　32–33. *with . . . along*] whom she accompanies.
　　34. *Go but on*] simply proceed.
　　37. *all your*] of all of you.
　　40. *resiant*] "resident" (H & S).
　　46. *watching after*] seeking.
　　47. *in . . . with*] currently hating.
　　49. *society*] membership.
　　50. *The rather*] all the more.
　　50. *seat*] position.

All to be present, to confirm 'em more.   55
The sight of such spirits hurt not, nor the store.

GABINIUS.

     I will not fail.

STATILIUS.   Nor I.

CURIUS.   Nor I.

CETHEGUS.   Would I
Had somewhat by myself apart to do.
I ha' no genius to these many councils.
Let me kill all the Senate for my share;   60
I'll do it at next sitting.

LENTULUS.   Worthy Caius,
Your presence will add much.

CETHEGUS.   I shall mar more.   [*Exeunt.*]

[IV.iv]   [*Enter*] Cicero, Sanga.

CICERO.

The state's beholden to you, Fabius Sanga,
For this great care, and those Allobroges
Are more than wretched if they lend a list'ning
To such persuasion.

SANGA.   They, most worthy Consul,
As men employ'd here from a grieved state   5
Groaning beneath a multitude of wrongs,
And being told there was small hope of ease
To be expected to their evils from hence,
Were willing at the first to give an ear
To anything that sounded liberty;   10
But since on better thoughts and my urg'd reasons
They are come about and won to the true side.
The fortune of the Commonwealth hath conquer'd.

62. S.D.] *Gifford.*   0.1.] *Gifford*; CICERO, SANGA,
[IV.iv]   ALLOBROGES. *Q, Ff.*
                               1. to] *Q, F1*; unto *F2.*

55. *confirm*] strengthen; cf. I.504, n.
56. *The sight . . . store*] Neither the sight nor the number of such people
will do any harm.
62. *mar*] spoil.
[IV.iv]
   9. *give an ear*] listen.
   10. *sounded*] spoke of.

CICERO.

    What is that same Umbrenus, was the agent?

SANGA.

    One that hath had negotiation   15

    In Gallia oft, and known unto their state.

CICERO.

    Are th'ambassadors come with you?

SANGA.   Yes.

CICERO.

    Well, bring 'em in; if they be firm and honest,

    Never had men the means so to deserve

    Of Rome as they.   [*Exit* Sanga.]

               A happy, wish'd occasion,   20

    And thrust into my hands, for the discovery

    And manifest conviction of these traitors.

    Be thank'd, O Jupiter.

            [*Re-enter* Sanga *with*] *the* Allobroges.

               My worthy lords,

    Confederates of the Senate, you are welcome.

    I understand by Quintus Fabius Sanga,   25

    Your careful patron here, you have been lately

    Solicited against the Commonwealth

    By one Umbrenus—take a seat, I pray you—

    From Publius Lentulus, to be associates

    In their intended war. I could advise   30

    That men whose fortunes are yet flourishing

    And are Rome's friends, would not without a cause

    Become her enemies and mix themselves

    And their estates with the lost hopes of Catiline

    Or Lentulus, whose mere despair doth arm 'em;   35

    That were to hazard certainties for air

---

17. th'ambassadors] *Ff*; the'Am-   23. S.D. *Re-enter* Sanga *with*] *Gifford*.
bassadors *Q*.   23. S.D. *the* Allobroges] *om. Q, F2*;
20. S.D.] *Gifford*.   *The Allobroges enter. F1*.

    14. *agent*] intermediary.

    15. *One . . . negotiation*] someone who has business transactions (Lat. *negotiatus*).

    18. *firm*] steadfast.

    24. *Confederates*] allies by treaty (Lat. *foederati*).

    26. *careful*] solicitous.

And undergo all danger for a voice.
Believe me, friends, loud tumults are not laid
With half the easiness that they are rais'd.
All may begin a war, but few can end it.   40
The Senate have decreed that my colleague
Shall lead their army against Catiline
And have declar'd both him and Manlius traitors.
Metellus Celer hath already given
Part of their troops defeat. Honors are promis'd   45
To all will quit 'em, and rewards propos'd
Even to slaves that can detect their courses.
Here in the city I have by the Praetors
And Tribunes plac'd my guards and watches so
That not a foot can tread, a breath can whisper,   50
But I have knowledge. And be sure the Senate
And people of Rome, of their accustom'd greatness,
Will sharply and severely vindicate
Not only any fact but any practice
Or purpose 'gainst the state. Therefore, my lords,   55
Consult of your own ways, and think which hand
Is best to take. You now are present suitors
For some redress of wrongs. I'll undertake
Not only that shall be assur'd you, but
What grace or privilege else, Senate or people   60
Can cast upon you, worthy such a service
As you have now the way and means to do 'em
If but your wills consent with my designs.

ALLOBROX.

We covet nothing more, most worthy Consul,
And howsoe'er we have been tempted lately   65
To a defection, that not makes us guilty;
We are not yet so wretched in our fortunes

---

38. *laid*] suppressed.
39. *rais'd*] started.
41. *colleague*] the other Consul, Antonius.
47. *detect*] inform against.
53. *vindicate*] "punish (Lat. *vindico*)" (H & S).
56. *hand*] direction.
63. *but . . . designs*] only your wishes are in agreement with my plans.
66. *defection*] abandonment of allegiance.

Nor in our wills so lost as to abandon
A friendship prodigally of that price
As is the Senate and the people of Rome's   70
For hopes that do precipitate themselves.

CICERO.

You then are wise and honest. Do but this, then:
When shall you speak with Lentulus and the rest?

ALLOBROX.

We are to meet anon at Brutus' house.

CICERO.

Who, Decius Brutus? He is not in Rome.   75

SANGA.

O, but his wife Sempronia.

CICERO.   You instruct me
She is a chief. Well, fail not you to meet 'em
And to express the best affection
You can put on to all that they intend.
Like it, applaud it, give the Commonwealth   80
And Senate lost to 'em. Promise any aids
By arms or counsel. What they can desire
I would have you prevent. Only say this,
You have had dispatch in private by the Consul
Of your affairs, and for the many fears   85
The state's now in, you are will'd by him this evening
To depart Rome, which you by all sought means
Will do of reason to decline suspicion.
Now for the more authority of the business
They have trusted to you, and to give it credit   90
With your own state at home, you would desire
Their letters to your Senate and your people,
Which shown, you durst engage both life and honor

---

69. *of that price*] so precious.
71. *precipitate*] destroy by impetuosity.
76. *instruct*] inform.
78. *affection*] partiality.
79. *put on*] apply.
80. *give*] allege.
84. *dispatch*] quick riddance.
85. *for*] because of.
88. *of . . . decline*] so as to avert.
93. *engage*] offer as security.

The rest should every way answer their hopes.
Those had, pretend sudden departure, you,   95
And as you give me notice at what port
You will go out, I'll ha' you intercepted
And all the letters taken with you, so
As you shall be redeem'd in all opinions
And they convicted of their manifest treason.   100
Ill deeds are well turn'd back upon their authors,
And 'gainst an injurer the revenge is just.
This must be done now.

ALLOBROX.   Cheerfully and firmly.
We are they, would rather haste to undertake it
Than stay to say so.

CICERO.   With that confidence, go;   105
Make yourselves happy while you make Rome so.
By Sanga let me have notice from you.

ALLOBROX.   Yes.   [*Exeunt.*]

[IV.v]   [*Enter*] Sempronia, Lentulus.

SEMPRONIA.

When come these creatures the ambassadors?
I would fain see 'em. Are they any scholars?

LENTULUS.

I think not, madam.

SEMPRONIA.   Ha' they no Greek?

LENTULUS.   No, surely.

SEMPRONIA.

Fie, what do I here waiting on 'em then,
If they be nothing but mere statesmen?

LENTULUS.   Yes,   5

107. S.D.] *Gifford*.   STATILIVS, LONGINVS, VOL-
[IV.v]   TVRTIVS, ALLOBROGES. *Q*,
0.1.] *Gifford*; SEMPRONIA, LEN-   *Ff*.
TVLVS, CETHEGVS, GABINIVS,

---

94. *The rest*] what follows.
95. *Those*] those letters being.
95. *pretend*] offer as an excuse (Lat. *praetendo*).
105. *confidence*] resoluteness.
[IV.v]
4. *waiting on*] in attendance on.

Your ladyship shall observe their gravity
And their reservedness, their many cautions
Fitting their persons.

SEMPRONIA.   I do wonder much
That states and commonwealths employ not women
To be ambassadors sometimes. We should   10
Do as good public service, and could make
As honorable spies, for so Thucydides
Calls all ambassadors.

                    [*Enter* Cethegus.]

                    Are they come, Cethegus?
CETHEGUS.
Do you ask me? Am I your scout or bawd?
LENTULUS.
O Caius, it is no such business.
CETHEGUS.   No?   15
What does a woman at it then?
SEMPRONIA.   Good sir,
There are of us can be as exquisite traitors
As e'er a male-conspirator of you all.
CETHEGUS.
Ay, at smock treason, matron, I believe you,
And if I were your husband; but when I   20
Trust to your cobweb-bosoms any other
Let me there die a fly and feast you, spider.
LENTULUS.
You are too sour and harsh, Cethegus.
CETHEGUS.   You
Are kind and courtly. I'd be torn in pieces

13. S.D., 31.1, 33. S.D.] *Gifford.*

---

6. *gravity*] worthiness.

7–8. *cautions . . . persons*] careful observances of protocol.

14. *scout*] spy.

17. *exquisite*] accomplished.

19. *smock treason*] treason by women, especially by use of their sexual attractiveness.

21. *cobweb-bosoms*] confidence that ensnares.

21. *any other*] i.e., kind of treason.

With wild Hippolytus, nay prove the death   25
Every limb over, ere I'd trust a woman
With wind, could I retain it.
SEMPRONIA.   Sir, they'll be trusted
With as good secrets yet as you have any,
And carry 'em too as close and as conceal'd
As you shall for your heart.
CETHEGUS.   I'll not contend with you   30
Either in tongue or carriage, good Calypso.

                    [*Enter* Longinus.]

LONGINUS.
Th'ambassadors are come.
CETHEGUS.   Thanks to thee, Mercury,
That so hast rescu'd me.

        [*Enter* Volturtius, *Statilius*, Gabinius, Allobroges.]

LENTULUS.   How now, Volturtius?
VOLTURTIUS.
They do desire some speech with you in private.
LENTULUS.
O, 'tis about the prophecy, belike,   35
And promise of the Sibyl's.
GABINIUS.   It may be.
SEMPRONIA.
Shun they to treat with me too?
GABINIUS.   No, good lady,
You may partake; I have told 'em who you are.
SEMPRONIA.
I should be loath to be left out, and here too.
CETHEGUS.
Can these or such be any aids to us?   40
Look they as they were built to shake the world
Or be a moment to our enterprise?

---

25. *prove*] undergo.
30. *for your heart*] despite all your resoluteness.
31. *tongue or carriage*] speech or behavior.
37. *treat*] negotiate.
38. *partake*] participate.
42. *moment*] "determining influence (Lat. *momentum*)" (H & S).

A thousand such as they are could not make
One atom of our souls. They should be men
Worth heaven's fear, that looking up but thus   45
Would make Jove stand upon his guard and draw
Himself within his thunder which, amaz'd,
He should discharge in vain, and they unhurt;
Or if they were like Capaneus at Thebes,
They should hang dead upon the highest spires   50
And ask the second bolt to be thrown down.
Why, Lentulus, talk you so long? This time
Had been enough t'have scatter'd all the stars,
T'have quench'd the sun and moon, and made the world
Despair of day, or any light but ours.   55

LENTULUS.

How do you like this spirit? In such men
Mankind doth live. They are such souls as these
That move the world.

SEMPRONIA.   Ay, though he bear me hard,
I yet must do him right. He is a spirit
Of the right Martian breed.

ALLBROX.   He is a Mars!   60
Would we had time to live here and admire him.

LENTULUS.

Well, I do see you would prevent the Consul,
And I commend your care: it was but reason
To ask our letters, and we had prepar'd them.
Go in and we will take an oath and seal 'em.   65
You shall have letters too to Catiline,
To visit him i'the way and to confirm
The association. This our friend Volturtius
Shall go along with you. Tell our great general

51. bolt] *Ff*; charge *Q*.   58. S.P. SEMPRONIA] *F2*; SEN. *Q*,
                                          F1.

---

44. *atom*] tiny particle.
58. *bear me hard*] finds me hard to bear.
59. *do him right*] give him credit.
61. *admire*] marvel at.
63. *commend your care*] praise your painstaking attention.
67. *i'the way*] on the way back to their country.
68. *association*] alliance.

That we are ready here, that Lucius Bestia 70
The Tribune is provided of a speech
To lay the envy of the war on Cicero,
That all but long for his approach and person;
And then you are made freemen as ourselves. [*Exeunt.*]

[IV.vi] [*Enter*] Cicero, Flaccus, Pomtinius.

CICERO.

I cannot fear the war but to succeed well,
Both for the honor of the cause and worth
Of him that doth command; for my colleague,
Being so ill affected with the gout,
Will not be able to be there in person, 5
And then Petreius, his lieutenant, must
Of need take charge o'the army, who is much
The better soldier, having been a Tribune,
Prefect, Lieutenant, Praetor in the war
These thirty years, so conversant i'the army 10
As he knows all the soldiers by their names.

FLACCUS.

They'll fight then bravely with him.

POMTINIUS. Ay, and he
Will lead 'em on as bravely.

CICERO. They have a foe
Will ask their braveries, whose necessities
Will arm him like a Fury. But however 15
I'll trust it to the manage and the fortune
Of good Petreius, who's a worthy patriot;

72. on] *Q*, *F1*; upon *F2*.
74. S.D.] *Gifford*.

[IV.vi]
0.1.] *Gifford*; CICERO, FLACCVS,
POMTINIVS, SANGA. *Q*, *Ff*.

71. *of*] with.
[IV.vi]
1. *fear . . . but*] doubt that the war will.
4. *affected with*] attacked by.
14. *ask*] require.
14. *necessities*] poverty.
16. *manage*] management.

Metellus Celer, with three legions, too,
Will stop their course for Gallia.

[*Enter* Sanga.]

                                    How now, Fabius?

SANGA.

The train hath taken. You must instantly   20
Dispose your guards upon the Milvian bridge,
For by that way they mean to come.

CICERO.   Then thither,

Pomtinius and Flaccus, I must pray you
To lead that force you have and seize them all;
Let not a person 'scape. Th'ambassadors   25
Will yield themselves. If there be any tumult
I'll send you aid.   [*Exeunt* Pomtinius *and* Flaccus.]
                    I in meantime will call
Lentulus to me, Gabinius and Cethegus,
Statilius, Ceparius, and all these
By several messengers, who no doubt will come   30
Without sense or suspicion. Prodigal men
Feel not their own stock wasting. When I have 'em
I'll place those guards upon 'em that they start not.

SANGA.

But what'll you do with Sempronia?

CICERO.   A state's anger   35

Should not take knowledge either of fools or women.
I do not know whether my joy or care
Ought to be greater that I have discover'd
So foul a treason, or must undergo

19, 27. S.D.] *Gifford.*   34. state's anger] *Ff*; State *Q.*

---

19. *stop their course*] halt their journey.
20. *train hath taken*] trick has worked; the metaphor comes, perhaps, from the ignition of a train of gunpowder leading to the main charge.
21. *Dispose*] arrange.
26. *tumult*] outburst.
30. *several*] separate.
31. *sense*] realization.
32. *stock wasting*] supplies diminishing.
33. *that . . . not*] so they won't escape.
35. *knowledge*] notice.

The envy of so many great men's fate.
But happen what there can, I will be just,   40
My fortune may forsake me, not my virtue;
That shall go with me and before me still,
And glad me doing well, though I hear ill.   [*Exeunt.*]

[IV.vii]

    [*Enter* Flaccus, Pomtinius, *Guards*], Allobroges, Volturtius.

FLACCUS.

    Stand, who goes there?
ALLOBROX.   We are th'Allobroges,
    And friends of Rome.
POMTINIUS.   If you be so, then yield
    Yourselves unto the Praetors, who in name
    Of the whole Senate and the people of Rome
    Yet, till you clear yourselves, charge you of practice   5
    Against the state.
VOLTURTIUS.   Die, friends, and be not taken.
FLACCUS.

    What voice is that? Down with 'em all.
ALLOBROX.   We yield.
POMTINIUS.

    What's he stands out? Kill him there.
VOLTURTIUS.   Hold, hold, hold.
    I yield upon conditions.
FLACCUS.   We give none
    To traitors; strike him down.
VOLTURTIUS.   My name's Volturtius,   10
    I know Pomtinius.
POMTINIUS.   But he knows not you
    While you stand out upon these traitorous terms.

43. S.D.] *Gifford.*   LOBROGES, VOLTVRTIVS. *Q,*
[IV.vii]   *Ff.*
0.1.] *Gifford;* PRAETORS, AL-

---

    39. *envy . . . fate*] ill-will caused by my having doomed so many great men.
    43. *glad*] gladden.
    43. *hear ill*] "am ill spoken of" (H & S).
[IV.vii]
    8. *stands out*] resists.

VOLTURTIUS.
    I'll yield upon the safety of my life.
POMTINIUS.
    If it be forfeited, we cannot save it.
VOLTURTIUS.
    Promise to do your best. I am not so guilty   15
    As many others I can name, and will
    If you will grant me favor.
POMTINIUS.   All we can
    Is to deliver you to the Consul. Take him,
    And thank the gods that thus have saved Rome.   [*Exeunt.*]
CHORUS.
              Now do our ears before our eyes   20
                  Like men in mists
              Discover who'd the state surprise,
                  And who resists?
              And as these clouds do yield to light
                  Now do we see   25
              Our thoughts of things, how they did fight,
                  Which seem'd t'agree?
              Of what strange pieces are we made
                  Who nothing know,
              But as new airs our ears invade   30
                  Still censure so,
              That now do hope and now do fear,
                  And now envy,
              And then do hate and then love dear,
                  But know not why,   35
              Or if we do, it is so late,
                  As our best mood
              Though true, is then thought out of date
                  And empty of good.

---

19. S.D.] *Gifford.*

13. *upon . . . life*] if you promise to save my life.
17. *favor*] leniency.
24. *yield*] give way to.
28. *strange pieces*] incompatible components.
30. *airs*] whispers.
31. *censure*] "judge" (H & S).
37. *best mood*] most correct opinion.

How have we chang'd and come about   40
    In every doom
Since wicked Catiline went out
    And quitted Rome?
One while we thought him innocent,
    And then w'accus'd   45
The Consul for his malice spent
    And power abus'd.
Since that we hear he is in arms
    We think not so,
Yet charge the Consul with our harms   50
    That let him go.
So in our censure of the state
    We still do wander,
And make the careful magistrate
    The mark of slander.   55
What age is this where honest men
    Plac'd at the helm,
A sea of some foul mouth or pen
    Shall overwhelm,
And call their diligence, deceit,   60
    Their virtue, vice,
Their watchfulness, but lying in wait,
    And blood the price.
O let us pluck this evil seed
    Out of our spirits,   65
And give to every noble deed
    The name it merits;
Lest we seem fall'n, if this endures,
    Into those times
To love disease, and brook the cures   70
    Worse than the crimes.

---

41. *doom*] judgment (rhymes with *Rome*, l. 43).

44. *while*] time.

46. *spent*] squandered.

50. *charge . . . with*] blame . . . for.

55. *mark*] target.

63. *price*] reward sought.

65–67. *spirits . . . merits*] The words rhymed.

[V.i]   [*Enter*] Petreius[, Soldiers].

PETREIUS.

It is my fortune and my glory, soldiers,
This day to lead you on, the worthy Consul
Kept from the honor of it by disease;
And I am proud to have so brave a cause
To exercise your arms in. We not now   5
Fight for how long, how broad, how great and large
Th'extent and bounds o'th' people of Rome shall be,
But to retain what our great ancestors
With all their labors, counsels, arts, and actions,
For us were purchasing so many years.   10
The quarrel is not now of fame, of tribute,
Or of wrongs done unto confederates,
For which the army of the people of Rome
Was wont to move, but for your own Republic,
For the rais'd temples of th'immortal gods,   15
For all your fortunes, altars, and your fires,
For the dear souls of your lov'd wives and children,
Your parents' tombs, your rites, laws, liberty,
And, briefly, for the safety of the world;
Against such men as only by their crimes   20
Are known, thrust out by riot, want, or rashness.
One sort, Sylla's old troops left here in Fesulae,
Who suddenly made rich in those dire times
Are since by their unbounded, vast expense,
Grown needy and poor, and have but left t'expect   25
From Catiline new bills and new proscriptions.
These men, they say, are valiant; yet I think 'em

V.i.] *Scene divisions in this Act follow*   0.1.] PETREIVS. THE ARMY. *Q*;
Gifford to the beginning of Scene vi, which   *The Armie.* PETREIVS. *Ff.*
he extends to the end of the Act.   11. of tribute] *Q*, *F1*; or tribute *F2*.

---

10. *purchasing*] gaining.
15. *rais'd*] lofty.
21. *thrust out*] made eminent.
24. *expense*] expenditure.
25. *but left t'expect*] nothing to wait for except.
26. *new bills . . . proscriptions*] cancellation of creditors' accounts and
further condemnation of individuals, with forfeiture of their property.

Not worth your pause, for either their old virtue
Is in their sloth and pleasures lost, or, if
It tarry with 'em, so ill match to yours 30
As they are short in number or in cause.
The second sort are of those, city-beasts
Rather than citizens, who whilst they reach
After our fortunes, have let fly their own;
These, whelm'd in wine, swell'd up with meats, and
    weaken'd 35
With hourly whoredoms, never left the side
Of Catiline in Rome, nor here are loos'd
From his embraces; such as, trust me, never
In riding or in using well their arms,
Watching or other military labor, 40
Did exercise their youth, but learn'd to love,
Drink, dance, and sing, make feasts, and be fine gamesters,
And these will wish more hurt to you than they bring you.
The rest are a mix'd kind, all sorts of Furies,
Adulterers, dicers, fencers, outlaws, thieves, 45
The murderers of their parents, all the sink
And plague of Italy met in one torrent
To take today from us the punishment
Due to their mischiefs for so many years.
And who in such a cause and 'gainst such fiends 50
Would not now wish himself all arm and weapon
To cut such poisons from the earth and let
Their blood out, to be drawn away in clouds
And pour'd on some inhabitable place
Where the hot sun and slime breeds nought but monsters? 55

---

28 *pause*] hesitation because of fear.

30–31 *so . . . cause*] as little equal to yours as is their small number or unworthy cause.

32. *city-beasts*] domestic animals (Lat. *si cives sunt potius quam pecudes*).

34. *let fly*] cast away.

35. *whelm'd*] overwhelmed.

41. *exercise*] employ.

54. *inhabitable*] "uninhabitable" (H & S).

55. *Where . . . monsters*] "when Perseus flew over the . . . desert after cutting off Medusa's head, the blood drops falling on the sand turned to . . . snakes" (H & S).

Chiefly, when this sure joy shall crown our side,
That the least man that falls upon our party
This day, as some must give their happy names
To fate and that eternal memory
Of the best death writ with it for their country,   60
Shall walk at pleasure in the tents of rest,
And see far off beneath him all their host
Tormented after life, and Catiline there
Walking a wretched and less ghost than he.
I'll urge no more; move forward with your eagles,   65
And trust the Senate's and Rome's cause to heaven.

SOLDIERS.

To thee, great father Mars, and greater Jove.   [*Exeunt.*]

[V.ii]   [*Enter*] Caesar, Crassus.

CAESAR.

I ever look'd for this of Lentulus
When Catiline was gone.

CRASSUS.   I gave 'em lost
Many days since.

CAESAR.   But wherefore did you bear
Their letter to the Consul that they sent you
To warn you from the city?

CRASSUS.   Did I know   5
Whether he made it? It might come from him
For aught I could assure me; if they meant
I should be safe among so many, they might
Have come as well as writ.

CAESAR.   There is no loss
In being secure. I have of late, too, plied him   10

67. S.P. SOLDIERS] *this edn.*; ARM.   67. S.D.] *Gifford.*
Q, Ff.

56. *sure*] inevitable.
57. *upon*] among.
[V.ii]
    1. *look'd for this of*] expected this from.
    2. *gave 'em*] thought them.
    5. *warn you from*] give you warning to leave.
    7. *assure*] ascertain for.
    8. *so many*] i.e., to be killed.

Thick with intelligences, but they have been
Of things he knew before.

CRASSUS.   A little serves
To keep a man upright on these state-bridges,
Although the passage were more dangerous.
Let us now take the standing part.

CAESAR.   We must,   15
And be as zealous for't as Cato. Yet
I would fain help these wretched men.

CRASSUS.   You cannot.
Who would save them that have betray'd themselves? [*Exeunt.*]

[V.iii]   [*Enter*] Cicero, Quintus, Cato.

CICERO.

I will not be wrought to it, brother Quintus.
There's no man's private enmity shall make
Me violate the dignity of another.
If there were proof 'gainst Caesar, or whoever,
To speak him guilty, I would so declare him,   5
But Quintus Catulus and Piso both
Shall know the Consul will not for their grudge
Have any man accus'd or named falsely.

QUINTUS.

Not falsely, but if any circumstance
By the Allobroges or from Volturtius   10
Would carry it.

CICERO.   That shall not be sought by me.
If it reveal itself, I would not spare
You, brother, if it pointed at you, trust me.

[V.ii]
18. S.D.] *Gifford.*

---

13. *state-bridges*] their conduct, seen as a span between the Ciceronian
and Catilinarian factions on which they balance precariously.

15. *take . . . part*] join the side that will survive.

[V.iii]

1. *wrought*] made to do it by coercion.

5. *speak him*] proclaim him to be.

9. *circumstance*] evidence.

11. *carry*] sustain.

CATO.

    Good Marcus Tullius, which is more than great,
    Thou hadst thy education with the gods.   15

CICERO.

    Send Lentulus forth, and bring away the rest.
    This office I am sorry, sir, to do you.   [*Exeunt.*]

[V.iv]

[*Enter* Cicero, Lictors, Cato, Quintus, Caesar, Crassus, Syllanus, *other members of*] the Senate.

CICERO.

    What may be happy still and fortunate
    To Rome and to this Senate. Please you, Fathers,
    To break these letters and to view them round.
    If that be not found in them which I fear,
    I yet entreat at such a time as this   5
    My diligence be not contemn'd.

                [*Enter* Pomtinius, Flaccus.]

                      Ha' you brought
    The weapons hither from Cethegus' house?

POMTINIUS.

    They are without.

CICERO.   Be ready with Volturtius
    To bring him when the Senate calls, and see
    None of the rest confer together.   [*Exeunt* Pomtinius, Flaccus.]
                      Fathers,   10
    What do you read? Is it yet worth your care,
    If not your fear, what you find practic'd there?

[V.iii]   8. S.P. POMTINIUS] *this edn.*; PRAE.
17. S.D.] *Gifford.*   *Q, Ff.*
[V.iv]   10. S.D., 29.1.] *Gifford.*
6. S.D.] *Gifford.*

---

16. *Send . . . rest*] Bring Lentulus to me and imprison the rest.
17. *This . . . you*] I regret giving you this task.
[V.iv]
  3. *break . . . round*] open these sealed letters and consider (Lat. *circumspicio*) them.
  10. *confer*] consult.
  11. *care*] anxiety.

CAESAR.
    It hath a face of horror.
CRASSUS.   I am amaz'd.
CATO.
    Look there.
SYLLANUS.   Gods! Can such men draw common air?
CICERO.
    Although the greatness of the mischief, Fathers,   15
    Hath often made my faith small in this Senate,
    Yet since my casting Catiline out (for now
    I do not fear the envy of the word,
    Unless the deed be rather to be fear'd
    That he went hence alive, when those I meant   20
    Should follow him, did not) I have spent both days
    And nights in watching what their fury and rage
    Was bent on, that so stay'd against my thought;
    And that I might but take 'em in that light
    Where, when you met their treason with your eyes,   25
    Your minds at length would think for your own safety:
    And now 'tis done. There are their hands and seals.
    Their persons too are safe, thanks to the gods.
    Bring in Volturtius and the Allobroges.

[*Re-enter* Pomtinius, Flaccus, *with* Volturtius, Allobroges, *guarded.*]

    These be the men were trusted with their letters.   30
VOLTURTIUS.
    Fathers, believe me, I knew nothing; I
    Was traveling for Gallia, and am sorry—
CICERO.
    Quake not, Volturtius, speak the truth and hope
    Well of this Senate on the Consul's word.
VOLTURTIUS.
    Then I knew all. But truly I was drawn in   35
    But t'other day.

---

    16. *my faith*] belief in me.
    23. *Was . . . thought*] was directed at, who remained in Rome contrary
to my intention.
    27. *hands*] handwriting.
    32. *for*] to.

CAESAR.   Say what thou know'st, and fear not.
　　　Thou hast the Senate's faith and Consul's word
　　　To fortify thee.
VOLTURTIUS (*He answers with fear and interruptions*).
　　　　　　　　　I was sent with letters—
　　　And had a message too—from Lentulus—
　　　To Catiline—that he should use all aids—   40
　　　Servants or others—and come with his army
　　　As soon unto the city as he could—
　　　For they were ready and but stay'd for him—
　　　To intercept those that should flee the fire—
　　　These men, the Allobroges, did hear it too.   45
ALLOBROX.
　　　Yes, Fathers, and they took an oath to us
　　　Besides their letters, that we should be free,
　　　And urg'd us for some present aid of horse.
CICERO.
　　　Nay, here be other testimonies, Fathers,
　　　Cethegus' armory.

　　　　　　　The weapons and arms are brought forth.

CRASSUS.   What, not all these?   50
CICERO.
　　　Here's not the hundred part. Call in the fencer
　　　That we may know the arms to all these weapons.

　　　　　　　[*Enter* Cethegus, *guarded.*]

　　　Come, my brave sword-player, to what active use
　　　Was all this steel provided?
CETHEGUS.   Had you ask'd
　　　In Sylla's days, it had been to cut throats,   55
　　　But now it was to look on only; I lov'd
　　　To see good blades and feel their edge and points,
　　　To put a helm upon a block and cleave it,
　　　And now and then to stab an armor through.

38. S.D.] *Ff*; *om. Q*.　　　　　52.1., 66. S.D.] *Gifford*.
50. S.D.] *om. Q*; *opp. l. 49, Ff*.

───────────────────────────────

37. *faith*] fidelity to its promises.
48. *urg'd*] asked.
48. *present . . . horse*] immediate . . . horses.
51. *hundred*] hundredth.
58. *helm*] helmet.

CICERO.

    Know you that paper? That will stab you through.   60
    Is it your hand? Hold, save the pieces. Traitor,
    Hath thy guilt wak'd thy fury?

CETHEGUS.   I did write

    I know not what, nor care not; that fool Lentulus
    Did dictate, and I t'other fool did sign it.

CICERO.

    Bring in Statilius; does he know his hand too?   65
    And Lentulus.

          [*Enter* Statilius *and* Lentulus, *guarded.*]

          Reach him that letter.

STATILIUS.   I

    Confess it all.

CICERO.   Know you that seal yet, Publius?

LENTULUS.

    Yes, it is mine.

CICERO.   Whose image is that on it?

LENTULUS.

    My grandfather's.

CICERO.   What, that renown'd good man

    That did so only embrace his country and lov'd   70
    His fellow citizens? Was not his picture,
    Though mute, of power to call thee from a fact
    So foul—

LENTULUS.   As what, impetuous Cicero?

CICERO.

    As thou art, for I do not know what's fouler.
    Look upon these. Do not these faces argue   75
    Thy guilt and impudence?

LENTULUS.   What are these to me?

    I know 'em not.

---

60. *paper*] document.

61. *Hold . . . pieces*] Gifford adds the S.D. "*Cethegus tears the letters.*"

66. *Reach*] hand over to.

69. *My grandfather's*] of P. Cornelius Lentulus, Consul in 162 B.C.; cf.
ll. 146–149. The older Lentulus, as *princeps senatus*, opposed C. Gracchus in
125 B.C.

70. *only embrace*] love uniquely (Lat. *unice amavit*).

75. *argue*] give evidence of.

ALLOBROX.   No, Publius? We were with you
     At Brutus' house.

VOLTURTIUS.   Last night.

LENTULUS.   What did you there?
     Who sent for you?

ALLOBROX.   Yourself did. We had letters
     From you, Cethegus, this Statilius here,   80
     Gabinius Cimber, all but from Longinus
     Who would not write because he was to come
     Shortly in person after us, he said,
     To take the charge o'the horse which we should levy.

CICERO.
     And he is fled to Catiline, I hear.   85

LENTULUS.
     Spies, spies!

ALLOBROX.   You told us too o'the Sibyl's books
     And how you were to be a king this year,
     The twentieth from the burning of the Capitol;
     That three Cornelii were to reign in Rome,
     Of which you were the last; and prais'd Cethegus   90
     And the great spirits were with you in the action.

CETHEGUS.
     These are your honorable ambassadors,
     My sovereign lord.

CATO.   Peace, that too bold Cethegus.

ALLOBROX.
     Besides Gabinius, your agent nam'd
     Autronius, Servius Sulla, Vargunteius,   95
     And divers others.

VOLTURTIUS.   I had letters from you
     To Catiline, and a message which I have told
     Unto the Senate truly, word for word,
     For which I hope they will be gracious to me.
     I was drawn in by that same wicked Cimber   100
     And thought no hurt at all.

CICERO.   Volturtius, peace.
     Where is thy visor or thy voice now, Lentulus?

95. Sulla] *Q, F1*; SYLLA *F2.*

---

101. *thought*] thought there would be.

Art thou confounded? Wherefore speak'st thou not?
Is all so clear, so plain, so manifest,
That both thy eloquence and impudence   105
And thy ill nature too have left thee at once?
Take him aside. There's yet one more, Gabinius,
The engineer of all.

[*Enter* Gabinius, *guarded.*]

                  Show him that paper,
If he do know it.
GABINIUS.   I know nothing.
CICERO.   No?
GABINIUS.
No. Neither will I know.
CATO.   Impudent head,   110
Stick it into his throat; were I the Consul
I'd make thee eat the mischief thou hast vented.
GABINIUS.
Is there a law for't, Cato?
CATO.   Dost thou ask
After a law, that wouldst have broke all laws
Of nature, manhood, conscience, and religion?   115
GABINIUS.
Yes, I may ask for't.
CATO.   No, pernicious Cimber.
Th'inquiring after good does not belong
Unto a wicked person.
GABINIUS.   Ay, but Cato
Does nothing but by law.
CRASSUS.   Take him aside.
There's proof enough, though he confess not.
GABINIUS.   Stay,   120
I will confess. All's true your spies have told you.
Make much of 'em.
CETHEGUS.   Yes, and reward 'em well
For fear you get no more such. See they do not
Die in a ditch and stink, now you ha' done with 'em,

108. S.D.] *Gifford.*   110. Neither will I] *Ff*; Nor I will
                                 not *Q*.

111. *Stick . . . throat*] force his words back down his throat.

Or beg o'the bridges here in Rome, whose arches   125
Their active industry hath sav'd.

CICERO.   See, Fathers,
What minds and spirits these are, that being convicted
Of such a treason and by such a cloud
Of witnesses, dare yet retain their boldness.
What would their rage have done if they had conquer'd?   130
I thought when I had thrust out Catiline
Neither the state nor I should need t'have fear'd
Lentulus' sleep here, or Longinus' fat,
Or this Cethegus' rashness; it was he
I only watch'd while he was in our walls   135
As one that had the brain, the hand, the heart.
But now we find the contrary. Where was there
A people griev'd or a state discontent,
Able to make or help a war 'gainst Rome,
But these, th'Allobroges, and those they found,   140
Whom had not the just gods been pleas'd to make
More friends unto our safety than their own,
As it then seem'd, neglecting these men's offers,
Where had we been, or where the Commonwealth,
When their great chief had been call'd home, this man,   145
Their absolute king, whose noble grandfather,
Arm'd in pursuit of the seditious Gracchus,
Took a brave wound for dear defense of that
Which he would spoil, had gather'd all his aids
Of ruffians, slaves, and other slaughter-men,   150
Given us up for murder to Cethegus,
The other rank of citizens to Gabinius,
The city to be fir'd by Cassius,
And Italy, nay the world, to be laid waste
By cursed Catiline and his complices?   155

---

150. ruffians] *Ff*; Ruffins *Q*.

---

125. *beg o'the bridges*] Bridges provided a favorite stand for beggars.
126. *industry*] toil.
143. *neglecting*] despising (Lat. *negligo*).
145. *been call'd home*] returned to Rome.
149. *he*] i.e., Catiline.
152. *other rank*] i.e., non-Senators.

Lay but the thought of it before you, Fathers,
Think but with me you saw this glorious city,
The light of all the earth, tower of all nations,
Suddenly falling in one flame. Imagine
You view'd your country buried with the heaps   160
Of slaughter'd citizens that had no grave;
This Lentulus here reigning, as he dream'd,
And those his purple Senate; Catiline come
With his fierce army; and the cries of matrons,
The flight of children, and the rape of virgins,   165
Shrieks of the living with the dying groans
On every side t'invade your sense; until
The blood of Rome were mixed with her ashes.
This was the spectacle these fiends intended
To please their malice.

CETHEGUS.   Ay, and it would   170
Have been a brave one, Consul. But your part
Had not then been so long as now it is:
I should have quite defeated your oration
And slit that fine rhetorical pipe of yours
I'the first scene.

CATO.   Insolent monster.

CICERO.   Fathers,   175
Is it your pleasures they shall be committed
Unto some safe but a free custody
Until the Senate can determine farther?

SENATORS.

It pleaseth well.

CICERO.   Then, Marcus Crassus,
Take you charge of Gabinius; send him home   180
Unto your house. You, Caesar, of Statilius.
Cethegus shall be sent to Cornificius

---

156. *Lay . . . before*] imagine (Lat. *propono*).

163. *purple*] dressed in purple (i.e., rich) garments; the suggestion is that the Senate would become like the court of a despot.

167. *invade your sense*] impinge on your hearing.

173. *defeated*] frustrated.

177. *free custody*] in the homes of individual citizens, instead of prison.

178. *determine*] decide.

And Lentulus to Publius Lentulus Spinther,
Who now is Aedile.

CATO.   It were best the Praetors
Carried 'em to their houses and delivered 'em.   185

CICERO.
Let it be so. Take 'em from hence.

CAESAR.   But first
Let Lentulus put off his Praetorship.

LENTULUS.
I do resign it here unto the Senate.

[*Exeunt* Pomtinius, Flaccus, *and Guards with* Lentulus, Cethegus,
Statilius, Gabinius.]

CAESAR.
So now there's no offense done to religion.

CATO.
Caesar, 'twas piously and timely urg'd.   190

CICERO.
What do you decree to th'Allobroges
That were the lights to this discovery?

CRASSUS.
A free grant from the state of all their suits.

CAESAR.
And a reward out of the public treasure.

CATO.
Ay, and the title of honest men to crown 'em.   195

CICERO.
What to Volturtius?

CAESAR.   Life and favor's well.

VOLTURTIUS.
I ask no more.

188.1–2.] *Gifford.*

---

185. *Carried 'em . . . 'em*] conveyed them under guard to their houses and
handed them over.

189. *offense . . . religion*] A magistrate could not be imprisoned while
holding office. The offense to religion would arise because Lentulus as
Praetor had the right of taking the auspices. Caesar is intervening as *Pontifex
Maximus* (chief priest of the state religion).

192. *were . . . to*] threw light on.

194. *treasure*] treasury.

196. *favor's*] favor is.

CATO.   Yes, yes, some money; thou need'st it.
    'Twill keep thee honest; want made thee a knave.

SYLLANUS.
    Let Flaccus and Pomtinius, the Praetors,
    Have public thanks, and Quintus Fabius Sanga,   200
    For their good service.

CRASSUS.   They deserve it all.

CATO.
    But what do we decree unto the Consul,
    Whose virtue, counsel, watchfulness, and wisdom
    Hath freed the Commonwealth, and without tumult,
    Slaughter, or blood, or scarce raising a force,   205
    Rescu'd us all out of the jaws of fate?

CRASSUS.
    We owe our lives unto him, and our fortunes.

CAESAR.
    Our wives, our children, parents, and our gods.

SYLLANUS.
    We all are saved by his fortitude.

CATO.
    The Commonwealth owes him a civic garland.   210
    He is the only father of his country.

CAESAR.
    Let there be public prayer to all the gods
    Made in that name for him.

CRASSUS.   And in these words:
    "For that he hath by his vigilance preserv'd
    Rome from the flame, the Senate from the sword,   215
    And all her citizens from massacre."

CICERO.
    How are my labors more than paid, grave Fathers,
    In these great titles and decreed honors,
    Such as to me first of the civil robe

---

209. *fortitude*] courage (Lat. *fortitudo*).
210. *civic garland*] *corona civica*, of oak leaves, the reward for saving the lives of citizens.
211. *father of his country*] *pater patriae*, a title of honor.
214. *For that*] because.
219. *of . . . robe*] (Lat. *togato*). All previous public prayers and thanksgiving had been decreed for military victories.

Of any man since Rome was Rome have happen'd,   220
And from this frequent Senate, which more glads me
That I now see yo'have sense of your own safety.
If those good days come no less grateful to us
Wherein we are preserv'd from some great danger
Than those wherein we are born and brought to light,   225
Because the gladness of our safety is certain
But the condition of our birth not so,
And that we are sav'd with pleasure but are born
Without the sense of joy; why should not then
This day to us and all posterity   230
Of ours be had in equal fame and honor
With that when Romulus first rear'd these walls,
When so much more is saved than he built?

CAESAR.

It ought.

CRASSUS.   Let it be added to our Fasti.

CICERO.

What tumult's that?

[*Re-enter* Flaccus.]

FLACCUS.   Here's one Tarquinius taken   235
Going to Catiline, and says he was sent
By Marcus Crassus, whom he names to be
Guilty of the conspiracy.

CICERO.   Some lying varlet.
Take him away to prison.

CRASSUS.   Bring him in
And let me see him.

CICERO.   He is not worth it, Crassus.   240
Keep him up close and hungry till he tell
By whose pernicious counsel he durst slander
So great and good a citizen.

CRASSUS [*aside*].   By yours

222. yo'have] *Ff*; you'have *Q*.   235, 243, 264. S.D.] *Gifford*.
225. we are] *F2*; w'are *Q*, *F1*.

---

223. *come . . . grateful*] are . . . pleasing.
230. *posterity*] descendants.
238. *varlet*] low fellow.
241. *Keep . . . close*] keep him in prison.

I fear 'twill prove.

SYLLANUS.   Some o'the traitors, sure,
    To give their action the more credit bid him   245
    Name you or any man.

CICERO.   I know myself
    By all the tracts and courses of this business
    Crassus is noble, just, and loves his country.

FLACCUS.
    Here is a libel too, accusing Caesar,
    From Lucius Vectius, and confirm'd by Curius.   250

CICERO.
    Away with all, throw it out o'the court.

CAESAR.
    A trick on me too?

CICERO.   It is some men's malice.
    I said to Curius I did not believe him.

CAESAR.
    Was not that Curius your spy that had
    Reward decreed upon him, the last Senate,   255
    With Fulvia, upon your private motion?

CICERO.
    Yes.

CAESAR. But he has not that reward yet?

CICERO.   No.
    Let not this trouble you, Caesar, none believes it.

CAESAR.
    It shall not if that he have no reward;
    But if he have, sure I shall think myself   260
    Very untimely and unsafely honest
    Where such as he is may have pay t'accuse me.

CICERO.
    You shall have no wrong done you, noble Caesar,
    But all contentment.

CAESAR.   Consul, I am silent.   [*Exeunt.*]

---

244. *prove*] turn out.
245. *credit*] credibility.
247. *tracts and courses*] sequence of events.
249. *libel*] "document (Lat. *libellus*)" (H & S).
256. *private motion*] Lat. *privilegium*, a bill relating to an individual.
261. *untimely . . . honest*] prematurely and uncertainly deemed reputable.
264. *contentment*] satisfaction.

[V.v]   [*Enter*] Catiline[, *Soldiers*].

CATILINE.

    I never yet knew, soldiers, that in fight
    Words added virtue unto valiant men,
    Or that a general's oration made
    An army fall or stand, but how much prowess
    Habitual or natural each man's breast   5
    Was owner of, so much in act it show'd.
    Whom neither glory or danger can excite
    'Tis vain t'attempt with speech, for the mind's fear
    Keeps all brave sounds from ent'ring at that ear.
    I yet would warn you some few things, my friends,   10
    And give you reason of my present counsels.
    You know no less than I what state, what point
    Our affairs stand in, and you all have heard
    What a calamitous misery the sloth
    And sleepiness of Lentulus hath pluck'd   15
    Both on himself and us; how whilst our aids
    There in the city look'd for are defeated,
    Our entrance into Gallia too is stop'd.
    Two armies wait us: one from Rome, the other
    From the Gaul provinces, and where we are,   20
    Although I most desire it, the great want
    Of corn and victual forbids longer stay,
    So that of need we must remove, but whither
    The sword must both direct and cut the passage.
    I only therefore wish you when you strike   25
    To have your valors and your souls about you,
    And think you carry in your laboring hands
    The things you seek: glory and liberty,
    Your country which you want now, with the Fates

0.1.] *this edn.*; CATILINE. THE   *Ff.*
ARMIE. *Q*; *The Armie.* CATILINE.   22. victual] *Q, F1*; victuals *F2.*

---

   4. *prowess*] military valor.
   5. *Habitual or natural*] formed by habit or nature.
  11. *reason . . . counsels*] reasons for my present plan of action.
  12. *point*] condition.
  19. *wait*] wait for.
  22. *corn and victual*] grain and (other) food.
  23. *of need . . . remove*] necessarily . . . change our location.

That are to be instructed by our swords.   30
If we can give the blow all will be safe to us:
We shall not want provision nor supplies,
The colonies and free towns will lie open;
Where if we yield to fear, expect no place
Nor friend to shelter those whom their own fortune   35
And ill-us'd arms have left without protection.
You might have liv'd in servitude or exile
Or safe at Rome depending on the great ones,
But that you thought those things unfit for men;
And in that thought you then were valiant,   40
For no man ever yet chang'd peace for war
But he that meant to conquer. Hold that purpose.
There's more necessity you should be such
In fighting for yourselves than they for others.
He's base that trusts his feet whose hands are arm'd.   45
Methinks I see death and the Furies waiting
What we will do, and all the heav'n at leisure
For the great spectacle. Draw then your swords,
And if our destiny envy our virtue
The honor of the day, yet let us care   50
To sell ourselves at such a price as may
Undo the world to buy us, and make Fate,
While she tempts ours, fear her own estate.   [*Exeunt.*]

[V.vi]
[*Enter Lictors,* Pomtinius, Cicero, Syllanus, Caesar, Cato, Crassus,
other members of] *the Senate.*

1 SENATOR.
    What means this hasty calling of the Senate?

47. heav'n] *this edn.*; heauen *Q, Ff.*   V.vi.] *All numbered S.P.s in this Scene*
53. S.D.] *Gifford.*   *where Q, Ff have* SEN., *follow Gifford*
                                               except as noted.

---

31. *give . . . to*] conquer, all will be secure for.
42. *Hold that purpose*] Keep that intention.
43. *such*] i.e., conquerors.
46. *waiting*] looking forward to.
47. *at leisure*] having ceased normal activities.
49. *virtue*] courage.
50. *care*] take care.
53. *tempts*] attacks.

2 SENATOR.

    We shall know straight. Wait till the Consul speaks.

POMTINIUS.

    Fathers Conscript, bethink you of your safeties
    And what to do with these conspirators;
    Some of their clients, their free'd men and slaves   5
    'Gin to make head; there is one of Lentulus' bawds
    Runs up and down the shops through every street
    With money to corrupt the poor artificers
    And needy tradesmen to their aid; Cethegus
    Hath sent, too, to his servants, who are many,   10
    Chosen, and exercis'd in bold attemptings,
    That forthwith they should arm themselves and prove
    His rescue; all will be in instant uproar
    If you prevent it not with present counsels.
    We have done what we can to meet the fury,   15
    And will do more. Be you good to yourselves.

CICERO.

    What is your pleasure, Fathers, shall be done?
    Syllanus, you are Consul next design'd;
    Your sentence of these men.

SYLLANUS.   'Tis short, and this.

    Since they have sought to blot the name of Rome   20
    Out of the world, and raze this glorious empire
    With her own hands and arms turn'd on herself,
    I think it fit they die, and could my breath
    Now execute 'em, they should not enjoy
    An article of time or eye of light   25
    Longer, to poison this our common air.

1 SENATOR.

    I think so too.

2 SENATOR.   And I.

---

   3. *bethink you of*] consider.
   6. *make head*] raise troops.
   8. *corrupt . . . artificers*] lure . . . artisans.
  11. *exercis'd . . . attemptings*] experienced . . . assaults.
  12. *prove*] attempt.
  18. *design'd*] elect (Lat. *designatus*).
  19. *sentence*] judgment (Lat. *sententia*).
  25. *article . . . eye*] moment of time or point.

3 SENATOR.   And I.
4 SENATOR.   And I.
CICERO.

    Your sentence, Caius Caesar.

CAESAR.   Conscript Fathers,
    In great affairs and doubtful, it behooves
    Men that are ask'd their sentence to be free   30
    From either hate or love, anger or pity,
    For where the least of these do hinder, there
    The mind not easily discerns the truth.
    I speak this to you in the name of Rome
    For whom you stand, and to the present cause: 35
    That this foul fact of Lentulus and the rest
    Weigh not more with you than your dignity,
    And you be more indulgent to your passion
    Than to your honor. If there could be found
    A pain or punishment equal to their crimes,   40
    I would devise and help; but if the greatness
    Of what they ha' done exceed all man's invention,
    I think it fit to stay where our laws do.
    Poor petty states may alter upon humor
    Where, if they offend with anger, few do know it   45
    Because they are obscure; their fame and fortune
    Is equal and the same. But they that are
    Head of the world and live in that seen height,
    All mankind knows their actions. So we see
    The greater fortune hath the lesser license.   50
    They must nor favor, hate, and least be angry,
    For what with others is call'd anger, there
    Is cruelty and pride. I know Syllanus
    Who spoke before me a just, valiant man,

---

29. *doubtful*] controversial.
35. *present cause*] case before us.
37. *Weigh*] prevail.
38. *passion*] anger.
41. *devise*] join in planning.
43. *stay*] stop.
44. *petty . . . humor*] minor countries can change policy on a whim.
46–47. *their . . . same*] They are no more well-known than they are great.
50. *license*] freedom of action.
51. *nor*] neither . . . nor.

A lover of the state, and one that would not   55
In such a business use or grace or hatred;
I know too, well, his manners and modesty,
Nor do I think his sentence cruel, for
'Gainst such delinquents, what can be too bloody,
But that it is abhorring from our state,   60
Since to a citizen of Rome offending,
Our laws give exile and not death. Why then
Decrees he that? 'Twere vain to think for fear,
When by the diligence of so worthy a Consul
All is made safe and certain. Is't for punishment?   65
Why, death's the end of evils, and a rest
Rather than torment; it dissolves all griefs,
And beyond that is neither care nor joy.
You hear my sentence would not have 'em die.
How then, set free and increase Catiline's army?   70
So will they, being but banish'd. No, grave Fathers,
I judge 'em first to have their states confiscate;
Then that their persons remain prisoners
I'the free towns far off from Rome and sever'd,
Where they might neither have relation   75
Hereafter to the Senate or the people,
Or if they had, those towns then to be mulcted
As enemies to the state, that had their guard.

1 SENATOR.

'Tis good and honorable, Caesar hath utter'd.

CICERO.

Fathers, I see your faces and your eyes   80

---

57. and] *Ff*; and his *Q*.   79. S.P.] *this edn.*; Omnes *Gifford.*

---

56. *grace*] judicial favor.

60. *abhorring from*] unacceptable to (Lat. *aliena ab*; Jonson has in mind the alternative *abhorrens ab*).

62. *give*] prescribe.

63. *vain*] superfluous.

65. *certain*] secure.

72. *confiscate*] confiscated.

74. *sever'd*] kept distant.

75–76. *relation . . . Senate*] Latin *referre* (supine *relatum*) *ad Senatum* was the technical term for putting a motion in the Senate. The original says that no one should hereafter put a motion in the Senate concerning them.

77. *mulcted*] fined.

All bent on me to note of these two censures
Which I incline to. Either of them are grave
And answering the dignity of the speakers,
The greatness of th'affair, and both severe.
One urgeth death, and he may well remember   85
This state hath punish'd wicked citizens so;
The other bonds, and those perpetual, which
He thinks found out for the more singular plague.
Decree which you shall please. You have a Consul
Not readier to obey than to defend   90
Whatever you shall act for the Republic,
And meet with willing shoulders any burden
Or any fortune with an even face,
Though it were death, which to a valiant man
Can never happen foul, nor to a Consul   95
Be immature, or to a wise man wretched.

SYLLANUS.

  Fathers, I spake but as I thought the needs
  O'th' Commonwealth requir'd.

CATO.   Excuse it not.

CICERO.

  Cato, speak you your sentence.

CATO.   This it is.

  You here dispute on kinds of punishment   100
And stand consulting what you should decree
'Gainst those of whom you rather should beware.
This mischief is not like those common facts
Which, when they are done, the laws may prosecute;
But this, if you provide not ere it happen,   105
When it is happen'd will not wait your judgment.
Good Caius Caesar here hath very well
And subtilly discours'd of life and death

---

81. *bent . . . note*] turned toward me to see.
82. *incline to*] prefer.
82. *Either*] both.
83. *answering*] corresponding to.
88. *found . . . plague*] devised as a specially appropriate punishment.
91. *act*] enact.
93. *an even face*] equanimity.
96. *immature*] premature (Lat. *immatura*).
108. *subtilly*] subtly; Jonson's spelling indicates a trisyllable.

As if he thought those things a pretty fable
That are deliver'd us of hell and Furies,   110
Or of the divers way that ill men go
From good to filthy, dark, and ugly places;
And therefore he would have these live, and long too,
But far from Rome and in the small free towns
Lest here they might have rescue, as if men   115
Fit for such acts were only in the city
And not throughout all Italy, or that boldness
Could not do more where it found least resistance.
'Tis a vain counsel if he think them dangerous,
Which if he do not, but that he alone   120
In so great fear of all men stand unfrighted,
He gives me cause, and you, more to fear him.
I am plain, Fathers. Here you look about
One at another, doubting what to do,
With faces as you trusted to the gods   125
That still have sav'd you; and they can do't, but
They are not wishings or base womanish prayers
Can draw their aids, but vigilance, counsel, action,
Which they will be ashamed to forsake.
'Tis sloth they hate, and cowardice. Here you have   130
The traitors in your houses, yet you stand
Fearing what to do with 'em; let 'em loose
And send 'em hence with arms too, that your mercy
May turn your misery as soon as't can.
O but they are great men and have offended,   135
But through ambition. We would spare their honor;
Ay, if themselves had spar'd it, or their fame,
Or modesty, or either god or man,
Then I would spare 'em, but as things now stand,

110. *deliver'd*] related to.
111. *ill*] evil.
119. *a vain counsel*] foolish advice.
120. *but that*] but.
121. *In*] amid (Latinate construction).
125. *as*] as if.
132. *Fearing*] doubting.
134. *turn*] become.

Fathers, to spare these men were to commit   140
A greater wickedness than you would revenge,
If there had been but time and place for you
To have repair'd this fault, you should have made it,
It should have been your punishment to have felt
Your tardy error; but necessity   145
Now bids me say, let 'em not live an hour
If you mean Rome should live a day. I have done.

1 SENATOR.

Cato hath spoken like an oracle.

CRASSUS.

Let it be so decreed.

2 SENATOR.   We are all fearful.

SYLLANUS.

And had been base, had not his virtue rais'd us.   150

3 SENATOR.

Go forth, most worthy Consul, we'll assist you.

CAESAR.

I am not yet chang'd in my sentence, Fathers.

CATO.

No matter.

[*Enter* Servant.]

                What be those?

SERVANT.   Letters for Caesar.

CATO.

From whom? Let 'em be read in open Senate.
Fathers, they come from the conspirators.   155
I crave to have 'em read, for the Republic.

CAESAR.

Cato, read you it. 'Tis a love-letter

---

149. are all] *Ff*; all were *Q*.   153. S.P. SERVANT] *Q*, *F1*; SEN.
153. S.D.] *Gifford*.   *F2*.

---

143. *repair'd*] corrected.
145. *tardy error*] error of being dilatory.
147. *done*] finished.

From your dear sister to me; though you hate me,
Do not discover it.

CATO.   Hold thee, drunkard. Consul,
Go forth, and confidently.

CAESAR.   You'll repent   160
This rashness, Cicero.

POMTINIUS.   Caesar shall repent it.

CICERO.
Hold, friends.

POMTINIUS.   He's scarce a friend unto the public.

CICERO.
No violence. Caesar, be safe. Lead on.
Where are the public executioners?
Bid 'em wait on us. On to Spinther's house.   [*Exeunt.*] 165

[V.vii]   [*Enter* Cicero, *Cato, Pomtinius, Lictors, Guards.*]

CICERO.
Bring Lentulus forth.

              [*Enter* Lentulus, *guarded.*]

                  Here, you, the sad revengers
Of capital crimes against the public, take
This man unto your justice: strangle him.

LENTULUS.
Thou dost well, Consul. 'Twas a cast at dice
In Fortune's hand not long since that thyself   5
Shouldst have heard these or other words as fatal.

CICERO.
Lead on to Quintus Cornificius' house.   [*Exeunt.*]

161, 162. S.P. POMTINIUS] *this edn.*;   [V.vii]
PRAE. *Q, Ff.*   1. S.D.] *Gifford.*

---

158. *sister*] Servilia, Cato's half-sister and mother of Caesar's assassin Brutus.

159. *Hold thee*] keep (the letter) for yourself.

163. *be safe*] you are safe.

[V.vii]

1. *sad*] grave.

4. *cast at dice*] matter of chance.

[V.viii]   [*Enter* Cicero, *Cato, Pomtinius, Lictors, Guards.*]

CICERO.

Bring forth Cethegus.

[*Enter* Cethegus, *guarded.*]

Take him to the due
Death that he hath deserv'd, and let it be
Said, "He was once."

CETHEGUS.   A beast or what is worse,
A slave, Cethegus. Let that be the name
For all that's base hereafter, that would let   5
This worm pronounce on him and not have trampled
His body into—ha, art thou not mov'd?

CICERO.

Justice is never angry; take him hence.

CETHEGUS.

O, the whore Fortune, and her bawds the Fates,
That put these tricks on men which knew the way   10
To death by a sword. Strangle me, I may sleep;
I shall grow angry with the gods else.

CICERO.   Lead

To Caius Caesar for Statilius.   [*Exeunt.*]

[V.ix]   [*Enter* Cicero, Cato, *Pomtinius, Lictors, Guards.*]

CICERO.

Bring him and rude Gabinius out.

[*Enter* Statilius *and* Gabinius, *guarded.*]

Here, take 'em
To your cold hands, and let 'em feel death from you.

[V.viii]   [V.ix]
1. S.D.] *Gifford.*   1. S.D., 3.1., 12. S.D.] *Gifford.*
13. Caesar] *Ff*; Cæsars *Q*.

[V.viii]
 1. *due*] appropriate.
 3. "*He was once*"] i.e., he existed once (and has now ceased to); but
Cethegus picks up his sentence as though it were incomplete.
 7. *mov'd*] angered.
 11. *I may*] so I may.
[V.ix]
 1. *rude*] savage.

GABINIUS.

    I thank you, you do me a pleasure.

STATILIUS.   And me too.

                    [*Exeunt* Statilius *and* Gabinius, *guarded.*]

CATO.

    So, Marcus Tullius, thou mayst now stand up
    And call it happy Rome, thou being Consul.   5
    Great parent of thy country, go and let
    The old men of the city, ere they die,
    Kiss thee; the matrons dwell about thy neck;
    The youths and maids lay up 'gainst they are old
    What kind of man thou wert to tell their nephews   10
    When such a year they read within our Fasti,
    Thy Consulship.

                    [*Enter* Petreius.]

                    Who's this, Petreius?

CICERO.   Welcome,

    Welcome, renowned soldier. What's the news?
    This face can bring no ill with't unto Rome.
    How does the worthy Consul, my colleague?   15

PETREIUS.

    As well as victory can make him, sir.
    He greets the Fathers, and to me hath trusted
    The sad relation of the civil strife,
    For in such war the conquest still is black.

CICERO.

    Shall we withdraw into the house of Concord?   20

CATO.

    No, happy Consul, here; let all ears take
    The benefit of this tale. If he had voice
    To spread unto the poles and strike it through
    The center to the Antipodes, it would ask it.

---

    5. *happy . . . Consul*] *thou being Consul* is an imitation of the Latin ablative
absolute construction. The whole line is suggested by Cicero's own verse,
o fortunatam natam me consule Roman.
    8. *dwell*] remain.
    9. *lay up*] store up.
    9. *'gainst*] for the time when.
    19. *conquest still*] even the conquest.
    20. *house*] temple.
    24. *it would ask it*] the tale would demand as much.

                              – 156 –

PETREIUS.

 The straits and needs of Catiline being such   25
 As he must fight with one of the two armies
 That then had near enclos'd him, it pleas'd Fate
 To make us th'object of his desperate choice
 Wherein the danger almost pois'd the honor,
 And as he riss, the day grew black with him   30
 And Fate descended nearer to the earth
 As if she meant to hide the name of things
 Under her wings and make the world her quarry.
 At this we rous'd, lest one small minute's stay
 Had left it to be inquir'd what Rome was;   35
 And, as we ought, arm'd in the confidence
 Of our great cause, in form of battle stood,
 Whilst Catiline came on, not with the face
 Of any man, but of a public ruin:
 His count'nance was a civil war itself,   40
 And all his host had standing in their looks
 The paleness of the death that was to come.
 Yet cried they out like vultures, and urg'd on
 As if they would precipitate our fates,
 Nor stay'd we longer for 'em, but himself   45
 Struck the first stroke, and with it fled a life;
 Which cut, it seem'd a narrow neck of land
 Had broke between two mighty seas, and either
 Flow'd into other, for so did the slaughter,
 And whirl'd about as when two violent tides   50
 Meet and not yield. The Furies stood on hills
 Circling the place, and trembled to see men
 Do more than they; whilst piety left the field,
 Griev'd for that side that in so bad a cause
 They knew not what a crime their valor was.   55

---

25. *straits*] difficulties.
29. *pois'd*] "balanced" (H & S).
30. *with*] because of.
34. *stay*] delay.
37. *form of battle*] battle formation.
38. *came on*] advanced.
41. *standing . . . looks*] showing in their faces.
45. *himself*] i.e., Catiline.
47. *Which cut*] which being cut.
48. *either*] each.

The sun stood still and was, behind the cloud
The battle made, seen sweating to drive up
His frighted horse whom still the noise drove backward,
And now had fierce Enyo, like a flame,
Consum'd all it could reach, and then itself,   60
Had not the fortune of the Commonwealth
Come Pallas-like to every Roman thought;
Which Catiline seeing, and that now his troops
Cover'd that earth they had fought on with their trunks,
Ambitious of great fame to crown his ill,   65
Collected all his fury and ran in,
Arm'd with a glory high as his despair,
Into our battle like a Libyan lion
Upon his hunters, scornful of our weapons,
Careless of wounds, plucking down lives about him   70
Till he had circled in himself with death;
Then fell he too, t'embrace it where it lay,
And as in that rebellion 'gainst the gods,
Minerva holding forth Medusa's head,
One of the giant brethren felt himself   75
Grow marble at the killing sight, and now
Almost made stone, began t'inquire what flint,
What rock it was that crept through all his limbs,
And ere he could think more, was that he fear'd;
So Catiline at the sight of Rome in us   80
Became his tomb, yet did his look retain
Some of his fierceness, and his hands still mov'd
As if he labor'd yet to grasp the state
With those rebellious parts.

CATO.   A brave bad death.
    Had this been honest now, and for his country   85
    As 'twas against it, who had e'er fallen greater?

CICERO.
    Honor'd Petreius, Rome, not I, must thank you.
    How modestly has he spoken of himself!

---

57. *sweating*] laboring.
65. *Ambitious of*] seeking.
74. *holding forth*] extending in her hands.
76. *killing*] fatal.
86. *e'er*] ever; but perhaps "ere," previously.

CATO.

   He did the more.

CICERO.   Thanks to the immortal gods,

   Romans, I now am paid for all my labors,   90

   My watchings, and my dangers. Here conclude

   Your praises, triumphs, honors, and rewards

   Decreed to me; only the memory

   Of this glad day, if I may know it live

   Within your thoughts, shall much affect my conscience,   95

   Which I must always study before fame.

   Though both be good, the latter yet is worst

   And ever is ill got without the first.   [*Exeunt.*]

THE END

This Tragedy was first
acted in the year
1611

By the King's Majesty's
Servants   5

The principal Tragedians were

Ric. Burbadge	Joh. Hemings
Alex. Cooke	Hen. Condel
Joh. Lowin	Joh. Underwood
Wil. Ostler	Nic. Tooly
Ric. Robinson	Wil. Eglestone

With the allowance of the Master of Revels

98. S.D.] *Gifford.*
[Cast list]
1–5. This . . . Servants] *F1*; *om. Q,*
F2.
6–11. The . . . Eglestone] *F1*; *om.*

Q; *following* The Persons of the Play
. . . Rome *F2.*
12. With . . . Revels] *F1*; *om. Q*; *on*
title page, F2.

95. *affect my conscience*] influence my inward thought.
96. *Which . . . before*] which (i.e., conscience) I must always make my aim
in preference to.

Appendix A

Glossary of Classical Names and Terms

Reference is given only for the first occurrence.

AEDILE (V.iv.184). Magistrate responsible primarily for maintenance of public order in Rome and control of markets.

ALLOBROGES (IV.i.0.1) (singular ALLOBROX). A Gallic tribe, living between the Rhône and the Isère, in the Roman province of Gallia Narbonensis. They had been under Roman rule since 121 B.C.; in 63 B.C. an embassy from the tribe was in Rome with a complaint against the governor of the province.

AMBROSIAC (I.112). Ambrosia was the food of the gods.

Gaius ANTONIUS *Hybrida* (I.447). Cicero's colleague in the consulship, and previously in the praetorship (66 B.C.). His incompetent and corrupt governorship of Macedonia led to his exile (59 B.C.). (Here as in other names, Jonson's form of the praenomen is Caius.)

APULIA (III.iii.70). A district in southeast Italy between the Appian Way and the Adriatic Sea.

ARPINUM (IV.ii.421). A town in central Italy, birthplace of Cicero.

ASIA (I.587). The Roman province, corresponding roughly to Western Turkey.

ATE (IV.ii.111). A goddess, frequent in Greek tragedy, personification of infatuation or moral blindness, who leads men to commit sin through presumption.

ATLAS (I.86). A mythological giant who held up the sky on his shoulders.

ATREUS (I.313). A legendary Greek who avenged himself on his brother Thyestes for the latter's attempt to usurp the throne by killing Thyestes' children and serving him their flesh at a banquet, at which event the sun turned back upon its course in horror. In an alternative version, Zeus caused the sun to turn back after the attempted usurpation as a sign that Thyestes was not the rightful king.

ATTALIC (I.386). Gold-embroidered. Attalus III of Pergamum was proverbial for his wealth and was traditionally credited with the introduction of gold-embroidered textiles.

ATTIC (I.384). From, or in the style of, Athens, whose territory was called Attica. Most of the statuary purchased would be late imitations of the productions of the best period (fifth–fourth century B.C.) of Athenian sculpture.

AUGURS (I.139). Official interpreters of omens and oracles. The augurate was a state priesthood held for life; at this period the "college" of augurs consisted of fifteen men.

AURELIA *Orestilla* (I.97.1). The wife of Catiline. It was generally believed that when she hesitated to marry him from fear of his grown-up son by a previous marriage, Catiline murdered his son.

AURELIAN WAY (IV.ii.323). A road running northwards from Rome along the west coast of Italy to Genoa.

Publius AUTRONIUS *Paetus* (I.156). He was elected Consul for 65 B.C., but disqualified on a charge of bribery; he subsequently joined the conspiracy.

BELGIA (III.iii.92). Northwest Gaul. Jonson may be guilty of an anachronism; this area was not yet a province or protectorate of the Roman Empire.

Lucius Calpurnius BESTIA (I.156). A supporter of Catiline, who took office as tribune for 62 B.C. on December 10th, 63.

BRUTI (II.391). The principal reference is probably to Lucius Junius Brutus, one of the first Consuls of Rome in 509 B.C. Other famous Bruti were the Consuls of 325 and 292 B.C. and Decimus Junius Brutus, Consul 138 B.C. and conqueror of part of Spain. See also DECIUS.

Gaius Julius CAESAR (II.100). Praetor-elect in 63 B.C. and a supporter of "popular" policies. He became Consul for the first time in 59 B.C., conquered Gaul 58–50 B.C., and seized supreme power in Rome after a civil war in which he defeated Pompey. There is no firm evidence for his complicity in the conspiracy.

CALYPSO (IV.v.31). The nymph who detained Odysseus on her island for seven years. The name is used here for its supposed connection with the Greek καλύπτω, "I hide."

CAMILLI (II.395). (1) Marcus Furius Camillus, in exile at the time of the capture of Rome by the Gauls (c. 390 B.C.), was recalled, levied an army, repulsed the Gauls, and recovered the gold paid to them by the Romans. (2) Lucius Furius Camillus, his son, as Consul in 349 B.C. defeated the Gauls. (3) Lucius Furius Camillus, son of (2), as Consul in 338 B.C. destroyed the Latin League.

CAPANEUS (IV.v. 49). One of the Seven against Thebes. He boasted that not even Zeus should prevent him from scaling the city walls, and in punishment for this arrogance he was blasted by a thunderbolt.

CAPITOL (I.321). The Capitoline Hill at Rome, on which stood the great temple of Jupiter, also sometimes called the Capitol. The Capitol was burned during the Civil Wars in 83 B.C.

CARTHAGE (III.iii.264). A powerful trading city in North Africa, which built up an empire in Spain and Sicily. Rome fought three major wars against Carthage between 264 and 146 B.C., in the second of which Hannibal invaded Italy. Carthage was destroyed in 146 B.C. but remained in tradition as one of Rome's most implacable enemies.

CASTOR (II.86). Twin brother of Pollux. The two, together known as the Dioscuri ("sons of Zeus") were worshipped as deities, exercising special protection over mariners. According to some traditions, Pollux was the son of Zeus but Castor of the mortal Tyndarus, achieving deification only after death. The oath "by Castor" was customarily used only by women.

CATILINE (*Lucius Sergius Catilina*) (passim) was born about 108 B.C. In 89 B.C., he was on the staff of the consul Gnaeus Pompeius Strabo (father of Pompey) during the war against the Italian allies. He was a lieutenant of Sylla during the civil war and the dictatorship of Sylla and was alleged personally to have committed murder in that capacity. In 73 B.C. he was accused of seduction of a Vestal virgin but was acquitted. His political career does not appear to have been adversely affected. His earlier offices are unrecorded, but he was a Praetor in 68 B.C. and subsequently governor of the province of Africa for two years. He was unable to stand for the consulship on his return in 66 B.C. because of an impending prosecution for peculation (not an uncommon charge against provincial governors); he was acquitted at his trial the following year. Jonson follows the major sources in alleging Catiline's participation in a plot to murder the incoming Consuls of 65 B.C. The tradition is hostile; modern opinion tends to the view that, if there was a plot, it was among an optimate faction and was intended to forestall the possibility of a coup by Pompey on the latter's return from the East. From what is known of Catiline's associations at this period, he appears to have been connected rather with the "popular" faction, which included the Consuls of 65, and Caesar and Crassus. Cicero himself in 65, at a time when he was anxious for the favor of Pompeian supporters, contemplated Catiline as a running mate for the consulship of 63. In the period 65–64, however, the tentative efforts of Caesar and Crassus to introduce a popular program and also to build up their own personal following, independently of Pompey, seems to have alienated Cicero.

Catiline was a candidate in 64 B.C. for the consulship of 63, with, it is thought, the financial backing of Crassus, who also supported Antonius. After his failure at the polls, Catiline probably lost Crassus' help. The precise time at which, and the reasons for which, he decided to resort to violence are unknown. Equally unanswerable is the question of the relative emphasis in the mind of Catiline, or of *populares* in general, on personal career ambition and a genuine desire for reform.

The ancient tradition relating to Catiline takes the standpoint of the senatorial oligarchy; moderns tend to draw attention to the classes of people from whom Catiline received support (cf. Catiline's speeches in Act I and Petreius' speech at V.i.22 ff.)—debtors, farmers dispossessed in the proscriptions, unemployed urban populace—as symptomatic of the current social and political problems of the Roman state, in which wealth was engrossed in the hands of a small ruling class, while small-scale agriculture languished and there was a lack of alternative employment. Catiline's revolutionary attempt could be regarded as an indictment of the failure of Roman senatorial government. Sallust (*Cat.* 35) quotes a letter allegedly from Catiline to Catulus part of which expresses the ambiguity of the position of the senatorial *popularis*: "I was provoked by the wrongs done me; and as I was bereft of the fruits of my painstaking labor and unable to maintain my status, I undertook the cause of the wretched, as I have been wont to do."

Marcus Porcius CATO (III.i.0.1). A staunchly conservative Senator, bitterly opposed both to the conspirators and to the "popular" policies of Caesar and Pompey later. He committed suicide in 46 B.C., once Caesar's victory in the civil war was certain.

Quintus Lutatius CATULUS (III.i.0.1). Born about 121 B.C., Praetor 81 B.C. Catiline had killed a certain Marius Gratidianus, on Sylla's orders, as a result of Catulus' demand for vengeance for his father's death. As Consul in 78 B.C., he opposed the revolutionary attempts of Lepidus. By 63 B.C. he was *princeps senatus*.

CAUCASUS (III.i.199). A range of mountains to the east of the Black Sea; to the Greeks, one of the remotest points of the known world.

CENTAURS (II.171). Mythical monsters, half-man, half-horse, generally represented as drunken and lascivious.

CENTURIES (II.98). Originally military divisions of the Roman people, graded according to wealth, the centuries at an early date acquired political function as well; at some time between 241 and 218 B.C. the centuries were in some way correlated with the tribes. The century was an electoral unit for some purposes, including the election of Consuls.

Marcus CEPARIUS (correctly, Caeparius) (III.iii.236). An associate of Catiline, from Terracina in Latium.

Gaius Cornelius CETHEGUS (I.140). A young Senator, the boldest and most headstrong of Catiline's associates.

CHARON (I.247). The mythical ferryman who conveyed the spirits of the dead over the river Styx.

CHARYBDIS (III.iii.164). Proverbially, a serious danger—from the legendary whirlpool of that name, thought to have been situate in the Straits of Messina, where Odysseus lost part of his fleet (Homer *Od.* 12. 101 ff.).

Marcus Tullius CICERO (II.108). The famous Roman orator and statesman, and leading legal pleader of his day; Consul in 63 B.C.

Quintus CICERO. See QUINTUS.

CIMBER. See GABINIUS.

CIMBRIAN WAR (III.iii.75). In 101 B.C. Marius inflicted a heavy defeat on the Cimbri (see GABINIUS) who had been attempting to invade Italy.

Lucius Cornelius CINNA (I.21). Consul in 87, 86, 85, and 84 B.C. He used military force to compel Marius' recall to Rome. He was killed in a mutiny while preparing to resist Sylla on the latter's return from Greece.

CIPI (II.392). A rhetorical plural. The story of Genucius Cipus is told by Ovid (*Met.* 15. 565 ff.). Horns sprouted on his forehead, a portent which the seers interpreted as meaning that he would become king if he re-entered Rome. To save the Republic, he voluntarily went into exile and was given a portion of farmland by the grateful people.

CIRCEI (I.390). A town on the west coast of Italy (modern Circello) the neighborhood of which produced excellent oysters.

Publius CLODIUS *Pulcher* (II.4). A young Roman noble, later notorious for the scandal involving Caesar's wife (61 B.C.), for his vendetta against Cicero and use of his tribunate to procure Cicero's exile (58 B.C.), and for occasioning riot and disorder in Rome subsequently until his murder in 52 B.C. Jonson appears to suppose a connection between Fulvia and the woman of the same name whom Clodius married, but there is no evidence for this.

CONCORD (V.ix.20). *Concordia*, civil harmony, personified and worshipped as a goddess. The temple of Concord was near the Forum.

CONSCRIPT FATHERS (IV.ii.6). The meaning of this term, applied to Senators, was in doubt among the Romans themselves. One explanation was that the formal mode of address to the Senate, *patres conscripti*, was originally *patres et conscripti*, there having been a distinction between the original patrician Senators and those later added to their number.

CONSUL (I.418). The chief civil and military executive officer of Rome. Two were elected annually for a term of one year.

CORINTHIAN (I.385). Of the most costly bronze work. According to tradition, at the sack of Corinth in 146 B.C. the metal from the statues which melted in the general conflagration produced an alloy of exceptional quality.

CORNELII (I.137). See SYLLA, LENTULUS, CINNA, CETHEGUS.

Gaius CORNELIUS (III.iii.214). A conspirator of equestrian rank, not otherwise known.

Quintus CORNIFICIUS (V.iv.182). One of the unsuccessful candidates for the consulship of 63 B.C. The conspirator Cethegus was assigned to custody in his house.

Marcus Licinius CRASSUS (II.100). Lieutenant under Sylla, Consul with Pompey in 70 B.C. Supporter of "popular" policies. A very wealthy and ambitious man, he formed a political alliance with Caesar and Pompey in 60 B.C.

Quintus CURIUS (I.149). An impoverished noble, privy to the plot.

CURTII (II.392). The hero of an etiological myth invented to explain the name of the *lacus Curtius*, a pit or cavity in the Roman Forum which was regarded as sacred. Three different stories are told. (1) It marked the spot where the Sabine Mettius Curtius and his horse struggled to safety from a swamp during the battle which resulted in the union of Sabines and Romans under Romulus. (2) Gaius Curtius, consul in 445 B.C., consecrated the spot after it was struck by lightning. (3) The best-known story made the eponymous hero Marcus, or Manius, Curtius who "devoted" himself in 362 B.C. by leaping, armed and on horseback, into a chasm which had appeared in the Forum. He did this in obedience to an oracle which said that Rome must secure her safety by sacrificing the source of her power.

CYCLOPS (I.144). Three one-eyed giants, the sons of Earth and Heaven, who worked as blacksmiths for the gods (not to be confused with the savage shepherds in Homer's *Odyssey*).

CYPRIS (II.278). A cult-title of the goddess Venus, with whose worship the island of Cyprus was particularly associated.

DANAE (II.182). Daughter of the king of Argos, who imprisoned her in a brazen tower because an oracle predicted that his grandson would cause his death. Jupiter visited her in the form of a shower of gold and she bore a son.

DECII (II.391). Three members of this family, Publius Decius Mus and his son and grandson of the same name, were said to have carried out "devotio," i.e., each as commander of an army vowed himself and the enemy to the infernal gods and deliberately charged to his death, to secure victory for his side—the first in 340 B.C., the second in 295 B.C. and the third in 279 B.C. If any of these is historical, it is probably the second.

DECIUS *Brutus* (correctly Decimus Junius Brutus) (IV.iv.75). Consul 77 B.C., husband of Sempronia; an elderly Senator, apparently not prominent in public life. His son was one of the assassins of Julius Caesar.

ENYO (V.ix.59). Another name for Bellona, goddess of war.

EPHESIAN (I.385). Ephesus in Asia Minor was noted for a school of "naturalistic" artists which had flourished particularly in the fourth century B.C.

EUROPA (II.181). She was carried off to Crete by Jupiter disguised as a bull.

FABII (II.396). (1) Quintus Fabius Maximus Rullianus, hero of the Samnite Wars (325–295 B.C.), Consul five times, dictator at least once. (2) Quintus Fabius Maximus Cunctator, author of Rome's delaying policy against Hannibal.

FASCES (I.472). A bundle of rods, bound together with an axe, traditional symbol of office of the Consuls at Rome.

FASTI (V.iv.234). The calendar of Rome, including dates of holy festivals, days of ill-omen, days of thanksgiving, etc.

FAUNS (II.170). Attendants on the god Faunus. As Faunus was often equated with the Greek Pan, the fauns would correspond to the satyrs of Greek mythology, wood-deities with the horns and hooves of goats, alleged to have very powerful sexual appetites.

FESULAE (correctly Faesulae) (III.iii.71). A city of Etruria, now Fiesole.

Lucius Valerius FLACCUS (III.iv.13). Praetor in 63 B.C., a man with extensive military experience.

FULVIA (II.0.1). A Roman lady who betrayed the conspiracy to Cicero; not to be confused with Clodius' wife.

Marcus FULVIUS *Nobilior* (I.208). A conspirator of equestrian rank. Not otherwise known.

FURIES (I.70). Malign spirits sent by the dead to harry the living.

Publius GABINIUS *Capito* (I.208). A conspirator of the equestrian order. Jonson, perhaps following Felicius, chap. 4, mistakenly takes "Cimber" (III.iii.236) as part of his name. Cicero (3 *Cat.* 6) referred to *scelerum improbissimum machinatorem Cimbrum Gabinium*, using the term not as a cognomen but as an ethnic, the Cimbri, a Germanic tribe who invaded Transalpine Gaul in the late second century B.C., being among the fiercest of Rome's enemies.

Publius Sulpicius GALBA (II.106). A candidate for the consulship of 63 B.C.

GALLA (II.0.1). A slave-girl. Her name indicates that she came from Gallia (Gaul).

GALLIA (IV.vi.19). Gaul, of which the part at this time belonging to the Roman empire consisted of two provinces, Gallia Cisalpina (the basin of the river Po), and Gallia Transalpina (modern Provence).

GAUL (III.iii.263). Inhabitant of Gallia. Jonson is probably thinking in III.iii.263 of the invasion of Rome itself by Gaulish armies in the early fourth century B.C. (see note on III.ii.230).

GRACCHI (I.21). The brothers Tiberius and Gaius Sempronius Gracchus, tribunes of the people respectively in 133 B.C. and 123–122 B.C.

Their attempts to introduce radical policies of reform resulted in their deaths by violence. The Gracchus referred to in V.iv.147 is Gaius.

HANNIBAL (I.24). A Carthaginian general who invaded Italy in 218 B.C. and campaigned there for sixteen years; to the Romans he was a byword for cruelty and treachery. There was a tradition that as a child he had at his father's instance sworn eternal hatred to Rome.

HERCULES (II.227). A legendary Greek hero, son of Jupiter, who was deified after his death because of his benefactions to mankind in slaying monsters. His name was commonly used as an oath by the Romans, though its use by women was regarded as improper.

HETRURIA (correctly, Etruria) (IV.ii.155). A large area of the Italian peninsula west of the river Tiber and the Apennines, extending westward to the coast and northward beyond the river Arno.

HIPPOLYTUS (IV.v.25). His stepmother avenged his rejection of her advances by killing herself and leaving a message alleging rape; his father therefore called on the sea-god to punish him. A bull sent from the sea frightened Hippolytus' horses as he was driving on the shore; they ran away, and he was entangled in the chariot reins and dragged to his death. He typifies disinclination toward physical love.

HYDRA (III.i.100). A monster slain by Hercules. It had nine heads, one of which was immortal, and for every head cut off, two new ones grew.

IDES (IV.ii.272). In the Roman calendar, the 13th day of the month (15th in March, July, October, and May). In each month, there were three fixed dates—the Kalends, Nones (5th or 7th) and the Ides; other dates were specified as a given number of days before the next fixed date.

JOVE (I.181). The ruler of the gods; also called Jupiter. One of the titles under which he was worshipped at Rome was Jupiter Stator ("Stayer," IV.ii.2) or protector of the city.

JUNO (I.181). A goddess, consort of Jove.

JUPITER (II.183). See JOVE.

KALENDS (IV.ii.187). The first day of the month in the Roman calendar.

LAIS (II.283). This name was borne by two famous courtesans of Corinth, one of whom lived in the latter part of the fifth century B.C., the other a century later.

LAR (I.383). The tutelary god of a Roman house.

Marcus Porcius LECCA (correctly, Laeca) (I.156). A Roman Senator, who joined the conspiracy at an early stage; a meeting was held at his house.

LEDA (II.181). A Spartan woman, seduced by Jupiter in the guise of a swan.

Publius Cornelius LENTULUS *Sura* (I.133). Consul 71 B.C., and Catiline's principal coadjutor in the conspiracy. He had been expelled from the Senate for immorality and secured re-entry by election as Praetor for 63.

Manius Aemilius LEPIDUS (IV.ii.276). Consul 66 B.C.

LICTORS (I.473). Official attendants on certain Roman magistrates.

Lucius Cassius LONGINUS (I.207). Praetor 66 B.C. He was one of the unsuccessful candidates for the consulship of 63 (Jonson says he withdrew—III.i.111), and later was one of the conspirators.

LUCRECE (II.283). Wife of Collatinus, she committed suicide, alleging rape by Sextus Tarquinius, son of the last king of Rome. The Tarquins were expelled from Rome and the Republic established, Collatinus being one of the first Consuls (509 B.C.).

LUCRINE (I.389). A lake at the north end of the Bay of Naples, famous for its oysters.

Lucius MANLIUS (IV.ii.324). A former officer of Sylla, who was to muster an army for Catiline in Etruria.

Gaius MARIUS (I.21). Born at Arpinum, of humble origins, his outstanding generalship earned him six consulships between 107 and 100 B.C., in alliance with the democratic or "popular" faction. Supported by Cinna, he started a civil war against Sylla in 87 B.C. and obtained a seventh consulship. His reign of terror was terminated by his death (January 13, 84 B.C.).

MARS (I.97). The Roman god of war.

MASSILIA (IV.iii.21). The modern Marseilles.

MAURETANIA (I.443). A country in North Africa, corresponding roughly to Western Algeria and Morocco.

MEDUSA (V.ix.74). Seduced by her grandfather. As punishment, Minerva turned her hair to serpents and gave her eyes the power to petrify whatever they looked at. After her decapitation, Medusa's head was worn as an emblem on the shield of Minerva.

MERCURY (IV.v.32). A god; herald of the gods, patron of thieves and traders, god of eloquence.

Quintus METELLUS *Celer* (IV.iv.44). *Praetor urbanus* in 63 B.C.

MILVIAN BRIDGE (IV.vi.21). A bridge across the Tiber above Rome, on the Via Flaminia.

MINERVA (V.ix.74). Originally a Roman goddess, patroness of the arts and crafts, identified with the Greek Pallas Athene, daughter of Zeus. The head of Medusa was conventionally represented as borne by Pallas on the aegis (originally a goat-skin mantle, later conventionalized into a shield).

MOOR (III.iii.263). Inhabitant of Mauretania. Jonson is probably thinking here of the protracted war against Mauretania in the second century B.C.

NECTAR (I.112). The drink of the gods.

NUCERINUS (I.444). Publius Sittius, from Nuceria in Campania. A bankrupt, turned mercenary officer, who went to Spain in 64 B.C. and from there to Mauretania, where he stayed in the service of the native king. During the Civil War, in 46 B.C., he gave help to Caesar, and was rewarded with territory in Africa. Jonson follows Sallust, *Cat.* 21, in making him a member of the conspiracy; this is denied by Cicero *pro Sulla* 56, and is not in any other ancient source.

ORESTILLA (I.107). See AURELIA.

PALLAS (V.ix.62). Pallas Athene, or Minerva, goddess of wisdom, and daughter of Zeus.

PATRICIANS (II.117). Members of the old Roman noble families.

Marcus PETREIUS (IV.vi.6). Ex-Praetor, served as lieutenant of Gaius Antonius against Catiline's forces in Etruria. Jonson repeats the outline of his career given by Sallust, *Cat.* 59. He subsequently served as Pompey's lieutenant in Spain 55–49 B.C. and led Pompeian forces in Greece and then in Africa in the Civil War 49–46 B.C.

PHASIS (I.388). A river at the eastern end of the Black Sea; for the Romans, at one of the remotest parts of the inhabited world. It was said to be a particular haunt of the pheasant, which takes its name from the river.

PHOEBUS (I.100). The sun god.

PICENE TERRITORY (III.iii.69). A district in northeast Italy, modern Ancona.

Gnaeus Calpurnius PISO (I.443). A Roman Senator, sent in 65 B.C. to govern one of the Spanish provinces. He had allegedly been involved in a conspiracy in late 66–early 65. He was murdered in Spain, as some believed by supporters of Pompey. Jonson follows Sall. 21, but at the time of the meeting at Catiline's house, Piso was already dead.

PLUTO (I.16). God of the underworld and ruler over the dead.

POLLUX (II.282). Twin brother of Castor.

POMPEY (Gnaeus Pompeius Magnus) (I.387). The Roman general and statesman, who at the time of the conspiracy was engaged in organizing the affairs of the eastern provinces after his defeat of Mithridates. A situation was already developing at Rome in which the Senators were dividing into factions according to their willingness or otherwise to support what were believed to be Pompey's ambitions.

Gaius POMTINIUS (correctly, Pomptinius) (III.iv.13.). Praetor 63 B.C. As governor of Transalpine Gaul, 62–61 B.C., he subdued a rebellion of the Allobroges, but was not allowed to celebrate a triumph for this till 54 B.C.

PONTIC WAR (I.90). The war against Mithridates (74–63 B.C.), ruler of the kingdom of Pontus on the south coast of the Black Sea. There is no evidence in the ancient sources that Catiline sought a command in this war, but a statement to this effect is found in the *Invectiva in Catilinam* attributed to Porcius Latro. Latro was a rhetorician who died in A.D. 4. There are no authenticated works by him; the *Invectiva* is thought to be a late forgery. It is printed, along with other works, in the edition of Sallust used by Jonson.

PRAENESTE (IV.ii.197). A town near Rome (modern Palestrina).

PRAETOR (I.471). At this period, eight Praetors were elected annually and acted as presidents of the courts of law at Rome. "The Praetor" (I.471) may refer particularly to the *praetor urbanus*, who acted as supreme judge in the civil court in cases between Roman citizens.

QUINTUS *Tullius Cicero* (III.iv.1). Brother of the orator Cicero. He reached the praetorship in 62 B.C. and governed Asia 61–58 B.C., but never attained the consulship.

Quintus Fabius SANGA (IV.i.40). A descendant of the Roman conqueror of the Allobroges. Because of this connection, he acted as the tribe's patron at Rome.

SATURNALS (III.iii.108). A festival celebrated in mid-December, characterized by license and revelry.

SCIPIO(s) (II.396). (1) Publius Cornelius Scipio, Consul 218 B.C., fought against Hannibal and died in Spain 211 B.C. (2) Publius Cornelius Scipio Africanus Maior, son of the above, was mainly responsible for the Roman victory over Hannibal in 202 B.C. (3) Publius Cornelius Scipio Aemilianus Africanus Minor Numantinus, son of Lucius Aemilius Paullus Macedonicus, was adopted by the elder son of (2) above. He destroyed Carthage in 146 B.C.

SEMPRONIA (II.32). The wife of Decimus Junius Brutus (Consul 77 B.C.); a high-born and accomplished Roman lady of indeterminate years, privy to the plot.

SENATE (I.38). The chief deliberative council at Rome, numbering about six hundred. There was a property qualification for membership, which was for life, though expulsion was possible. Entry was automatic on election to the lowest grade of state magistracy, the quaestorship.

SERGIUS (I.283). See CATILINE.

Servius Cornelius SULLA (V.iv.95). A Senator, member of the conspiracy.

SIBYL (I.135). A legendary prophetess. A collection of oracles purporting to have been given by her to king Tarquin was kept at Rome and consulted when the national interest was felt to demand it. Spurious prophecies were sometimes put about for political purposes.

Publius Cornelius Lentulus SPINTHER (V.iv.183). Aedile in 63 B.C. As Consul in 57 B.C. he worked for Cicero's return from exile and he took Pompey's side in the Civil War. The conspirator Lentulus was put in custody in his house.

Lucius STATILIUS (III.iii.141). A conspirator of equestrian rank, not otherwise known.

STYGIAN SOUND (I.11). The river Styx, over which the spirits of the dead had to pass to reach the underworld.

Lucius Cornelius SYLLA (correctly, Sulla) (I.3). Dictator of Rome 82–80 B.C. after civil war against Cinna and Marius. His opponents were put to death and their property confiscated for the benefit of himself and his followers. The severity of these proscriptions made his name a byword for cruelty.

Decimus Junius SYLLANUS (correctly, Silanus) (V.vi.18). Consul-elect in 63 B.C. for 62, and one of the college of priests at Rome.

TANTALUS (IV.ii.294). A legendary king who repaid the kindness of Zeus by attempted theft from the gods' table. As punishment, he was condemned to everlasting hunger and thirst, in the presence of inaccessible water and fruit. He is one of the persons regularly depicted in accounts of the tortures of the damned in the underworld.

TARQUIN (1) III.iii.156. The last king of Rome, Tarquinius Superbus. According to Livy I. 54, his son Sextus Tarquinius sent to ask his father's advice on how to secure his power in the town of Gabii. His father said nothing; but Sextus took the hint from his messenger's report of his gestures, and had the leading citizens of the town killed or exiled. (2) II.286. Sextus Tarquinius, son of Tarquinius Superbus. His alleged rape of Lucrece, wife of a Roman noble, precipitated the expulsion of the king and his family.

Lucius TARQUINIUS (V.iv.235). A supporter of Catiline, arrested while conveying a message to him. Not otherwise known.

TERENTIA (III.ii.110). Wife of Cicero. Divorced by him in 46 B.C., she is said subsequently to have been married to Sallust and then to Messalla Corvinus (Consul 31 B.C.).

THEBES (IV.v.49). Chief city of Boeotia, in central Greece.

THUCYDIDES (IV.v.12). An Athenian (c. 460–400 B.C.) who wrote a history of the Peloponnesian War; the work is incomplete but covers the first twenty years of the war, 431–411 B.C. The remark attributed to him by Sempronia does not occur in the extant works.

TIBER (I.7). The river on which Rome stands; it used frequently to flood parts of the city.

TITAN (III.iii.53). The Titans, in Greek mythology, were the gigantic offspring of Air, or Uranus, and Earth. "Potter Titan" refers to Prometheus, who was said to have molded mankind from clay. Prometheus was punished by Zeus for stealing fire from heaven for the benefit of mankind (see also III.i.196–200).

TITYUS (IV.ii.294). A giant; like Tantalus, he was one of those condemned to everlasting torment. His punishment was to have a vulture constantly feed on his liver, which was constantly renewed.

TRIBES (II.97). Each Roman citizen was enrolled in one of the tribes, which at this time were thirty-five in number. The tribe was a voting unit for certain purposes.

TRIBUNE (III.ii.79). *Tribunus plebis*; a Roman magistrate, of whom ten were elected annually. They convened assemblies of the people and had the power of veto over other magistrates.

Marcus TULLIUS (III.i.56). See CICERO.

Lucius Volcatius TULLUS (IV.ii.276). Consul 66 B.C.

TYRIAN (I.384). Tinted with purple, the most expensive of ancient dyes, of which the principal center of production was the city of Tyre, on the coast of Phoenicia.

Publius UMBRENUS (IV.iii.39). A merchant who acted as agent for Lentulus in approaching the Allobroges. Not otherwise known.

Lucius VARGUNTEIUS (I.156). A Senator, in the conspiracy. Not otherwise known.

Lucius VECTIUS (correctly, Vettius) (V.iv.250). A Roman knight, member of the conspiracy. He may have given information to Cicero in 63 B.C.; in 62 he denounced several conspirators and attempted also to implicate Caesar. In 59 B.C. he offered information of a plot to assassinate Pompey, and died mysteriously in prison.

VENUS (II.87). The Roman goddess of love.

VESTAL (I.31). A woman, usually of noble family, dedicated to the service of Vesta, goddess of the hearth, and vowed to chastity. A fire was kept burning in the temple of Vesta: its extinction would be taken as an omen of danger to the State.

Titus VOLTURTIUS (IV.v.33). A conspirator, from Crotona in South Italy.

Appendix B

Jonson's Classical Sources

JONSON'S USE OF CLASSICAL SOURCES

The action and events of *Catiline*, and to a great extent the very words, are closely tied to classical sources,[1] and from the amount of direct translation in the play, it is clear that Jonson consulted the two major sources, Sallust and Cicero, at first hand. These and the minor sources are cited directly in our serial list; the use of an intermediary cannot, however, be ruled out, especially for the minor sources.

Jonson's copy of Sallust's works is now in the library of Clare College, Cambridge. It is a folio volume, containing the following: a text of Sallust, with voluminous commentaries on the *Catilina* by nine Renaissance scholars; a speech ascribed to Sallust, attacking Cicero, and one ascribed to Cicero, attacking Sallust; Cicero's four Catilinarian Orations; Julius Exsuperantius, *de bellis civilibus*, thought to be an epitome of Sallust's *Histories*; the *declamatio contra L. Sergium Catilinam*, allegedly by the famous first-century B.C. rhetorician Porcius Latro but not attested before the second half of the fifteenth century; and the *Historia coniurationis Catilinariae* of Constantius Felicius Durantinus

---

[1] The fullest and most comprehensive work on the sources of *Catiline* is Alice P. Wright, "A Study of Ben Jonson's *Catiline* with Special Reference to its Sources" (Ph.D. dissertation, Yale, 1907). The importance of this dissertation to our study is such that, in regard to it, we have made an exception to our general practice of citing only published works. See also A. Vogt, *Ben Jonsons Tragödie "Catiline his Conspiracy" und ihre Quellen* (Halle, 1903); W. D. Briggs, "Source-Material for Jonson's Plays," *MLN*, XXXI (1916), 195–202; L. H. Harris, "Local Color in Ben Jonson's *Catiline* and Historical Accuracy of the Play," *Classical Philology*, XIV (1919), 273–283; idem, "Lucan's *Pharsalia* and Jonson's *Catiline*," *MLN*, XXXIV (1919), 397–402; idem, "Three Notes on Ben Jonson. 1: The Influence of Seneca on 'Catiline'," *MP*, XVII (1920), 679–685; idem, introduction and notes to *Catiline his Conspiracy*, Yale Studies in English, LIII (New York, 1916); E. M. T. Duffy, "Ben Jonson's Debt to Renaissance Scholarship in 'Sejanus' and 'Catiline'," *MLR*, XLII (1947), 24–30; H & S, X (1950), 117–165.

(first edition 1518). By and large, the minor sources cited in the list are to be found quoted in the commentaries on Sallust in Jonson's copy; Jonson may have derived their evidence from these commentaries and not at first hand. Felicius' history is little more than a cento of the classical sources. Occasionally he will express an opinion of his own on a doubtful point, for instance the drinking of a murdered man's blood (or eating of his flesh, which Felicius believes), or the complicity of Caesar and Crassus, where Felicius inclines to treat as fact what Jonson also treats as fact—but the former as a historian, the latter, we would say, for dramatic reasons. Such resemblances as these we would not regard as in themselves constituting evidence of direct use of Felicius by Jonson.

There is, nonetheless, some evidence that Jonson did make direct use of Felicius (although in our view none of the passages cited by Duffy[2] proves the use of Felicius rather than an original source). At II.105–112, the specification of four candidates who are likely to withdraw follows Felicius, not Asconius; only Felicius couples together Longinus and Statilius, as at III.iii.236; the actual words and order of thought in the speeches at IV.vii.46–63 and V.i.5–49 follow Felicius very closely. Places where an odd detail seems to come from Felicius are IV.ii.323, "Aurelian Way," where Cicero 1 *Cat.* 24 has *forum Aurelii*; and IV.ii.408, where Jonson uses "vomits," which is in the speech as given in Felicius but not in Sallust 31. The name Cimber (see Glossary) at III.iii.236 may not come directly from Cicero; Felicius made the mistake (chap. 4). Catiline's candidature for the Pontic command (I.90), found in no securely attested ancient source, is mentioned in Felicius, chapter 3; it is also found in Porcius Latro 7, and Jonson did make direct use of Porcius (IV.ii.61–62). At I.447–448, Jonson directly follows Sallust, whom Felicius paraphrases inaccurately. There is, then, some evidence for the use of Felicius, but not to the exclusion of consultation of original sources.

Jonson in the main follows his ancient sources. He accepts the account they give of Catiline's supposed involvement in an earlier conspiracy, which modern historical criticism has tended to reject. Where Jonson seems to have departed slightly from his sources, as in the acceptance of the involvement of Caesar and Crassus as fact, it is for dramatic reasons, although these reasons have not always been appreciated; and indeed this apparent divergence brings Jonson's

2 Duffy, "Ben Jonson's Debt," 24–26, 29–30.

treatment of the conspiracy closer in spirit to that of Sallust than the latter's own partisanship of Caesar. The point has been well taken by Bryant.[3] Sallust's famous introduction to his monograph (13 out of 61 chapters) puts Catiline and the conspiracy very firmly into what, for Sallust, was the proper perspective, and he summarizes his view at the beginning of chapter 14: *in tanta tamque corrupta civitate*—Catiline was the corrupt product of a corrupt society. Sallust, 53–54, felt obliged to except his admired Caesar, as well as Cato, from the general corruption; Jonson, by making Caesar's complicity explicit, prevents this play from being the combat of a hero and a villain, and turns it into "the tragedy of a whole state."[4]

Jonson's use of classical sources is not confined to matters of fact and verbal borrowings from speeches, direct or reported. He makes considerable use of a small but significant group of Latin verse writers: Lucan, Seneca, Petronius, and Juvenal. All are from the century after the Catilinarian conspiracy. All belong to a period in which the favored Latin style was highly wrought and "pointed"; all write with moral passion of the corrupt state of society. The various subjects of which they treat are also relevant. Jonson draws on Petronius and Juvenal for attacks on extravagance and self-indulgence; on Lucan for the vivid expression of the horrors of civil war; and on Seneca in particular for the theme of human rebellion against the gods and the natural order.

Jonson's classical reading further supplies him not only with occasional apt reminiscences (for instance, of Horace, Statius, and Ovid), but also with the numerous allusions to details of Roman life and manners[5] by means of which he is at pains to give the play an "atmosphere" of historical verisimilitude.

His language, both in translations and in passages of his own invention, contributes to the maintenance of a consistently Roman atmosphere. Jonson appears to fall naturally into Latinate constructions, e.g., IV.vi.1, "I cannot fear the war but to succeed well" (*vereri non possum quin*); V.vi.60, "abhorring from" (where his original has *aliena ab*); I.416, "Use me your general" (*imperatore me utimini*); and IV.vi.43, "glad me doing well, though I hear ill," where both the participial

---

[3] J. A. Bryant, Jr., "*Catiline* and the Nature of Jonson's Tragic Fable," *PMLA*, LXIX (1954), 265–277.

[4] Ibid., p. 276.

[5] Listed in Wright, "A Study of . . . *Catiline*," chap. 6, pp. 98–104; see also Harris, "Local Color," p. 279, and *Catiline his Conspiracy*, pp. l–li.

construction and the idiom "hear ill" are Latinate. Single words which are derivatives or equivalents of Latin words are frequently found used in their original Latin sense rather than that they normally bear in English, e.g., "consent" (IV.ii.384), "convince" (IV.ii.79), "frequency" (IV.ii.296), "note" (IV.ii.257), "virtue" I.205).[6]

This Latinate character of Jonson's English makes possible very close translations of his originals; see, for instance, IV.ii.220–223:

> These I behold, being Consul; nay, I ask
> Their counsels of the state, as from good patriots,
> Whom it were fit the axe should hew in pieces,
> I not so much as wound, yet, with my voice,

which corresponds to Cic. 1 *Cat.* 9:

> *hos ego video consul et de re publica sententiam rogo, et quos ferro trucidari oportebat, eos nondum voce volnero.*

Jonson preserves the appositional construction of *consul*; "ask counsels of" corresponds *to rogo sententiam de*; and, most striking, he places, like Cicero, the relative clause before its antecedent, and so succeeds in retaining the dramatic emphasis of Cicero's concluding *voce volnero*.

The method does not always work. "Have relation" (V.vi.75) is downright obscure, until one realizes that it is derived (though not directly translated) from the original *neu quis de his postea ad senatum referat* (Sall. 51)—"that no one should bring a motion concerning them in the Senate."

Notorious is IV.ii.116: "Whither at length wilt thou abuse our patience?" Here Jonson has "translated" the first few words of the original by English words which, as single words, are possible renderings, but which are inappropriate in this context. The effect is as of a schoolboy rendering, so childishly literal and inflexible as to be ludicrous. Yet Jonson's skill as a translator is in general such that we cannot readily accuse him of error or slovenliness here. Alice Wright, speaking of Jonson's use of individual English words in their original Latin sense, says: "in [the reader extraordinary's] mind he hopes the Anglicized Latin words will rouse the memories and associations connected with their Latin use,"[7] and we think that here Jonson's intention was similar. The line in question occurs—in Jonson—in the *middle* of one of Cicero's speeches; but it is in fact a version of the *first*

---

[6] A long list is given by Wright, "A Study of . . . *Catiline*," pp. 111–113.
[7] Ibid., p. 43.

line of one of Cicero's speeches, and a first line which (like the opening words of Plato's *Republic*) was traditionally cited as an example of the author's extreme care in arrangement of words. It was one of the most famous tags in Latin literature. By the blatant badness of his rendering, Jonson is surely deliberately calling attention to the fact that here begins *his* version of a famous speech, a version of which, his address to the "reader in ordinary" indicates, he was not a little proud.

In a passage quoted *in extenso* by L. H. Harris, Alice Wright summarizes Jonson's salient characteristics as a translator,[8] with illustration from Sall. 20 and Cic. 1 *Cat.*, the former in rather more detail than the latter. It would not be without value to take this investigation a little farther and conduct a more detailed comparison between a piece of Latin and Jonson's version of it, with special regard to the arrangement of thought, to syntactical correspondences and divergencies, to the vocabulary and to other stylistic matter, in particular to those alterations and additions made by Jonson to suit his own conception of the character and the dramatic situation.

Let us consider V.vi.100–147, the speech of Cato in the senatorial debate on the fate of the captured conspirators; this is based on Sall. 52. Part of Sallust's text is printed below; those portions used by Jonson are in italics.

Longe mihi alia mens est, patres conscripti, cum res atque pericula considero, et cum sententias nonnullorum mecum ipse reputo. *Illi mihi disseruisse videntur de poena eorum, qui patriae, parentibus, aris atque focis suis bellum paravere: res autem monet, cavere ab illis, quam, quid in illis statuamus, consultare. Nam cetera maleficia tum persequare, ubi facta sunt; hoc nisi provideris ne accidat ubi evenit frustra judicia implores;* capta urbe nihil fit reliqui victis. Sed, per deos immortales, vos ego appello . . . omnes perditum eant. *Bene et composite C. Caesar paullo ante in hoc ordine de vita et morte disseruit, credo, falsa existimans ea quae de inferis memorantur; diverso itinere malos a bonis loca taetra, inculta, foeda atque formidolosa habere. Itaque censuit* "pecunias eorum publicandas, *ipsos per municipia in custodiis habendos";* videlicet timens ne si Romae sint, aut a popularibus coniurationis aut a multitudine conducta, *per vim eripiantur. Quasi vero mali atque scelesti tantummodo in urbe, et non per totam Italiam sint; aut non ibi plus possit audacia, ubi ad defendendum opes minores sunt.*

---

[8] Harris, *Catiline his Conspiracy*, pp. xxvii–xxxv; Wright, "A Study of . . . *Catiline*," pp. 34–45.

Quare vanum hoc consilium est, si periculum ex illis metuit; sin in tanto omnium metu solus non timet, eo magis refert me mihi atque vobis timere. Quare, cum de P. Lentulo ceterisque statuetis ... dux hostium supra caput est; *vos cunctamini etiam nunc, quid intra moenia deprehensis hostibus faciatis? Miseramini censeo—deliquere homines adulescentuli per ambitionem—atque etiam armatos dimittatis. Nae ista vobis mansuetudo et misericordia, si illi arma ceperint, in miseriam vertet. Scilicet res ipsa aspera est; sed vos non timetis eam. Immo vero maxime*; sed inertia et mollitia animi *alius alium exspectantes cunctamini, dis immortalibus confisi, qui hanc rempublicam in maximis saepe periculis servavere. Non votis neque suppliciis muliebribus auxilia deorum parantur: vigilando, agendo, bene consulendo, prospera omnia cedunt: secordiae te tradideris, nequidquam deos implores; irati infestique sunt.* Apud maiores nostros ... huic sceleri obstat. *Verum parcite dignitati* Lentuli, *si ipse pudicitiae, si famae suae, si dis aut hominibus unquam ullis pepercit:* ignoscite Cethegi ... de republica habuissent. *Postremo, patres conscripti, si mehercule peccato locus esset facile paterer vos ipsa re corrigi,* quoniam verba contemnitis .... *quo magis properandum est.* Quare ita censeo: cum nefario consilio sceleratorum civium *respublica in maxima pericula venerit,* hique indicio T. Volturcii et legatorum Allobrogum convicti confessique sint caedem, incendia, alia foeda atque crudelia facinora in cives patriamque paravisse, de confessis, sicuti de manifestis rerum capitalium, more maiorum, supplicium sumendum.

Cato was great-grandson of the Censor of 184 B.C., and tradition credited him, like his ancestor, with a stern and austere morality and —in part a reflection of this—a terse, unadorned rhetorical style. It should be noticed first that Jonson has omitted large sections of the speech Sallust gives to Cato, especially *sed, per deos immortales .... perditum eant* and *quare cum de P. Lentulo .... supra caput est.* These passages are rhetorical commonplaces, general in content, and used by Sallust to limn in the picture of the constant enemy and critic of Roman extravagance and corruption and the deleterious effects of prosperity on private morality and the welfare of the state. Jonson has treated the theme of corruption by wealth elsewhere and in another fashion. He omits these passages. Instead, he renders the rigidity and austerity of the man through the style of his speech; there is little or no overtly moralistic content. In Sallust, the style is already plain. Only the simplest rhetorical figures are used, and those sparingly; there is a

notable absence of periodic structure and asyndeton is frequent. In
the main, Jonson follows Sallust closely and in a style as plain. He
makes, however, certain additions and verbal changes which express
the character more vividly.

Cato begins, abruptly, "This it is," and ends, as abruptly, "I have
done." Jonson here is surely making a deliberate contrast with the
prooemium and *peroratio* of developed rhetorical theory, for which
elaborate rules were devised.

There is also a certain "toning down" of Sallust's already restrained
vocabulary and phraseology. The patriotic cliché *patriae, parentibus,
aris atque focis* ("fatherland, parents, altars, and hearths") has totally
disappeared; "those" (l. 102) is unqualified. *Frustra implores* ("one
would beg in vain") is reduced to "will not wait" (l. 106). *Taetra,
inculta, foeda atque formidolosa* ("vile, waste, foul, and frightful") appears as "filthy, dark, and ugly"; the Latin phrase, especially because
of the addition of the emotional *formidolosa*, has a poetic tinge absent
in the English, which expresses only disgust. *Mali atque scelesti* ("bad
and wicked") becomes "fit for such acts" (l. 116).

There are two other places in which Jonson's changes heighten the
contemptuousness of Cato's tone. *Falsa* is replaced by "pretty fable"
(l. 109); note the economy with which in two words Jonson exposes
the conflict between the old morality and the new sophistication. The
abstract notions of *inertia et mollitia animi* ("inaction and indecisive-
ness") give way to "Look about/ With faces as you trusted" (ll. 123–
125), summoning up a concrete, and contemptible, spectacle.

As far as the structure of the piece is concerned, Jonson in most
places follows closely the arrangement of thought in the Latin. Occasionally he alters it, usually in the direction of greater conciseness.
The first three lines are an example; Sallust, by contrast, is repetitive
and diffuse in his expression of the same thoughts. His version, roughly
paraphrased, runs, "You are considering/ how to punish/ the crimi-
nals./ The situation requires/ that you should take precautions/
rather than consider/ how to punish." This circularity, returning to
its starting point, is abandoned by Jonson. Two lines are given to the
actual and dilatory behavior of the senators; the third is a straight
contrast, and puts the warning, which is the chief point of the sentence, in the most emphatic position, at the end. "Stand consulting"
well conveys the bumbling inactivity of the senators; here, the sound
of the Latin, rather than its sense, may have suggested the phrase
(*statuamus, consultare*).

In the following four lines (103–106) Jonson translates closely Sallust's *nam cetera . . . implores*. Significantly, he omits the repetitious hammering home of the point in *capta urbe . . . victis*.

Lines 107–122 are very close to Sallust; the changes (apart from those already mentioned in lines 109, 112, 116) consist in the removal of prosaic technicalities of Roman politics: "have these live, and long too," instead of *pecunias eorum publicandas* ("confiscation of their property by the state") and "might have rescue" instead of *aut a popularibus . . . eripiantur* ("be forcibly rescued by associates of the conspiracy or by a hired mob"). These technical expressions are unnecessary for verisimilitude here and would obscure the main point. The rest of lines 107–122 could scarcely be closer to the actual syntax and vocabulary of Sallust.

In lines 123–147 Jonson alters Sallust's order. Lines 123–130 correspond to *sed inertia . . . infestique sunt;* 131–134 go back to *vos cunctamini . . . in miseriam vertet*; 135–137 correspond to *verum parcite . . . circumventi sumus*. That is, in Sallust the order of ideas is "treatment of the conspirators—attitude of the gods—treatment of the conspirators." Jonson simplifies this to "attitude of the gods—treatment of the prisoners."

In the concluding lines, however, Jonson reverses his previous procedure and uses a more elaborate and rhetorical treatment than Sallust. Lines 140–144 are Jonson's expansion of the notion contained in *si peccato locus esset* ("if there were room for fault"), and an extension of *peccato*; for Jonson's Cato, the Roman Senators would not merely be making a mistake, but—since they have been told the truth— deliberately committing a crime against the state in sparing the conspirators. From this it follows that *corrigi* is rendered not as "correction" but "punishment." In lines 145–147, the notions of urgency (*quo magis properandum est*—"therefore haste is all the more necessary") and crisis (*respublica in maxima pericula venerit*—"the state has come into extreme danger") are picked up and turned into a dramatic closure of Jonson's own invention, instead of the formal phraseology of a senatorial motion, with which Sallust ends.

Jonson, in *Catiline*, followed his sources. His "discrepancies" are minor and amount to stating as fact what was reported as suspicion. We have suggested (see Glossary, *s.v.* "Catiline") that the real Catiline perhaps had more to be said in his favor than the sources allow. Of the Catiline of tradition, Rice Holmes wrote: "Neither the portrait drawn

by the historian nor the invective of the orator enables us to understand him. A list of qualities, an inventory of vices, a catalogue of
crimes, do not recreate a character: even Plutarch could not make
more of Catiline than a conventional villain of melodrama."[9] Is this
true of the Catiline of Jonson's play? It would be difficult to find passages to support any contention that Catiline is represented as a *sym-
pathetic* character; nevertheless, Jonson's delineation is of no mere
bloodthirsty monster, but of someone more subtle and complex than
the "conventional villain of melodrama."

The most detailed portrayal of Catiline is in the first Act. The
murderer and libertine is there (ll. 30–42, 115–116), the man of in-
sensate ambition (e.g., in the rodomontade of ll. 73–78). Jonson,
however, perhaps taking hints from Cicero *pro Caelio* 12–14 and Sallust
14, presents also a calculating, cool, altogether more dangerous man.
In the scene with Aurelia, the springs of Catiline's ambition are
shown. The identification of himself and Aurelia with the Olympians,
together with the contemptuous references to his associates who are
his instruments, indicates that Catiline is one of those who regard
themselves as by nature superior to the common run, as entitled by that
superiority to recognition and power and as not bound by the laws
that restrain others. Not bloodlust but pride is his motive force. This
conception is not melodramatic, and it is not (as the opening of the
play is) Senecan; but it is classical. The Ate which smote the heroes
of classical Greek tragedy was a kind of moral blindness; it manifested
itself in a failure to "think human thoughts," and so presumption and
rebellion against the rule of the gods.

The conspirators arrive. We know, from his conversation with
Aurelia, what Catiline really thinks of them. We are therefore in a
position to judge the sincerity of his dealings with them. The characters of Lentulus and Cethegus are created by Jonson from mere
phrases in the original sources (especially *P. Lentuli somnium . . . C.
Cethegi furiosam temeritatem*, Cic. 3 *Cat.* 16). Cethegus' choleric aggres-
siveness is encouraged by Catiline, who praises and eggs him on,
capping (ll. 229 ff.) his fantasies of atrocities. At line 254 he turns his
attention to the booby Lentulus, flattering his dull pride outrageously
and soothing his timidity. The "trio," lines 283–292, concludes the
passage and marks the success of his manipulation. With the arrival
of the other conspirators, Catiline has to change from stirring up

[9] T. Rice Holmes, *The Roman Republic*, I (Oxford, 1923), p. 233.

Cethegus to dampening down the fire he has raised so that the meeting can come to order.

Catiline's speech to the conspirators draws in part upon Sallust. The *luxuria* and corruption of a ruling clique are attacked; but it is clear that the main appeal to the conspirators is not to a desire for social justice, but to envy and cupidity. Still, they are weak tools; Catiline has to stiffen their spirits (ll. 430 ff.), to such effect that the scene ends with the ominous salute, "God-like Catiline."

Catiline appears less, and says less, in the rest of the play. He dissimulates his chagrin (III.i), settles details of organization (III.iii) and makes a formal speech to his troops (V.v); apart from that he has little to do save interject resentful remarks. The soliloquy at III.iii.225–265 is virtually a restatement of the main themes of the first Act, but Jonson's Catiline is given little chance to display them in practice. After the first Act, he is almost a background character. The nature of the disease in the state has been described; the rest of the play shows the efforts of the body politic to deal with the distressing symptoms.

Catiline as individual receives attention again at the end of the play through the classical device of the messenger's speech. In Petreius' description of Catiline's end (V.ix.25–84), the Medusa passage is of key importance. Jonson here uses the classical formula—the great man guilty of impiety and ruined by the gods—and at the same time returns to the principal recurrent image in the play, of the rebellion of giants against the gods (see Introduction, pp. xx–xxi).

There are other, structural, aspects in which Jonson's play has at least a partial claim to be called classical in form. He uses a Chorus, but in the manner of Seneca rather than of the Greek tragedians; the Chorus comments on the action at the end of each Act, but takes virtually no direct part in it. The catastrophe does not take place on stage but is narrated by Petreius. Unity of place, however, is by no means observed; neither is unity of time, but it is notable that Jonson has so ordered things as to give the impression that events which covered several months (at least eighteen in Sallust) follow closely upon each other within a period of two or three days.[10] The time

---

[10] M. Buland, *The Presentation of Time in the Elizabethan Drama*, Yale Studies in English, XLIV (New York, 1912), 148–150; H & S, X (1950), 120–121.

indications are more precise in the last three Acts than in the first two, but an impression of fairly close continuity of action is given throughout.

The compression of the sequence of events has advantages: it ensures concentration and dramatic tension. Crisis is quickly established; the struggle takes up most of the play; catastrophe ends it. It has also the advantage of removing the apparent time-lag which the narrative of Sallust, our most precise informant on the role of Fulvia (though he says nothing of her motives), introduces between the betrayal of the plot to Cicero and the taking of effective action against the conspirators.

However, the device has serious disadvantages. Jonson is following closely his sources, and these sources contain allusions to events which took place over a period of months. Many of these allusions Jonson has incorporated into his text, although they are incompatible with a time scheme of a few days. The most blatant example is Cicero's speech in IV.ii, in the main a translation of the first Catilinarian Oration, which incorporates a number of such allusions. Cicero has "of late spoke often in the Senate/ Touching this argument" (IV.ii. 15–16). The reference in 1 *Cat.* 4 to the passing of the emergency decree twenty days before is kept (1. 145), although in Jonson the decree is not proposed until the end of this meeting (ll. 456–459). The conspirators' army is "daily increasing" (1. 156). In ll. 182 ff., Cicero makes numerous references to earlier events and to the content of earlier speeches, all translated by Jonson directly from 1 *Cat.* There are awkwardnesses for the action, too. In Act I, for instance, the conspirators arrive for a prearranged meeting immediately after what appears to be the moment of Catiline's decision to resort to conspiracy and violence. Jonson has not altogether managed to make a happy marriage between dramatic urgency and fidelity to his historical sources.

So direct, and so extensive, is Jonson's dependence on his sources, both for the lines of the plot and for the dialogue, that some surprise must be occasioned by the assertion that *Catiline* is "a self-justifying parallelograph on the Powder Plot," as Dr. B. N. de Luna insists.[11] The thesis of Dr. de Luna's book is that Jonson wrote *Catiline*, with certain subtle distortions of history, as a covert means of simultaneously denigrating the conspirators in the Gunpowder Plot of 1605

[11] B. N. de Luna, *Jonson's Romish Plot* (Oxford, 1967), p. 143.

and excusing himself for having—as she alleges—been privy to the plot and played informer.

First, she holds that Jonson and his contemporaries were peculiarly alive to the use of historical parallels as a means of covert political commentary on current events. She cites half a dozen instances of identification of the Gunpowder Plot with the Catilinarian conspiracy, all of which anticipate Jonson; yet the establishment of this as a regular identification would render the theme unsuitable as a means of covert propaganda.

In two chapters (2 and 8), Dr. de Luna attempts to show that certain elements in *Catiline* are inappropriate to the conspiracy of 63 B.C., but appropriate to the Powder Plot, and, less directly, that Jonson's language is full of covert allusions to the Powder Plot. For the latter, more elusive, thesis her evidence can in the nature of things amount only to suspicion based on what might be mere verbal coincidence. The major evidence for the former thesis is the incidence of turns of phrase suggesting gunpowder. Though some of the alleged instances are very doubtful, a number of her examples must be accepted. This alone, however, does not prove Jonson's *intent* to write a *roman à clef* about the Powder Plot; it could be that Jonson's imagination seized on the nature and effects of gunpowder, suggested to him by the 1605 Plot, as a vivid vein of imagery to render the intended effect of the Catilinarian Plot.

Another line of her argument is that Jonson "skewed" events and characters to fit the Gunpowder Plot. Such is Jonson's adherence to his sources that the evidence Dr. de Luna can collect is unconvincing, much of it resting on coincidental similarities. In her "identification" of individual conspirators of 1605 with participants in the plot of 63 B.C., she more than once argues from the known nature of the latter persons to the supposed nature of the former. In at least one instance [12] she has overlooked the plain statement of Sall. 40 and Cic. 3 *Cat.* 14.

[12] That of Gabinius, who is a distinct person from Umbrenus (*pace* de Luna, *Jonson's Romish Plot*, p. 218). Dr. de Luna realizes that the reference to Gabinius as "the engineer of all" (V.iv.108) is a translation from Cic. 3 *Cat.* 6; she is, however, surely guilty of a *petitio principi* when, in defense of her equation Gabinius = Guy Fawkes, she says: "While Cicero may have had some now-buried reason for the epithet he gave him, Jonson's play provides not the slightest justification for its rough English counterpart" (p. 216), and therefore draws the conclusion that the justification must lie outside the play and its classical sources.

In short, Dr. de Luna's thesis rests too much on conjecture, coincidence, and unproven assumptions about the degree of familiarity with the classics among Jonson's contemporaries, to carry conviction. Where her work is valuable is in drawing attention to certain aspects of Jonson's dramatic handling of the story. Some of these we have already mentioned—the drinking of the slave's blood, the complicity of Caesar, the characterization of Cethegus and Lentulus. To these we might add (without adopting her conclusions) the passionate outbursts of Cato in IV.ii. However, these do not amount to departures from the evidence, although they heighten the dramatic color. Secondly (as with the "gunpowder" imagery), her work has value in drawing our attention to a contemporary event, with some resemblances to Catiline's plot, which might have influenced Jonson's imaginative treatment. To say, however, that some of these resemblances might have been heightened by Jonson's choice of language, as a way of increasing the contemporary interest and relevance of the play, is a very far cry from accepting the view that the *raison d'être* of the *Catiline* was the plot of 1605.

SERIAL LIST OF SOURCES

[I]

0.1. For Sylla's ghost, cf. Lucan 1. 580–581; the influence on Catiline of Sylla's precedent is mentioned in Sall. 5.

9. Virgil *Aen.* 6. 522.

11–12, 14. Sen. *Thyest.* 87–89.

24. Florus 2. 12. 2.

29. Sall. 5.

31. Ascon. 82.

32 ff. Sall. 15; Cic. 1 *Cat.* 14.

35–36. Plut. *Cic.* 10; Ascon. 82.

37–38. "knights": Q. Cic. 9–10, cf. Ascon. 75.

38–40. Plut. *Cic.* 10, *Sulla* 32.

42. Q. Cic. 9.

47. Sall. 18; Cic. 1 *Cat.* 15; Ascon. 83.

55–63. Sen. *Thyest.* 29–32, 48–49, 51.

79–80. Sen. *Agam.* 115.

90. Porcius 7; Felicius, chap. 3.

92 ff. Lucan 1. 2–3.

124. Sall. 35.

126. Cf. Hor. *Carm.* 1. 1. 36.

131. Cic. *pro Caelio* 13.

135 ff. Sall. 47; Plut. *Cic.* 17; Cic. 3 *Cat.* 9.

143. Sen. *Medea* 424–425.

149–150. Curius: Sall. 23. Lentulus: Plut. *Cic.* 17.

153. Cf. Cic. 2 *Cat.* 9.

157. Sall. 28.

159–180. Sall. 14.

226. Lucan 1. 365.

230. Ibid., 2. 101.

232–234. Ibid., 2. 149, 151, 145.

235 ff. Ibid., 2. 100.

239–241. Ibid., 104, 101, 106, 105.

244. Ibid., 109.

245–246. Ibid., 110–111.

247–250. Cf. ibid., 3. 16; Petron. 121. 117–120.

250–253. Lucan 2. 153, 152.

278–282. Cf. Lucan 1. 556–557.

292.1–3. Sall. 17.

312. Sen. *Thyest*. 892.
314. Lucan 1. 549.
318. Ibid., 1. 486.
320. Ibid., 1. 572–574.
326–420. Based on Sall. 20.
356. Hor. *Epist*. 1. 2. 27.
388–390. Petron. 119. 34–37.
391. Ibid., 33.
397–400. Ibid., 120. 85 ff.
425. Lucan 1. 281.
426–428, 441–445, 447–448. Sall. 21.
446. Ibid., 26.
453–473. Ibid., 21.
483 ff. Ibid., 22; cf. Florus 2. 12. 4.
501. "new fellow," cf. on II.115–116.
505–512. Cf. Sall. 14.
515. Ibid., 21.
519. Lucan 1. 259.
531–590. Mainly from Petron. 119–120.
531–535. Petron. 120. 80–84.
536. Hor. *Ep*. 16. 2.
544. Petron. 120. 85.
545. Ibid., 119. 1.
551–555. Ibid., 120. 87, 89, 90–94.
563–564. Ibid., 119. 24.
566. Juv. 11. 123.
576–577. Sall. 10.
579–590. Petron. 119. 39–45, 49–51.

[II] This is mainly of Jonson's own devising, worked up from remarks in Sall. 23 and 25.
4. Plut. *Ant*. 10; Jonson's misidentification.
34 ff. Sall. 25.
65. Juv. 6. 462.
74. Ovid *R.A*. 344.
105 ff. Ascon. 73; Felicius, chap. 7.
115–116. Sall. 31.
137. Plut. *Cic*. 4.
227. Sen. *de Ira* 2. 36.
253 ff. Ovid. *A.A*. 3. 601 ff.
301. Sall. 23.
353–354. Philostr. 13 (59).
391 ff. Val. Max. 5. 6 cites as examples of *pietas erga patriam*, in the

following order, Brutus, Curtius, Genucius Cipus, the Decii, Scipio Africanus Maior. For Cipus, see also Ovid *Met*. 15. 565 ff.; for Curtius, cf. Livy, 7. 6.
394. Hor. *Carm*. 4. 9. 39.

[III.i]
1. Varro 5. 73.
11. Cic. 2 *leg. agr*. 5.
15–16. Juv. 8. 5.
21. Cic. *pro Mur*. 17.
24–25. Cic. 2 *leg. agr*. 3.
26–31. Ibid., 4.
32–35. Ibid., 5.
38–41. Ibid., 6.
47–52. Ibid., 8.
54–56. Sall. 23.
83. *ignavi numerant tempore, laude boni*. anon.
85. Cic. 2 *leg. agr*. 9.
110. Ascon. 73.
112–113. Plut. *Cic*. 17.
115. Cic. *in Pis*. 6; Vell. Pat. 2. 43.
120–122. Juv. 10. 347–350.
128 ff. The following sources report suspicions of the involvement of Caesar and Crassus: Sall. 48, 49; Suet. *D.J*. 17; Plut. *Caes*. 7–8, *Crass*. 13, *Cic*. 20.
166. Ascon. 84.
179. Sen. *Thyest*. 883–884; cf. Pliny 6. 20. 17.
193. Lucan 1. 150.
219–221. Cic. *pro Mur*. 51.

[III.ii] Mainly from Sall. 23.
1–4. Sen. *Phaedra* 671–674.
14–15. Tac. 4. 6.
26–28. Porcius 4.
30. Cic. 4 *Cat*. 7, *pro Mur*. 80.
32–37. Cic. 2 *Cat*. 7, 8.
46–47. Lucan 5. 274.
51–53. Florus 2. 12. 4.
63–65. Cic. 2 *Phil*. 114.
81 ff. Sall. 26.
134. Sen. *Octavia* 441.
216–217. Florus 2. 12. 6.
237–239. Plut. *Cic*. 12.

243. Sall. 26.
246. Juv. 10. 141–142.

[III.iii]
1–39 is developed by Jonson from the rumor in the sources of Caesar's complicity (see on III.i.128 ff.).
15–16. Sen. *Herc. Fur.* 251–252.
40 ff. The content of the meeting is found in Cic. 3 *Cat.* 8–10, 1 *Cat.* 9, Sall. 27–28, 47, Plut. *Cic.* 18.
45. Sall. 24.
52–53. Juv. 14. 34–35.
54. Sall. 27–28; Cic. 1 *Cat.* 8. See explanatory note to III.iii (p. 74).
63. Sall. 19; Ascon. 83.
66. Plut. *Cic.* 18.
69–72. Sall. 27.
74. Cic. 1 *Cat.* 24, 2 *Cat.* 13; Sall. 59.
84. Sall. 47, Cic. 3 *Cat.* 9.
98–99. Sall. 27.
108. Cic. 3 *Cat.* 10.
110. Sall. 43.
141. Felicius, chap. 16, gives Longinus and Statilius; Cic. 3 *Cat.* 14 gives Longinus; Sall. 43 Statilius (and Gabinius).
144. Sall. 43.
145–150. Plut. *Cic.* 18.
153–155. Ibid.
156. Livy 1. 54. 6.
171–172. Sall. 27, Cic. 1 *Cat.* 9.
175–176. Sen. *Herc. Fur.* 644.
194. Cic. 3 *Cat.* 16.
213. Sall. 28.
236. "Cimber": Felicius, chap. 4; cf. Cic. 3 *Cat.* 6.

[III.iv] Mainly from Sall. 28, Plut. *Cic.* 16.
8–9. Cic. 1 *Cat.* 10.
34. Plut. *Cic.* 15, *Crass.* 13.

[III.v] Mainly from Cic. 1 *Cat.* 10, Sall. 28.
20–22. Cic. 1 *Cat.* 6.
23–24. Ibid., 8.
25–26. Cic. 2 *Cat.* 6.
27. Ibid., 25.

30–31. Cic. 2 *Cat.* 21.
65. Sall. 11.

[IV.i] Mainly from Sall. 40–41, Plut. *Cic.* 18.
7–10. Possible reminiscences of Juv. 13. 223–224, Ovid, *Met.* 1. 84–85, Lucr. 1. 62–70.
19–23. Juv. 8. 121–124.
30–32. Hor. *Carm.* 3. 3. 7–8.

[IV.ii] Mainly from Sall. 31.
2. Cic. 2 *Cat.* 12, Plut. *Cic.* 16.
16–18. Cic. 3 *Cat.* 4.
29. Cic. 1 *Cat.* 11.
31. Cic. 2 *Cat.* 27.
33. Cic. *pro Mur.* 52; Dio 37. 29; Plut. *Cic.* 14. Jonson transfers the incident from Campus Martius to the Senate.
61–62. Porcius chap. 4.
63–66. Q. Cic. 9.
70–73. Cic. *pro Caelio* 14.
82.1. Cic. 1 *Cat.* 16; Plut. *Cic.* 16.
92–95. Plut. *Cic.* 14; cf. Cic. *pro Mur.* 51.
116–402. Cic. 1 *Cat.*, omitting parts of 9 and 10, end of 11, 12, part of 17, all 18, 19, 21, 23, 25, 26, half of 27, 28.
323. Felicius, chap. 20.
406–411. Sall. 31.
408. anon., quoted by Felicius, chap. 19.
420. Sall. 31.
421. Juv. 8. 237.
422–425. Lucan, 3. 137–140.
427. Ovid *Met.* 1. 7.
435–436, 438–440. Lucan 3. 134–137.
442–451. Catiline's lines, Sall. 31.
457–458. Cic. 1 *Cat.* 2, Sall. 29, Plut. *Cic.* 15.
471–473. Plut. *Cic.* 20.

[IV.iii]
7–10. Sall. 32.
11–13. Sall. 44, Cic. 3 *Cat.* 12.

20–25. Sall. 34.
39–49. Ibid., 40.
51–52. Cic. 3 *Cat.* 9.

[IV.iv] Mainly from Sall. 41.
13. Ibid., 41.
15–16. Ibid., 40.
30–40. Felicius, chap. 26.
41–43. Sall. 36.
44–45. Ibid., 42.
45–47. Ibid., 30.
54–55. Cic. 2 *Cat.* 27.
74–76. Sall. 40.
77–81. Ibid., 41.

[IV.v] Mainly from Sall. 44.
10. There is no such remark in Thucydides.
49. Stat. 10. 935–939.
64–69. Sall. 44.
70–72. Ibid., 43.

[IV.vi]
3–11. Sall. 59.
18–19. Ibid., 57.
21–24. Ibid., 45.
28–29. Ibid., 46 (cf. Cic. 3 *Cat.* 3).

[IV.vii]
1–19. Sall. 45.
20–71. For fickleness of popular opinion at Rome see Sall. 37 and 48.
30. Cic. *pro Mur.* 35.
45–63. Felicius, chap. 22.
70–71. Livy *praef.* 9.

[V.i] The fact of Petreius' exhortation to the troops is recorded in Sall. 59. Jonson's version, ll. 5–49, follows very closely the text of Felicius, chap. 57.
5–21. Felicius includes reminiscences of Sall. 52, Cic. 2 *Cat.* 24, 4 *Cat.* 18.
22–49. Worked up by Felicius from part of Cic. 2 *Cat.* 17–23.

[V.ii]
1. Cic. 3 *Cat.* 16.
4. Plut. *Cic.* 15.
11. Suet. 17.

[V.iii]
4–8. Sall. 49.

[V.iv] Mainly from Cic. 3 *Cat.* 6–16.
4–6. 3 *Cat.* 7.
15–26. Translated from 3 *Cat.* 3–4.
31–35. Sall. 47.
38–44. 3 *Cat.* 8.
46–48. Ibid., 9.
57, 69–73. Ibid., 10.
86–91. Ibid., 9.
94–96. Sall. 47.
107. 3 *Cat.* 6.
108–109. Ibid., 12.
125. Juv. 14. 134.
131–135. 3 *Cat.* 16.
137–142. 3 *Cat.* 22.
146–148, 151–155. Cic. 4 *Cat.* 13.
157–165. Ibid., 11–12.
180–184. Sall. 47.
187–189. 3 *Cat.* 15.
191–198. Sall. 50.
199–201, 203. 3 *Cat.* 14.
210–211. Cic. *in Pis.* 6.
212–216, 219–220. 3 *Cat.* 15.
223–233. 3 *Cat.* 2.
235–244. Sall. 48.
249–264. Suet. 17.

[V.v] Translated closely from Sall. 58.

[V.vi] Mainly from Sall. 50–55 and Cic. 4 *Cat.*
96. Plut. *Cic.* 21.
153–159. Plut. *Cato Minor* 24.

[V.vii, viii] Mainly from Sall. 55; Plut. *Cic.* 22.

[V.ix]
1–3. Sall. 55.
5. Cic. *de cons. suo*, fragment.
35. Lucan 7. 132.

41–42. Ibid., 129–130.
47–51. Ibid., 1. 100–106.
54–55. Ibid., 6. 147–148.
64. Sall. 61.

66, 68–70. Lucan 1. 206–207, 212.
73–79. Claudian 91–101.
81–82. Sall. 61.
84–86. Florus 2. 12. 12.

ALPHABETICAL LIST OF SOURCES (with Abbreviations)

Ascon.	Q. Asconius Pedianus, *in orationem Ciceronis in senatu in toga candida enarratio*
Cic.	M. Tullius Cicero
pro Caelio	*oratio pro M. Caelio*
1, 2, 3, 4 *Cat.*	*oratio in Catilinam prima*, etc.
de cons. suo	*de consulatu suo poema*
2 *leg. agr.*	*oratio secunda de lege agraria contra Rullum*
pro Mur.	*oratio pro Murena*
Off.	*de Officiis*
2 *Phil.*	*in M. Antonium oratio Philippica II*
in Pis.	*oratio in Pisonem*
pro Sulla	*oratio pro Sulla*
Q. Cic.	Q. Tullius Cicero, *de petitione consulatus*
Claudian	Claudius Claudianus, *Gigantomachia*
Dio	Cassius Dio Cocceianus, *Roman History*
Felicius	Constantius Felicius Durantinus, *de coniuratione L. Catilinae liber* (1518)
Florus	L. Annaeus Florus, *Epitome bellorum omnium annorum DCC*
Homer *Od.*	Homer, *Odyssey*
Hor.	Q. Horatius Flaccus
Ep.	*Epodi*
Epist.	*Epistulae*
Carm.	*Carmina*
Sat.	*Satirae*
Juv.	D. Junius Juvenalis, *Satirae*
Livy	Titus Livius, *ab urbe condita libri* (history of Rome)
Lucan	M. Annaeus Lucanus, *Pharsalia*, or *Belli civilis libri decem*
Lucr.	T. Lucretius Carus, *de rerum natura libri sex*

Ovid.	P. Ovidius Naso
A.A.	*Ars Amatoria*
Met.	*Metamorphoses*
R.A.	*Remedia Amoris*
Petron.	Petronius Arbiter, *Satiricon*
Philostr.	Flavius Philostratus, *Erotic Epistles*
Pliny	C. Plinius Caecilius Secundus, *Epistulae*
Plut.	Plutarch
Ant.	*Life of Antony*
Caes.	*Life of Caesar*
Cato Minor	*Life of the younger Cato*
Cic.	*Life of Cicero*
Crass.	*Life of Crassus*
Sulla	*Life of Sulla*
Porcius	M. Porcius Latro, *declamatio contra L. Sergium Catilinam* (first attested in 15th century A.D.; real author unknown)
Sall.	C. Sallustius Crispus, *Catilina*
Sen.	L. Annaeus Seneca
Agam.	*Agamemnon*
de ira	*de ira*
Herc. Fur.	*Hercules Furens*
Octavia	*Octavia*
Phaedra	*Phaedra*
Thyest.	*Thyestes*
Stat.	P. Papinius Statius, *Thebais*
Suet.	C. Suetonius Tranquillus, *Divus Julius*
Varro	M. Terentius Varro, *de lingua Latina libri XXV*
Tac.	Cornelius Tacitus, *Historiarum libri*
Val. Max.	Valerius Maximus, *Factorum ac dictorum memorabilium libri IX*
Vell. Pat.	C. Velleius Paterculus, *Historiae Romanae*
Virgil *Aen.*	P. Vergilius Maro, *Aeneis*

Appendix C

Chronology

Approximate years are indicated by *, occurrences in doubt by (?).

Political and Literary Events	Life and Works of Ben Jonson

1558.
Accession of Queen Elizabeth I.
Robert Greene born.
Thomas Kyd born.

1560
George Chapman born.

1561
Francis Bacon born.

1564
Shakespeare born.
Christopher Marlowe born.

1572
Thomas Dekker born.*
John Donne born.
Massacre of St. Batholomew's Day.

1573

Benjamin Jonson born in London, about June 11, posthumous son of a clergyman. His mother remarried a bricklayer.

1574
Thomas Heywood born.*

1576
The Theatre, the first permanent public theater in London, established by James Burbage.
John Marston born.

1577

The Curtain theater opened.
Holinshed's *Chronicles of England, Scotland and Ireland.*
Drake begins the circumnavigation of the earth; completed 1580.

1578

John Lyly's *Euphues: The Anatomy of Wit.*

1579

John Fletcher born.
Sir Thomas North's translation of Plutarch's *Lives.*

1580

Thomas Middleton born.

1583

Philip Massinger born.

1584

Francis Beaumont born.*

1586

Death of Sir Philip Sidney.
John Ford born.
Kyd's *THE SPANISH TRAGEDY.*

1587

The Rose theater opened by Henslowe.
Marlowe's *TAMBURLAINE*, Part I.*
Execution of Mary, Queen of Scots.
Drake raids Cadiz.

Attends Westminster School, studying under William Camden, one of the most learned men in England.*

1588

Defeat of the Spanish Armada.
Marlowe's *TAMBURLAINE*, Part II.*

Leaves Westminster School; apprenticed as bricklayer.*

1589

Greene's *FRIAR BACON AND FRIAR BUNGAY.*
Marlowe's *THE JEW OF MALTA.*

1590

Spenser's *Faerie Queene* (Books I–III) published.
Sidney's *Arcadia* published.

Shakespeare's *HENRY VI*, Parts I–III,* *TITUS ANDRONICUS.*

1591
Shakespeare's *RICHARD III.*

Serves as a soldier in the Low Countries (1591–1592).

1592
Marlowe's *DOCTOR FAUSTUS* and *EDWARD II.*
Shakespeare's *TAMING OF THE SHREW* and *THE COMEDY OF ERRORS.*
Death of Greene.

1593
Shakespeare's *LOVE'S LABOR'S LOST*;* *Venus and Adonis* published.
Death of Marlowe.
Theaters closed on account of plague.

1594.
Shakespeare's *TWO GENTLEMEN OF VERONA*;* *The Rape of Lucrece* published.
Shakespeare's company becomes Lord Chamberlain's Men.
Death of Kyd.

Marries Anne Lewis.

1595
The Swan theater built.
Sidney's *Defense of Poesy* published.
Shakespeare's *ROMEO AND JULIET*,* *A MIDSUMMER NIGHT'S DREAM*,* *RICHARD II.*
Raleigh's first expedition to Guiana.

Serves as an actor in one of the London companies.*

1596
Spenser's *Faerie Queene* (Books IV–VI) published.
Shakespeare's *MERCHANT OF VENICE*,* *KING JOHN.*
James Shirley born.

Collaborated on plays, some for the Admiral's Men.*

1597
Bacon's *Essays* (first edition).
Shakespeare's *HENRY IV*, Part I.*

Imprisoned for part authorship of a lost play, *THE ISLE OF DOGS.*

1598
Demolition of The Theatre.
Shakespeare's *MUCH ADO ABOUT*

THE CASE IS ALTERED (Children of Chapel Royal).*

NOTHING, *HENRY IV*, Part II.*
Seven books of Chapman's translation of Homer's *Iliad* published.

EVERY MAN IN HIS HUMOR
(Lord Chamberlain's Men).
Kills Gabriel Spencer, a fellow actor, in a duel; imprisoned but freed on plea of benefit of clergy; converted to Roman Catholicism while in jail.

1599
The Paul's Boys reopen their theater.
The Globe theater opened.
Shakespeare's *AS YOU LIKE IT,* *HENRY V, JULIUS CAESAR.*
Marston's *ANTONIO AND MEL-LIDA,* Parts I and II.
Dekker's *THE SHOEMAKERS' HOLIDAY.*
Death of Spenser.

EVERY MAN OUT OF HIS HU-MOR (Lord Chamberlain's Men) starts a vogue in satiric comedy.

1600
Shakespeare's *TWELFTH NIGHT.*
The Fortune theater built by Alleyn.
The Children of the Chapel begin to play at the Blackfriars.

CYNTHIA'S REVELS (Children of Chapel Royal).

1601
Shakespeare's *HAMLET,* *MERRY WIVES OF WINDSOR.*
Insurrection and execution of the Earl of Essex.

POETASTER (Children of Chapel Royal).
Publicly feuds with Marston and Dekker in the War of the Theaters.

1602
Shakespeare's *TROILUS AND CRESSIDA.*

1603
Death of Queen Elizabeth I; accession of James VI of Scotland as James I.
Florio's translation of Montaigne's *Essays* published.
Shakespeare's *ALL'S WELL THAT ENDS WELL.*
Heywood's *A WOMAN KILLED WITH KINDNESS.*
Marston's *THE MALCONTENT.*
Shakespeare's company becomes the King's Men.

SEJANUS (King's Men) hissed off the stage.
Son Benjamin dies, aged six.
Forms "The Mermaid Club" and gathers a coterie about him.

1604

Shakespeare's *MEASURE FOR MEASURE*,* *OTHELLO*.*
Marston's *THE FAWN*.*
Chapman's *BUSSY D'AMBOIS*.*

1605

Shakespeare's *KING LEAR*.*
Marston's *THE DUTCH COURTE-SAN*.*
Bacon's *Advancement of Learning* published.
The Gunpowder Plot.

Early masque at court, *THE MASQUE OF BLACKNESS*.
EASTWARD HO, in collaboration with Chapman and Marston (Children of the Queen's Revels); Jonson and Chapman imprisoned because of alleged derogatory allusions to King James.

1606

Shakespeare's *MACBETH*.*
Tourneur's *REVENGER'S TRAG-EDY*.*
The Red Bull theater built.
Death of John Lyly.

VOLPONE (King's Men).*

1607

Shakespeare's *ANTONY AND CLEOPATRA*.*
Beaumont's *KNIGHT OF THE BURNING PESTLE*.*
Settlement of Jamestown, Virginia.

VOLPONE performed at Oxford and Cambridge.*

1608

Shakespeare's *CORIOLANUS*,* *TIMON OF ATHENS*,* *PERICLES*.*
Chapman's *CONSPIRACY AND TRAGEDY OF CHARLES, DUKE OF BYRON*.*
Richard Burbage leases Blackfriars Theatre for King's company.
John Milton born.

1609

Shakespeare's *CYMBELINE*;* *Sonnets* published.
Dekker's *Gull's Hornbook* published.

EPICOENE (Children of the Queen's Revels).

1610

Chapman's *REVENGE OF BUSSY D'AMBOIS.**

Richard Crashaw born.

THE ALCHEMIST (King's Men). Returns to Anglican religion.*

1611

Authorized (King James) Version of the Bible published.

Shakespeare's *THE WINTER'S TALE,* *THE TEMPEST.**

Beaumont and Fletcher's *A KING AND NO KING.*

Middleton's *A CHASTE MAID IN CHEAPSIDE.**

Tourneur's *ATHEIST'S TRAGEDY.**

Chapman's translation of *Iliad* completed.

CATILINE (King's Men) damned by theater audiences, but later greatly respected by readers.

Writing masques for Court entertainments regularly up to 1625.

1612

Webster's *THE WHITE DEVIL.**

Travels in France as tutor to son of Sir Walter Raleigh (1612–1613).

1613

The Globe theater burned.

Shakespeare's *HENRY VIII* (with Fletcher).

Webster's *THE DUCHESS OF MALFI.**

Sir Thomas Overbury murdered.

1614

The Globe theater rebuilt.

The Hope Theatre built.

BARTHOLOMEW FAIR (Lady Elizabeth's Men).

1616

Chapman's *Whole Works of Homer.*

Death of Shakespeare.

Death of Beaumont.

THE DEVIL IS AN ASS (King's Men).

Publication of Folio edition of *Works* ridiculed for its pretension.

Receives royal pension, and henceforth he is considered poet laureate, although he never styled himself such.

1618

Outbreak of Thirty Years War.

Execution of Raleigh.

Journeys on foot to Scotland; visits there with William Drummond (1618–1619).

1619

Given honorary M.A. by Oxford University.

1620
Settlement of Plymouth, Massachusetts.

1621
Middleton's *WOMEN BEWARE WOMEN.**
Robert Burton's *Anatomy of Melancholy* published.
Andrew Marvell born.

1622
Middleton and Rowley's *THE CHANGELING.**
Henry Vaughan born.

1623
Publication of Folio edition of Shakespeare's *COMEDIES, HISTORIES, AND TRAGEDIES.*

Lectures on rhetoric at Gresham College in London(?).
Books and manuscripts lost when lodgings burn.

1625
Death of King James I; accession of Charles I.
Death of Fletcher.

1626
Death of Tourneur.
Death of Bacon.

THE STAPLE OF NEWS (King's Men).

1627
Death of Middleton.

1628
Ford's *THE LOVER'S MELANCHOLY.*
Petition of Right.
Buckingham assassinated.

Paralyzed by a stroke.
Appointed chronologer of the City of London.

1629

THE NEW INN (King's Men).

1631
Shirley's *THE TRAITOR.*
Death of Donne.
John Dryden born.

Quarrels with Inigo Jones.

1632
Massinger's *THE CITY MADAM*.*

THE MAGNETIC LADY (King's Men).

1633
Donne's *Poems* published.
Death of George Herbert.

A TALE OF A TUB, revised from an earlier play (Queen Henrietta's Men).

1634
Death of Chapman, Marston, Webster.*
Publication of *THE TWO NOBLE KINSMEN*, with title-page attribution to Shakespeare and Fletcher.
Milton's *Comus*.

A final "entertainment," *LOVE'S WELCOME TO BOLSOVER*.

1635
Sir Thomas Browne's *Religio Medici*.

1637

Jonson dies in Westminster, August 6; buried in Westminster Abbey, August 9.

1638

Jonsonus Virbius, a memorial volume, published.

1639
First Bishops' War.
Death of Carew.*

1640
Short Parliament.
Long Parliament impeaches Laud.
Death of Massinger, Burton.

Works published, two volumes, folio, by Sir Kenelm Digby (1640–1641).

1641
Irish rebel.
Death of Heywood.

1642
Charles I leaves London; Civil War breaks out.
Shirley's *COURT SECRET*.
All theaters closed by Act of Parliament.

1643
Parliament swears to the Solemn
League and Covenant.

1645
Ordinance for New Model Army
enacted.

1646
End of First Civil War.

1647
Army occupies London.
Charles I forms alliance with Scots.
Publication of Folio edition of Beaumont and Fletcher's *COMEDIES
AND TRAGEDIES*.

1648
Second Civil War.

1649
Execution of Charles I.

1650
Jeremy Collier born.

1651
Hobbes' *Leviathan* published.

1652
First Dutch War begins (ended
1654).
Thomas Otway born.

1653
Nathaniel Lee born.*

1656
D'Avenant's *THE SIEGE OF
RHODES* performed at Rutland
House.

1657
John Dennis born.

1658
Death of Oliver Cromwell.
D'Avenant's *THE CRUELTY OF
THE SPANIARDS IN PERU* performed at the Cockpit.

1660
Restoration of Charles II.

Theatrical patents granted to Thomas Killigrew and Sir William D'Avenant, authorizing them to form, respectively, the King's and the Duke of York's Companies.

1661

Cowley's *THE CUTTER OF COLEMAN STREET*.

D'Avenant's *THE SIEGE OF RHODES* (expanded to two parts).

1662

Charter granted to the Royal Society.

1663

Dryden's *THE WILD GALLANT*.

Tuke's *THE ADVENTURES OF FIVE HOURS*.

1664

Sir John Vanbrugh born.

Dryden's *THE RIVAL LADIES*.

Dryden and Howard's *THE INDIAN QUEEN*.

Etherege's *THE COMICAL REVENGE*.

1665

Second Dutch War begins (ended 1667).

Great Plague.

Dryden's *THE INDIAN EMPEROR*.

Orrery's *MUSTAPHA*.

1666

Fire of London.

Death of James Shirley.